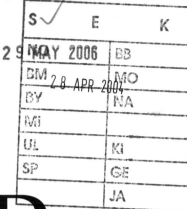
CAR
WARS

CAR WARS

How the car won our hearts
and conquered our cities

GRAEME DAVISON
with
Sheryl Yelland

ALLEN&UNWIN

First published in 2004

Allen & Unwin
83 Alexander Street
Crows Nest NSW 2065
Australia
Phone: (61 2) 8425 0100
Fax: (61 2) 9906 2218
Email: info@allenandunwin.com
Web: www.allenandunwin.com

National Library of Australia
Cataloguing-in-Publication entry:

Davison, Graeme, 1940- .
  Car wars : How the car won our hearts and conquered our cities

  Bibliography.
  Includes index.
  ISBN 1 74114 207 5.

  1. Automobiles - Social aspects. 2. Automobiles -
  Psychological aspects. 3. Automobiles - History. I. Title.

303.4832

Frontispiece: *From Prospect Hill Road.* (Photo Mark Strizic, 1967)
Set in 11/14 pt Plantin Light by Midland Typesetters, Victoria
Printed by SRM Production Services Sdn Bhd, Malaysia

10 9 8 7 6 5 4 3 2 1

In memory of George Davison
1911–1998

Contents

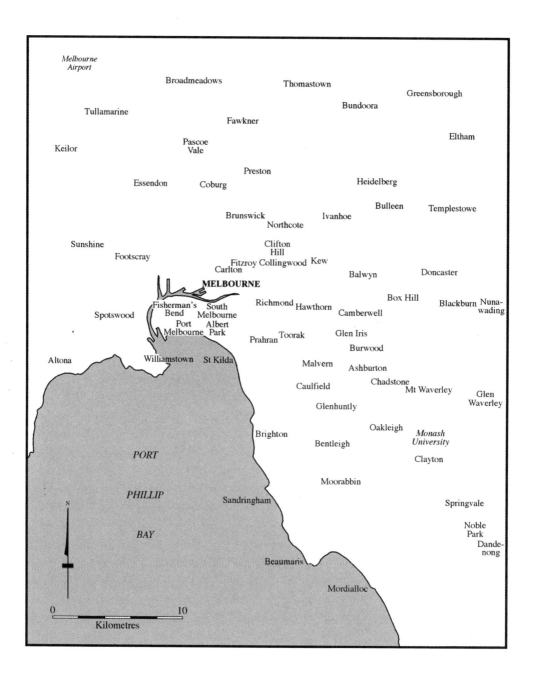

Melbourne suburbs

Introduction

The history of our times is written not only in words, but in things. We live in a materialistic age, and much of our lives is occupied with the pursuit of material things. Yet every age takes pride in the things it makes, and invests them with more than material significance. Medieval society built cathedrals, the rise of the modern state was made concrete in palaces and parliaments, the industrial age was inseparable from canals, railways and satanic mills. If an earthquake or atomic holocaust should suddenly destroy our own civilisation, future archaeologists will surely find no more significant ruins than the highway flyovers and clover leafs, parking stations and drive-in shopping malls of a society whose most valued tool, and most powerful status symbol, is the automobile.

Cars are everywhere. They take us to work, shop and play. They monopolise our streets and roadways and mould the landscape to their insistent demands. They are homes away from home, little oases of privacy, where drivers sit alone with their thoughts amidst the hum of traffic or couples cling together in dark side streets. In the battle of the sexes, cars are also powerful weapons. They are love objects and status symbols; also symbols of danger and sudden death.

From their first appearance during the Edwardian era, cars won attention for how they looked as much as what they did. By the 1960s, car owners as well as manufacturers and car salesmen recognised that the automobile was a 'status symbol', an essential prop in the search for social recognition that American sociologists saw as the ruling principle of postwar suburbia. 'No other piece of machinery is a greater status symbol or a means of emancipation for the average person than the ownership of a motor car', declared the Victorian motoring magazine *Royalauto* in 1966.[1]

DESIRE

If car worship had a heyday it was surely in the decades after World War II. Contemporary poets and novelists reached for high-flown metaphors of love or religious ecstacy to describe the mystic union between car and driver. In his satirical poem 'The Brides' (1951) A. D. Hope likened the movement of the car down the assembly line to a bridal procession:

> *Down the assembly line they roll and pass*
> *Complete at last, a miracle of design;*
> *Their chromium fenders, the unbreakable glass,*
> *The fashionable curve, the air-flow line.*
>
> *Grease to the elbows Mum and Dad enthuse,*
> *Pocket their spanners and survey the bride;*
> *Murmur: A sweet job! All she needs is juice!*
> *Built for a life-time—sleek as a fish. Inside*
>
> *'He will find every comfort: the full set*
> *Of gadgets; knobs that answer to the touch*
> *For light and music; a place for his cigarette:*
> *Room for his knees; a honey of a clutch.*[2]

Historians and cultural critics have fashioned the playful metaphor of the poet into theories. Cars, they suggest, were not just symbols of success but sex symbols too. 'Powerful cars', writes Stephen Bayley in his *Sex, Drink and Fast Cars* (1986), 'are not transport, they are aphrodisiacs. They are sold as costumes and worn for sexual display.'[3] Other writers liken them to sacred icons. 'A visitor from a different planet would have no trouble in describing the car as the central feature of an almost universal religion', say the authors of *Driving Passion* (1986), elaborating the observation with a catalogue of the vestments, rituals and iconography of the car-owning cult.[4] The automobile, writes Wolfgang Sachs, in his perceptive *For Love of the Automobile* (1992), 'is much more than a mere means of transportation; rather it is wholly imbued with feelings and desires that raise it to the level of cultural symbol'.[5] For Sachs the automobile is above all a symbol of modernism, and its appeal lies in its capacity to represent the modern ideals of efficiency, functionality, speed, mobility and beauty. Recent Australian writers follow obediently in this tradition. Charles Pickett, curator of the Powerhouse Museum's recent exhibition, *Cars and Culture*, sees both sexual and religious overtones in Australians' affection for their cars; it is a 'fetish', a 'cult'.

By stressing the symbolism of the automobile the critics suggest that there was something irrational, or at least excessive, in the devotion of motorists to their cars. 'Love', Sachs declares, 'only rarely listens to reason'. Cars, says Pickett, are 'functional objects, but they do not appeal primarily to reason and rationality'.[6] Since the oil crisis of the 1970s, when gas-guzzling cars were declared public enemies, it became common to picture the motorist as the dupe of oil companies and motor manufacturers. By seductive styling and advertising, they had persuaded him (car worship was seen primarily as a male cult) that without a car he was a nobody. Critics of the automobile often adopt a lofty, ironic attitude towards its devotees. They leap easily from analysis of the stylistic excesses of Detroit and the psychological subtexts of car advertisements to sweeping generalisations about the ego-gratification of the ordinary motorist. They often confuse the symbolism used to sell cars, or to enhance the appeal of a particular model, with the utility and appeal of the car itself.

The trouble with such interpretations is not that they exaggerate the symbolism of the car, nor even that they underestimate its utility. It lies in the false opposition that the critics erect between symbol and use, desire and reason. If cars were worshipped, and sometimes dressed up in extravagant ways, it was largely because they delivered real benefits and enlarged their owners' lives in highly valued ways. The freedoms that came with the car were real freedoms. They can only be understood if we first appreciate the more limited and regulated world from which the car delivered us.

Terrace-dwelling intellectuals occasionally sneer at the delight of suburban Australians in their cars. Yet it does no service to the cause of environmentalism or better cities to suggest that most people can give up their cars and take public transport—even if good public transport were on offer—and experience no significant loss in personal wellbeing. Automobilism—the liberty promised by the car to travel where, when and as often as we like—may be ultimately self-defeating and unsustainable. It may have to be curbed in the interests of our children and the health of the planet. But there is no point in trying to tell those who will suffer that limitation that it is really no loss at all. If we want to understand Australians' attachment to their cars, therefore, we must make an honest and open-minded appraisal of how cars have both enriched and impoverished our lives. We must resist the instinct to draw up a balance sheet until we have allowed all the interests that cluster around the car to speak of their experience, and give voice to their aspirations and regrets, their pleasures and pains.

Like a human love affair, our love affair with the car unfolded, step by step, from its first moment of distant admiration through casual acquaintance, infatuation and deep bonding to taken-for-granted familiarity. Sometimes, alas, the affair cooled or dissolved into irreconcilable differences. In tracing the impact of the car on the postwar city, we are tracing perhaps the most significant thread in the city's encounter with the project we sometimes call 'modernity'. 'To be modern', writes Marshall Berman, 'is to find ourselves in an environment that promises us adventure, power, joy, growth, transformation of ourselves and the world—and, at the same time, threatens to destroy everything we have, everything we know, everything we are'.[7] Mass motorisation was a kind of Faustian bargain. It promised its followers much, but the promises were often negated by the unanticipated consequences of their fulfilment. By attempting to universalise individual mobility the car created congestion. By building freeways to bring communities closer together it often endangered the cohesion of the communities themselves. By feeding the desire for speed it caused death and injury. Now, it seems, like Dr Faustus, we are so deeply in thrall that we cannot escape the bonds of the car, even if we wished to. Are we too far down the on-ramp to turn back?

CONFLICT

The car was not only an object of desire, but a subject of sometimes bitter conflict. *Car Wars* is a history of those conflicts. Cars were weapons in the battle of the sexes and in the revolt of the young against their parents. They generated fiscal struggles over taxation and road

finance. They challenged pedestrians and other road users for possession of the road. They caused death and injury on a scale equalled only
by war. They posed deep and still-unresolved conflicts between our
competing desires for access and amenity, self-expression and personal
safety, progress and continuity, individual rights and community
cohesion, material improvement and the conservation of the natural
environment. It was through the struggle to resolve these conflicts that
the modern metropolis was shaped.

In the following chapters I have sought to explore each of these
dimensions of conflict. I give special emphasis, however, to the four
decades from 1945 to the early 1980s that culminated in the prolonged
battle over the 1969 Melbourne Metropolitan Transportation Plan and
its proposals for an extensive system of urban freeways. Most Western
cities faced the challenge of mass automobilisation in the decades after
World War II. Melbourne's experience was similar to that of other
Australian cities, and the first half of the book is essentially an Australian
story. The political response to these developments inevitably took on a
more local character, and in later chapters I give special emphasis to the
prolonged battle over the ambitious plan to provide Melbourne with
the nation's most extensive and expensive freeway network. While I
touch on aspects of the history of public transport, especially its defensive responses to motorisation, and on the history of road haulage, this
is avowedly a study of the impact of the private car, not a comprehensive history of metropolitan transport. The urban freeway, I argue in
Chapter 7, was the pre-eminent expression of the modernist dream of
a city remade around the principle of automobilism. The conflicts it
generated reached a climax with the barricading by resident action
groups of the F19 (or Eastern) freeway in 1977, the most dramatic,
though not the final, test of that experiment. In telling its story I have
been fortunate to draw on the memories of veterans from both sides of
the conflict. I have tried to approach this, as other aspects of the study,
with an open mind, alert to its ironies and complexities, and respectful
of the strong commitment to the public good that I believe generally
inspired both state officials and local activists.

In the heat of battle each side attacked the other as ignorant, wicked
or self-interested. If urban conflicts were always so simple it would make
their history easier to tell, but also less instructive. The story of the car
and the city is not primarily a story of good people in conflict with bad
ones, or even of bad technology or corporations in conflict with good

people and harmonious communities. Cities are by their very nature complex systems in which the desires and interests of groups and individuals, each good according to their point of view, clash with those of others. We each inhabit our own familiar place within the city but we construct the metropolis as a whole from our own vantage point, as men and women, rich or poor, inner city dwellers or suburbanites, motorists, public transport users or pedestrians. Ideology simplifies and reinforces these differences. Car wars, like other wars, are trials of strength between competing interests, but—like other wars too—they are often precipitated by professional myopia, local loyalties, technical miscalculation and limited foresight.

In *The Rise and Fall of Marvellous Melbourne* I examined an earlier phase in the evolution of Melbourne as a modern metropolis, the great land boom and bust of the 1880s and 1890s. I saw that history as illustrative of a more general theme, 'the evolution of a provincial city towards the competitive, bureaucratic structures of an authentic metropolis'.[8] *Car Wars* returns to this theme, now in the context of a metropolis responding to a new phase in the evolution of modern capitalism. In the 1950s and 1960s Melbourne experienced a second boom. Its growth briefly rivalled that of its bigger competitor, Sydney. It became the principal beachhead of American investment and innovation, especially in cars, electronics and other new manufacturing industries. Under the ebullient Premier Henry Bolte, the Victorian Government pursued Keynesian policies of economic management, high foreign immigration, state planning and welfare and encouraged Fordist systems of industrial and social organisation.[9]

Writing *Car Wars*, however, has presented some new challenges from that earlier study, for the half-century since the arrival of mass motorisation overlaps with my own lifetime. I witnessed many of the events and movements I describe in these pages as passenger, driver, resident and citizen. I shared, and was myself a beneficiary, of the great modernist dream of growth and material betterment that came with the 1950s and 1960s, and I have wrestled, as have all my generation, with the dimming of many of those hopes in the 1970s and 1980s.

The study, as I first conceived it, concentrated on the high noon of modernism in Melbourne, from 1945 to 1980. By the early 1990s, however, it was clear that a new phase of urban and political development was under way. In 1992 a newly elected state Liberal government, under Premier Jeff Kennett, sought to propel the city on to a new growth path.

'On the Move' was the new motto on the state's numberplates. The accelerated movement of people, capital, goods and information became the hallmark of this new age. The 'Kennett Revolution', as some called it, promised a return to the Bolte era of economic prosperity. But it sought a new accommodation with the global forces of technological change, tourism and economic rationalism. It overturned the Keynesian models of state planning and development in favour of free-market doctrines of privatisation, corporatisation and outsourcing. The most striking monuments of this revolution were Crown Casino, a towering new gambling and entertainment complex on the south side of the Yarra, and CityLink, a privately owned and operated electronic toll road linking the city, its airport and its eastern and western industrial nodes. CityLink deserves a history of its own; in the concluding chapter of *Car Wars* I offer a brief reflection on the continuities and discontinuities it represents between these two eras of the city's postwar history.

MEMORY AND HISTORY

I look back, now, through these decades of change, to an auspicious afternoon in 1950. I am walking home from primary school along Buckley Street, Essendon, with my friend Maurice Johnson. Like schoolboys everywhere we like to spot new cars. It is Maurice who notices the

George Davison with the Chev, Hall's Gap, Victoria, c. 1952. (AUTHOR'S PHOTO)

approach of the brand-new Chevrolet utility with the cream duco and wide chromium grille, but I am the one who cries out in surprise as I recognise my own father at the wheel.

Dad had been a motorist since his twenties when he scrounged the funds for his first car, a Rugby panel van, purchased second-hand from the pioneering film studio Efftee Productions. His second, an old milk van, provoked girlish banter from my mother's sisters when he arrived to take her out, still displaying the dairyman's sign: 'Families Supplied'. By the time my father purchased his third car, a 1928 Essex, he and Mum were engaged. Soon it was wartime and the promised family was on the way. But it was not until the late 1940s that Dad was able to reopen the garage doors, lower the Essex from the wooden blocks on which it had rested during the long years of petrol rationing, and take to the road again.

By the early 1950s the building trade was picking up again and Dad, a plumber working for spec builders along Melbourne's northern frontier, was looking for something newer than the ancient Essex. For months, it seemed, we scrutinised brochures, compared models, prices and delivery dates. Would our new car be a British Bedford (Dad, the son of British immigrants, had a lingering loyalty to the Old Country) or would it be one of the new Holdens, 'Australia's Own Car'? But the Bedford was too small, and Holden didn't yet offer a utility truck. So, with the encouragement of his accommodating bank manager, Dad took the plunge and bought the magnificent Chev.

I find it hard, now, to think of those years without the 'ute', as we called it. It was not only the workhorse of the family business, but with a canvas canopy and one of the old Essex's horsehair-filled seats in the back it doubled as the family car. With a caravan hitched behind, it took us on holiday to Phillip Island, Marysville and Lakes Entrance. It took my junior cricket team to away matches. It carted furniture and garden rubbish. It extended our horizons, diversified our choices, consolidated our sense of family togetherness.

We were only one of the millions of Australian families who experienced the advent of mass motoring as a moment of liberation. Not until the early 1960s, when I paid £100 to Uncle Jack for his magnificent but dilapidated 1948 Triumph Roadster, did I own a car of my own. With Dad's help I replaced the tattered canvas hood, reconditioned the engine and repainted the duco British racing green in a brave, but vain, bid to realise the youthful dreams outlined in Chapter 3. I later exchanged it for an FJ Holden, but soon wrote that off in a reckless head-on crash, my first and only serious experience of the subject of Chapter 6. In the early 1970s I discovered, first-hand, the difficulties of living as a one-car household in a suburb without trains or trams. In the late 1970s, when the opening of the F19 freeway provoked some of my old Melbourne University students and colleagues to revolt, I sympathised with their cause, but soon found myself making the daily commute along another freeway towards Monash, Australia's first drive-in university.

This book is a delayed response to the shift of perspective occasioned by that move from Parkville to Clayton. I had long been accustomed, like most intellectuals, to looking at the city from the inside out. Working at Monash has gradually persuaded me to look at it, as most Melburnians do, from the outside in. I owe much to the stimulus of my Monash colleagues, especially Tony Dingle, Andrew Brown-May and Seamus O'Hanlon who joined me—and our Deakin colleague Renate Howe—in a collaborative project on the history of postwar Melbourne. I am grateful to the Australian Research Council for a grant towards this project. From an early stage we decided that the project should focus squarely on the 'cream brick frontier' of postwar suburbs, giving close attention to its most conspicuous material features, the house, the car and the neighbourhood.[10] I have been fortunate to draw on some of the interviews we jointly conducted with veterans of the postwar suburban boom.

The title page records a special, and sadly unrepayable, debt to another member of our group, Sheryl Yelland. Sheryl joined the project as a research assistant but soon assumed wider responsibilities. She collected much of the material from the daily press and motoring magazines for this volume and we jointly conducted most of the interviews with traffic engineers and anti-freeway activists used in Chapters 7 to 9. As a young wife and mother in the outer suburbs in the 1960s, she had vivid recollections of many of the issues examined in Chapter 2; we agreed that she should interview a number of female drivers and write the first draft. It has since been revised to add new material and merge the contents with the rest of the book, but many of the arguments of that chapter are hers. Sadly, Sheryl's untimely death in June 1999 meant that she did not give the completed manuscript the critical reading we both expected that she would. Elegant, efficient, and kind, Sheryl's passion for history expressed her own deep sense of social justice. Her contribution to this book is but a small part of her legacy.

I also wish to thank other scholars whose work and conversations have helped to shape my ideas, especially Bruce Bennett, Ray Brindle, Renate Howe, Ken Jackson, Paul Mees, Amanda Moore, Kevin O'Connor, Seamus O'Hanlon, Mark Peel, Peter Spearritt, Patrick Troy and Dean Wilson. I am grateful to the following people whose memories of the period I have drawn upon in the book: Olive Barker, Ted Barton, John Bayley, David Beauchamp, Dr John Birrell, Sally Browne, Joe Delaney, Ursula Draper, Neil Guerin, Clem and Nina Harris, Brian Howe, Trevor Huggard, Denise and Brian Hurley, Don and Shirley Knights, Andrew McCutcheon, Marion Miller, Baillieu Myer, Jessie Reed, Bill Saggers, Neil Underwood, David Yencken. I also thank several interviewees who wished to remain anonymous. The interpretation I have placed upon their words is of course my own. Tony Dingle kindly read and commented on draft chapters, and colleagues in the History program at

The End of the Horse-and-Buggy Era. Melbourne's last horse-drawn cab.
(Photo Mark Strizic, 1957)

the Australian National University offered me hospitality when I was drafting chapters of the book.

I have a special obligation to John Iremonger who, as publisher and friend, has supported the project throughout, offering timely suggestions, encouragement and incisive comments on the chapter outline and several chapters. His death, shortly before the book was completed in September 2002, robs Australia of one of its most gifted public intellectuals. His colleagues at Allen & Unwin, Rebecca Kaiser and Colette Vella, have been meticulous and supportive editors.

For permission to consult or reproduce original materials I thank The Age Company Limited, ARRB Transport Research, Australian War Memorial, Carringbush Library, Coles Myer Archives, Cushen Clothing Company, Mrs Patricia Davies, Mr Bruce Dawe, Ford Australia, Ford Discovery Centre, Exxon Mobil, the Gandel Group of Companies, Mr Jack Hibberd, the estate of A. D. Hope, Holden Ltd, Mr Michael Leunig, Mr Gary Morgan and the staff of the Morgan Research Centre, Museum Victoria, National Archives of Australia, Oakleigh Motel, the Public Record Office of Victoria, the Royal Automobile Club of Victoria, Shell Australia, Professor Barry Smith, the State Library of Victoria, University of Melbourne Archives and Vicroads. I am especially grateful to Wolfgang Sievers and Mark Strizic, the pre-eminent photographers of postwar Melbourne, for permission to reproduce some of their brilliant images.

Rosemary Johnston has helped me to find space for research and writing during years when administrative work threatened to displace them.

Barbara Davison has been the closest companion of my journeys for more than 30 years. In this, as in everything else, she has been an unfailing source of loving and practical support.

GD
January 2003

1
Dream Machines

War snuffs out lives and begets dreams. For servicemen and civilians alike, World War II was a time of deferred hopes and frustrated desires. For half a decade normal life was suspended, while people put their plans on hold. No sooner had the threat of defeat receded, however, than all the pent-up longings of the war years—sexual, scientific and material—were released. The 1940s and early 1950s were a time of new dreams in Australian society. 'If you don't have a dream, how you gonna make your dream come true?' asks Bloody Mary in Rogers and Hammerstein's 1949 musical *South Pacific*. While General MacArthur's troops were still fighting their way from island to island, politicians and planners conjured dreams of a happier future. Hollywood created the 'dream girl'. Newspapers held competitions to design the postwar 'dream home'. Detroit engineers drew plans of streamlined futuristic 'dream cars'. The war had shown how science and technology could be used to produce death and destruction; now there was a chance to show how they could be used for human betterment.[1]

War-weary Melburnians turned, in psychic compensation, to the quieter, safer lives they hoped to live once the conflict had ended. Their urban dreaming was strongly shaped, both positively and negatively, by the preceding decade of depression and war. They looked, not for a restoration of the pre-war world, but a radical remaking of it. Memories of dole queues and evictions were still painfully vivid in many minds. The war had relieved unemployment but the possibility of its return was still a lurking fear. Housing remained in short supply, there were tight

1

controls on rents and many families now lived in decrepit and over-crowded accommodation. Probably more than one-third of households contained boarders, old folk or young marrieds unable to find homes of their own.

Winning the war had required a drastic curtailment of people's freedoms, including their freedom of movement. Soldiers and civilians subject to manpower controls travelled far from home to work or fight. Army trains and convoys of trucks had priority on rail and road. Yet for almost everyone else travel was strictly rationed. 'Is your journey really necessary?' a large billboard asked travellers arriving at Melbourne railway stations. From mid-1942 a permit was required for any journey beyond the metropolitan area. Petrol was rationed and the owners of private cars were limited to 2000 miles of travel a year; many car owners simply garaged their vehicles, hoisting them on blocks and taking off the wheels until the war was over.[2] Within the metropolis itself the war had disrupted and constricted peacetime patterns of movement. Rationing forced many motorists to take to the train or tram, while more than one-third of wage-earners still walked or biked to work. Young women

During the war years, with most private cars off the road, Melbourne's public transport was stretched to breaking point. (PHOTO AUSTRALIAN WAR MEMORIAL)

from the eastern suburbs commuted across the city, through suburbs they had never glimpsed before, to work in the munitions factories of Maribyrnong and Deer Park.[3]

During the war, public transport patronage in Melbourne reached an all-time peak.[4] Since services were cut back to conserve fuel and labour, trains and trams were always overcrowded. At the main city terminals, passengers waited in ticket queues, and fought the crush of peak-time crowds on platforms and in subways. Workers who stood all day, and sometimes all night, to labour on lathes and assembly lines, continued to stand—or hung wearily on straps—as they made the long journey home. Even when the war was over, train and tram services were often halted by strikes and stoppages. Socialists looked forward to a time when public transport would be improved so that no-one had to stand or wait. But for Liberals, and an increasing number of ordinary citizens, public transport was forever associated with discomfort and regimentation. No wonder, then, that they craved the independence, privacy and mobility of the automobile. The attractions of the car were already strong enough; a decade of austerity had made them irresistible.

1945–1955: SEEING BUT NOT HAVING

Public opinion polls, an innovation of the war years, enable us to tap the public mood. In 1943 the Australian people were asked to rank their personal goals and expectations for the postwar period. Jobs came first, closely followed by better housing, and—much farther down the list, but still a lively presence in the imagination—a new car.[5] War Bonds posters urged thrifty Australians to save for a new postwar car, picturing a sleek red sedan of boldly futuristic design. In November 1944, when victory was certain if not yet in sight, the *Argus*, following the example of the New York Times, invited its readers to imagine their ideal postwar car. 'My idea of the postwar car', a typical correspondent replied, 'is that it should be a family car'. 'A medium powered car should be most suitable for Australian conditions', agreed another. Roomier and more powerful than the pre-war English Morrises, Austins and Singers, yet smaller and less ostentatious than the American Chevrolets, Fords and Buicks, the ideal Australian car would have a sturdy chassis suitable for rough Australian roads, a four- to six-cylinder engine of no more than 14 to 20 horsepower, a closed metal body rather than a canvas hood, and a roomy boot for carrying luggage and household equipment. The gear shift should be mounted on the steering column, rather than the floor, so as to accommodate two passengers as well as the driver across the front seat. Most correspondents were more interested in the utilitarian features of the ideal car than its styling. The car should be 'plain', 'practical', 'simple' and constructed on 'proven' and 'reliable' mechanical principles. Like the modern house, the modern car, with its clean straight lines, stripped of useless ornament, was a response as much to material scarcity as to international fashion.[6] 'Streamlining', rear engines and other modern design features were all very well, but not if they added to the cost or detracted from the reliability of the new vehicle. The new Australian car should cost no more than economy models elsewhere. 'Let's have a car in keeping with the English and American price, few can afford £400 or £500', one reader urged.

A few idealists put forward their own designs, arguing that Australia had the opportunity to take the best of the world's automotive technology, European as well as British and American, and produce a car that was ideally suited to Australian conditions. While eager to embrace modernist design principles, such as 'streamlining', they justified them on functional rather than aesthetic grounds. Rather than reinforcing the pre-war hierarchy of classes and styles, many writers sought to promote a democratic automobilism, embodied, for example, in the European people's cars such as the German Volkswagen and the Czech Tatra, often preferring their rational rear-engined layout to the allegedly unsafe and uneconomic front-engined American and British models.[7]

From the late 1940s Australian motoring magazines carried regular feature articles on 'Dream Cars' or 'Cars of the Future' describing the latest design fantasies from the drawing boards of Bristol or Detroit. The 'visioneers'—the engineers and designers who attempted to chart the future of the car—often took their inspiration from the newest frontier of travel, the skies. Where aeroplane designers had recently gone the car designer, they anticipated, would soon follow. By the early 1950s British car manufacturers were experimenting with gas turbines and predicting that the average motorist would be driving a jet car within ten years.[8] By the middle of the decade the latest models from Detroit were sprouting fins, wings and tails like jet fighters. Perhaps cars would even turn into planes, some designers thought. In 1955 the Bristol Car company outlined its plans for a 'helicar', a car with rotor blades like a helicopter, which would enable the hard-pressed businessman to escape

Cars in a 100 years time!

THEY MAY TRAVEL ON LAND SEA AND IN THE AIR

In the expansive 1950s the 'visioneers' of Detroit imagined a new generation of cars capable of travelling on water and in the air, as well as on land. (ROYALAUTO, 1957)

traffic jams by literally taking off. 'Cars in 100 Years Time! THEY MAY TRAVEL ON LAND, SEA AND IN THE AIR' the *Royalauto* predicted in 1957. An accompanying illustration depicts a jet-powered float plane approaching a giant space dome, as guests arrive at a party in the year 2050. In 1958 Ford had announced its 'Glideair Project', with the objective of producing a car without wheels that would glide up to 100 feet in the air on cushions of air or 'levapads'. Soon, it seemed, American motorists would be able to drive across the Atlantic to Europe, provided, of course, the driver had a little 'navigational background'.[9]

In an age of austerity, the 'dream car' was also a symbol of comfort. British luxury cars of the 1920s and 1930s, with their shiny black paint-work, deep leather seats and walnut-panelled dashboards, maintained the craftsmanship of the high-class coach-builder. Quality and comfort were necessarily for the few who could afford these rare and costly vehicles. American car manufacturers of the 1940s and 1950s took a different approach. They applied the techniques of mass production to provide mechanical luxuries for everyone. '1948 Car May Even Wash Itself' an American correspondent predicted in 1945. The future car would have seats that could be adjusted up and down as well as backwards and forwards, built-in jacks to hoist them from the ground at the touch of a button, built-in radios, picnic refrigerators and even televisions. Luxury was redefined as provision of 'labour-saving' gadgets.[10]

Melburnians had to wait almost half a decade for these paper dreams of automotive progress to be realised. The first postwar Melbourne Motor Show opened in the Exhibition Buildings in May 1949. Its organiser was the pioneer motorist and motoring journalist Horrie Harrison. Harrison, 'the man behind the wheel', had long been a force in the Melbourne motor business. He claimed to be the third person in Victoria to have driven a petrol-powered vehicle, later worked as a public relations man for the Vacuum Oil Company and had organised every Melbourne Motor Show since 1925. The dollar shortage, which had restricted car imports, had thwarted his ambition to revive the show in 1947 and 1948, but at last 'the man behind the wheel' had his way. The city was still emerging from wartime austerity and the organisers had to negotiate an exemption from the electricity restrictions occasioned by strikes on the New South Wales coalfields for the show to open at night. More than 20 000 people queued up on opening day to hear Lieutenant-Governor Sir Edmund Herring pay tribute to the car as the unsung hero of the war. 'The enemy was defeated because the Allies had better vehicles', he declared. In peacetime too, the car was to be an index of national progress. 'The Australian standard of living depends on the sort of motor transport available', Herring added.[11]

Since the 1920s Australian motorists had shown a strong preference for American cars. They were bigger, more powerful, more rugged and better suited to Australian conditions than British makes. But in 1949 only a few American models, including a low-slung Hudson and a new Buick, were exempted from the Australian Government's effective ban on American imports. So more than 90 per cent of the exhibits were British. 'Streamlining Comes Belatedly to British Cars', a journalist covering the show observed, somewhat begrudgingly.[12] The Rolls-Royce Silver Wraith, its design previously unchanged for more than twenty years, had acquired more flowing lines while the sleek new Bristol sports saloon was based on a modernistic Italian design. Compared with the dream cars glimpsed in American magazines, however, the standard

British models—the Ford Anglia, the Morris Minor, the Austin A40 and the Singer—seemed cramped and boxy. Prices, even for the cheapest models, were high and customers were obliged to wait for anything between six months and two years before delivery. More exciting, but with a higher price tag and an even longer waiting list, was 'Australia's Own Car', the brand-new Holden.

For most of the 200 000 visitors who passed through the turnstiles over the following weeks, the motor show remained an occasion for daydreaming rather than turning dreams into reality. 'It was a day of wonder, of seeing, but not having', a journalist shrewdly observed. On Family Day the children clambered excitedly over the shiny new models. Dad slid behind the wheel and sank appreciatively into the soft leather upholstery. Mum nervously clutched her purse, not daring to hope, not willing to dispel his dreams. 'Well, I'll think it over', dad would say at last, knowing that until prices fell or his wages rose, their dreams must remain unfulfilled.[13]

Horrie Harrison appreciated their dilemma: 'Makers say they are satisfying the people's needs, but I believe present-day models have too much tinsel and cost too much', the veteran motorist declared. 'Con Rod', writing in the Royal Automobile Club of Victoria (RACV) *Radiator*, agreed. 'At a time when so many thousands of people desire transport rather than trappings it is little short of amazing that so much "styling", glamor, glisten and gadgetry has been permitted to retard volume production and to enhance costs.'[14]

'Dream cars' for a few or 'people's cars' for the million? The question had appeared in many guises during the early postwar years as businessmen and politicians sought to balance the pressure of rising material expectations with democratic demands for social equality. Labor had sought to restrain demand and promote social equality by rationing petrol and building materials, limiting the size of new dwellings and restricting car imports. The Liberals, who would take power at the end of 1949, yearned to take off the controls, to allow demand and supply to find their own level. The sooner the middle class got their cars the quicker the workingman would get his, they thought. 'A car is as essential to a middle class man as a radio or a refrigerator', E. J. Harrison, the Liberals' Transport spokesman asserted in 1947.[15]

Yet in 1949 car ownership was still a prize far beyond the reach of most workingmen. An increasing number of Australians knew how to drive. In 1951 almost two-thirds (64 per cent) of Australian men and one-fifth (19 per cent) of women held driver's licences and only a year later the proportions had increased to 75 per cent and 25 per cent. But the supply of cars lagged far behind the numbers of drivers. In 1945 there were two and a half licensed Victorian drivers for every private vehicle and it was not until the mid-1950s that the ratio fell below two to one.[16] A survey of family expenditure commissioned by the economist Colin Clark, then official statistician to the Queensland Government, found that no other form of consumption was as income-dependent as motoring. 'The motor car is, as yet, a rich man's hobby', he concluded.[17] In 1951 barely one Melburnian in eight, or roughly one household in three, owned a car. A survey of metropolitan travelling habits carried out in that year showed that only 15 per cent of journeys to work were made by car. (Compare 26 per cent by train; 22 per cent by tram, 8 per cent by bus and 10 per cent by bicycle or on foot.)[18]

Many would-be motorists' hopes centred on the production of a small, low-cost 'people's car'. Early in 1949 hundreds of Melburnians replied to an advertisement by the Commonwealth Disposals Commission offering two captured 1940 model Volkswagens, or 'German People's Cars'. Although the Lieutenant-Governor attributed the Allies' victory to their better vehicles, many people thought the Allies had something to learn from the 'Hitler Car', as one newspaper dubbed it.[19] In 1946 Laurence Hartnett, former managing director of General Motors Holden (GMH) and Commonwealth Director of Ordnance Production, had actually travelled to Germany at the suggestion of Labor's Minister of Postwar Reconstruction, John Dedman. Dedman had learnt that the Volkswagen plant at Wolfsburg, formerly owned by the Nazi Party, was up for sale to meet the cost of German war reparations. Could he buy the plant, ship it out, and make the VW in Australia?, Dedman enquired. After three weeks Hartnett concluded the plan was unworkable: the Volkswagen could be produced cheaply only with very high volume production, much higher than the small Australian market could support. But the dream of a people's car remained with Hartnett. He imported a prototype small car designed by a Frenchman, J. A. Grégoire, and took the Prime Minister, Ben Chifley, for a spin. 'It's a bit small', Chifley remarked, 'but that probably doesn't matter. Let's make it the working-man's car.' Plans to build a manufacturing plant for the 'Hartnett' car at Frankston won initial support from the Victorian Liberal and Commonwealth Labor governments but the venture collapsed under the combined weight of financial, technical and political difficulties.

But Hartnett's was not the only attempt to produce an Australian people's car. In 1945 the Collingwood company Die Casters had unveiled plans for a 10-horsepower Australian-made saloon. Ten years later, two Oakleigh engineers, Harper and Gray, launched the 'Edith', a three-wheeler with a rear-mounted two-stroke engine—ideal, so it was claimed, as second car for the suburban housewife. In 1958 the Goggomobile, 'Australia's first mass-produced fibreglass car', was launched.[20]

Once the war was over, popular opinion consolidated around the idea of the medium-sized, medium-priced 'family sedan'. The 'hundreds' of replies to a reader survey by the *Australian Monthly Motor Manual* in 1946 showed that most people favoured a four-door, 25-hp six-passenger sedan with a top speed of about 70 mph. The body should be 'naturally streamlined', with a bulging rear trunk, engine at the front, built-in headlamps and a steel rather than canvas roof. Black with green upholstery was the favourite colour scheme.

Prime Minister Chifley launches the first Holden, 'Australia's Own Car', at Fisherman's Bend, 1948. (NATIONAL ARCHIVES OF AUSTRALIA)

The ideal car should cost no more than £400–500 and its would-be owner expected to keep it for about five years. Like the *Argus* correspondents, those surveyed overrepresented the well-to-do minority of car owners and enthusiasts; but their opinions were so nearly unanimous that it probably represents a fair consensus of wider opinion.[21]

The Holden, launched by Prime Minister Ben Chifley at Fisherman's Bend on 29 November 1948—was a striking realisation of Australians' wartime dreams. Six cylinders, four doors, five or six passengers, 20 horsepower, column gear shift, robust chassis and suspension, 'a conservatively streamlined body which is unlikely to be outmoded by new models'—only the relatively high price (£760) would have disappointed the dreamers of 1944.[22] 'We have sought to design a car for Australian conditions somewhere between the big American car and the small English car, with an eye on economical operation in view of the high price of petrol here', explained Mr. J. R. Holden, a director of GMH.[23]

The 'family car' was a concept that chimed nicely with the ideals of the 1950s, when prosperity, domestic privacy and the postwar baby boom had refocused people's aspirations around the suburban family as a unit of consumption as well as social organisation. The seating plan of the family sedan—dad in the driver's seat, mum beside him, and the kids in the back—was as powerful a symbol of domesticity as Australians had known since the 1850s when father had taken up his traditional place at the head of the dining table to carve the Sunday joint. According to a popular American radio program, the family that prayed together stayed together. But in the 1950s and 1960s, as millions of Australian families took to the road, the Sunday drive was quickly supplanting the Sunday church service as the favourite celebration of family togetherness.

STRETCHING, DOUBLING UP AND MAKING DO

For more than a decade after the war, far more people wanted cars than could afford or obtain them. Britain had emerged from the war heavily indebted to the United States, and for half a decade trade between sterling countries like Australia and the United States was curbed by a shortage of American dollars. All imported goods, especially luxury goods from the United States such as cinema films and high-priced

During the postwar US dollar shortage, Australian families were obliged to cut their dreams to the austere proportions of an English saloon. (Author's copy)

cars, were in short supply or simply unobtainable. In the 1920s American cars had outsold British cars in Australia by five or six to one but in the late 1940s English cars outsold American.[24] Morris Minors, Triumphs, Hillmans and Singers were more numerous than Chevs and

Fords. In John Brack's 1955 painting *The Car* a suburban family look out through the windows, not of an FX Holden, but of a British-built Triumph Mayflower.

Import controls and the pegging of prices on new and old vehicles created a long backlog of demand and a vigorous black market in used cars. In 1948 there were more than 73 000 outstanding applications for imported cars and more than 90 per cent of used cars were estimated to be sold on the black market. To compound the motorist's worries, petrol was still rationed. Only at the end of 1949, after the courts had upheld appeals by car dealers against the import regulations, did the federal Labor government finally lift them, and only in February 1950, after the Menzies Liberal Government came to power, was petrol rationing finally abolished.[25]

Throughout the 1950s motoring organisations upheld two contradictory propositions—that motoring was no longer a luxury but a necessity, and that the costs of motoring were too high for the average family man. A car was something that the family needed, even though they could not afford it. Governments might make cars more affordable by lowering the taxes on imports, fuel and third-party insurance. In the meantime the ordinary motorist could resolve this contradiction between what he desired, or needed, and what he could afford, by either economising— for example, by riding a motorcycle or driving an old bomb—by cutting other items of expenditure, such as housing, food or alcohol, or by buying a car on terms.

Two wheels were considerably cheaper than four, and a motorcycle might satisfy the desire for mobility and speed almost as well as a car. But it was obviously less comfortable, less commodious and more dangerous. The late 1940s saw a brief upsurge in motorcycle registrations. In 1947 the *Australian Monthly Motor Manual* observed the appearance of 'a new type of motor cyclist . . . the would-be motorist who cannot get a car and takes the next line of action, the cycle. Many sedate travellers, shorn of a petrol allowance during the war years have again become accustomed to the open air of the open road.'[26] But the revival of motorcycling as a form of mass transport was a trend that did not last. By the early 1950s, as wages rose and vehicles became more affordable, the cyclists quickly became drivers again.

For the family man, an old car was better than a new bike. In 1952 when a new Holden cost £1200, or more than twice a workingman's yearly wages, he could buy a pre-war Humber or Studebaker or a three-year-old Morris Minor or Vauxhall for less than half that sum.[27] For more than a decade after the war the old bomb was almost as common a sight on the city's roads as the new 'dream car'. In 1955 nearly 30 per cent of Australian cars were prewar models and five years later about 19 per cent were still more than ten years old.[28] A few enthusiasts professed to prefer their old bombs to the shiny new models. Harry Pollock, a keen fisherman, boasted that his old prewar tourer ran better on unmade roads, and was cheaper to run than a newer model. He could sit on the running board to eat his lunch and throw his freshly caught fish on the back seat without fear of spoiling the upholstery. To the lucky owners of new cars, such claims were mere rationalisations. 'We can't all be millionaires', Jonathan Edwards agreed. 'I don't mind admitting I've owned old cars in the past, because then I couldn't afford a new one. But as soon as I had enough cash to cast off those worn out old heaps I bought a new one as fast as I could get into the nearest showroom.' How could the old rattletrap compare with the new sedan with its quiet engine, wind-up windows, comfortable upholstery and heating?[29]

Old bombs, their critics said, were a hazard to other road users as well as to their owners. 'The Government should force dangerous jalopies off the road', urged the secretary of the Automobile Chamber of Commerce. But when an old bomb was all that many workingmen could afford, the prospect of its banishment from the road touched a raw nerve. The Labor deputy premier John Galvin refused to 'set up class distinction among motorists' by putting old bombs off the road. The police commissioner Selwyn Porter even paid a tribute to the bomb owner as a 'genuine car lover who loves a car for what it is, and not because it is a piece of jewellery to adorn his wife or a method of increasing his popularity'. Contrary to the myth, police car tests had shown that the owners of old cars were often more careful drivers, and knew more about the mechanical side of driving, than new car owners. 'Often a bomb owner is a family man', Porter explained. 'He has not a big income. What he has is carefully applied to bringing up his family and giving them the pleasure of a week-end outing which ends in a wholesome picnic or fishing expedition.'[30]

Middle-class, middle-aged males were overrepresented among new car owners. Market research carried out by Roy Morgan for GMH in the early 1950s showed that professional, managerial and small businessmen comprised about 33 per cent of new Holden owners (though only 16 per cent of the polled population), while white-collar workers (22 per cent of new Holden owners) were represented approximately in proportion to the poll sample (23 per cent). Skilled tradesmen (18 per cent of new owners, 28 per cent of the workforce), on the other hand, were only two-thirds as likely, and semi-skilled and unskilled workers half as likely (10 per cent of new owners and 22 per cent of the workforce) to buy a new model of 'Australia's Own Car'. Only 10 per cent of the new owners were under 30 and 22 per cent over 50. Only one in twenty was a female.[31]

Melbourne, a city of far-flung suburbs, appears to have embraced the automobile more eagerly than Sydney, with its stronger public transport network and higher housing densities. In 1953 a poll conducted for GMH found that 38 per cent of a random sample of Sydney men and women had a car compared with 51 per cent of Melburnians.[32]

Many people who had witnessed the evictions and foreclosures of the Depression years were loath to put themselves in debt, especially in order to finance a depreciating asset like a car. Until the mid-1950s fears of inflation had kept the supply of consumer credit under stringent control. Finance companies often required a deposit of 33 to 40 per cent or more on the purchase of a new car. Australians remained wary of hire-purchase, except for lower-priced consumer items, such as refrigerators and washing machines, which could be paid off quickly. In 1953 a Gallup poll found that almost twice as many people approved of buying a car on terms (59 per cent) as disapproved (35 per cent).[33] Yet only 5 per cent of those polled were actually buying a car on terms. While Australians and Americans devoted a similar proportion of their personal incomes to hire-purchase of household consumer items, Americans spent more than four times as much of their incomes on car repayments as Australians.[34] In the mid-1950s, however, there was a rapid expansion in the availability of consumer credit. Now it was possible to buy a car, new or used, on a deposit of no more than 10 or 20 per cent with payments spread over several years. By 1958 more than four out of ten Australians polled were buying some item on terms—usually a home (23 per cent), more rarely a refrigerator (10 per cent) or a car (9 per cent). Almost 40 per cent of new cars were purchased on terms.[35] Few of the eager new buyers stopped to calculate the real cost of their purchase. A typical loan on a £1000 car on a 25 per cent deposit repaid over two years added £284 to the purchase price and left the owner with an asset worth perhaps £650–700 at the end of the period—a total real cost of almost £600. Then the car had to be insured and maintained. Some purchasers were tempted by low deposits and easy terms into overcommitting themselves.[36] If the unwary buyer fell behind in his payments, a pair of burly men in ill-fitting suits might arrive on his door with a writ of repossession and take his prize away.

1955–1960: THE PURSUIT OF STYLE AND STATUS

The 1940s had been a period of high suppressed demand and limited choice. During the following two decades the pendulum swung strongly in the consumer's favour. Cars rapidly became more affordable. Between 1950 and 1960 a new Holden rose gradually in price from £900 to £1200 (33 per cent), much slower than the retail price index (60 per cent). Meanwhile average weekly male earnings more than quadrupled.[37] Throughout this period Australians remained, next to Americans and Canadians, the most automobilised people on earth.

By 1953 motor car ownership had risen to one Australian in five; by 1962 it was almost one in three. The ratio of cars to licensed drivers improved more slowly: after rising from 35 to 60 per cent in the late 1940s it remained fairly stable throughout the 1950s and early 1960s. The one-car family and the family car were becoming the norm. Market surveys of the early 1960s show that it was dad who generally drove, though mum might have a licence and 'borrow' the car for shopping or important social occasions. In 1957 more Australian men drove cars to work (51 per cent) than travelled by public transport (40 per cent), but working women were still more than twice as likely to travel by train, tram or bus (70 per cent) as to drive or be driven (30 per cent). The suburban housewife remained largely a captive of the house and her immediate neighbourhood. In 1960 most Melbourne housewives' weekday outings were made either by walking (40 per cent) or public transport (20 per cent) or in a car driven by someone else (10–12 per cent). Only about 10 per cent of women seem to have regularly driven themselves, although on Fridays—the traditional shopping day—it rose to 20 per cent.[38]

In the late 1940s people were captivated by dream cars, but framed their expectations around the economical, unadorned family car. As this suppressed demand was gradually satisfied, and the manufacturers' production capacity increased, the balance swung back in favour of consumers who now became fussier about looks and comfort. A 1960 survey of Australian car buyers' preferences found that the modest requirements expressed by contributors to the *Argus*'s ideal car competition in 1944 had been far exceeded. 'Better-looking' and more 'comfortable' were the now more important characteristics than fuel economy, power or size.[39]

In the late 1950s, as penetration of the market neared saturation point, American manufacturers had begun to anticipate a fall-off in demand, and their Australian counterparts soon echoed their fears.[40] The cost of producing a luxury car, with the full repertoire of gadgets and styling features, was only marginally greater than the cost of the standard model, but motorists were often prepared, or could be persuaded, to pay much more. This was the economic logic behind the otherwise bizarre stylistic gyrations of the late 1950s. 'Under-simplification' was the obverse of overproduction.[41]

In 1950 the majority of new Australian cars were still British-made, but by the mid-1950s the majority were either American-made or made in Australia by one of the two major American firms, General Motors and Ford, which had established local assembly plants. In September 1960, twelve years after General Motors had launched its first Australian-made car, the Holden, its American rival Ford launched a glamorous competitor, the Falcon. 'The invader has fired the first publicity shots and the great car war—Ford Falcon v. Holden—is well and truly on', noted one observer. Compared with the sober ceremony at Fisherman's Bend in 1948 the launch of the Falcon was a flamboyant affair with scantily clad dancing girls, a ten-piece orchestra and generous supplies of food and drink for members of the motoring press.[42]

The most publicised, if not the most powerful, weapon in the new car war was style. Styling enabled manufacturers to reconcile the standardisation required for mass production with the demands of an increasingly status-conscious motoring public. Under Robert Menzies' Liberals, Australians were encouraged to reorient their social identity from the traditional focus of the political parties—the relations of production—to the relations of consumption—the private world of family, home and suburb.[43] Rather than fretting about the gulf between boss and worker, the suburban family man was offered a new dignity based upon his status as defined by the style of his own home, car and repertoire of consumer goods. The more alienated his working life, the more frenetic his pursuit of status symbols. The American sociologist Vance Packard had written of 1950s suburbia as a society of status-seekers. Car manufacturers had catered to the desire for consumerist definitions of status by developing a totem pole of brands and models rising from the humble Chev and Ford through the middle-class Dodge and Studebaker to the bloated magnificence of the Lincoln and Cadillac.[44]

The Australian car market was too small to support the astonishing variety of makes and models available to the American or European motorist. But local manufacturers sought, in modest ways, to follow the same logic. When cars became status objects, each make, model, colour and style could express something about the identity of its owner. The 'featurism' that architect Robin Boyd had seen as the besetting sin of Australian architecture had its counterpart in the motorist's desire to individualise his mass-produced car by the addition of personally chosen paint colours, seat covers, cabin accessories and chromium adornments. 'Today we have the age of features', the *Sun* remarked in

Launched in 1960 with American-style ballyhoo, Ford's Falcon sedan was a glamorous rival to the dominant Holden. (FORD DISCOVERY CENTRE)

1956, noting the range of new technical features—power steering, automatic transmission, radios and other accessories available as extras with the new car. But as Boyd complained, it was the 'multi-coloured effects' rather than the new technical features that became the prime selling points on new Australian-built cars.[45]

Journalists covering the Melbourne Motor Show were increasingly interested in the look of the cars on display. 'Glamorous', 'stylish', 'dazzling', 'colourful', 'sleek', 'futuristic'—often coupled with the word 'American'—were the standard descriptions. 'Styling—or the car's appearance—has become the biggest selling feature of automobiles in America today', the American correspondent of *Wheels* observed in 1955. 'It is said that a dollar spent on styling features is worth five on technical improvements.'[46] Australian motor manufacturers noted that, as the market reached saturation point, prospective customers became 'choosier'.[47] In the late 1940s designers had anticipated that new technology would make cars that were faster, more versatile, more economical and more comfortable. By the 1950s it was already clear that the space age had more to do with the style than the performance of the American automobile. 'In bodywork the trend is towards aerodynamic designs with high stabiliser fins and "jet" intakes and exhausts', a journalist observed in 1956. The 'Firebird' and the 'Golden Rocket' competed with the 'Strato-Streak'. Ford's experimental car, the X-100, which had starred opposite Lauren Bacall in the 1955 Cinemascope movie *Woman's World*, was codenamed like an experimental space vehicle. Modernists had expected the logic of mass production to spawn a new aesthetic of simple, functional forms but, as the critic Reyner Banham perceived in 1955, it was the symbolism, rather than the engineering principles, of the machine that most influenced the appearance of the automobile.[48]

While Australian motor magazines eagerly followed American trends, and their readers may have enjoyed the chance to daydream about their future car, there was a bluntly realistic tone in Australian responses to the 'dream car'. 'So far as the various American cars of the future are concerned, they're likely to remain in the future so far as most Australian motorists are concerned, and a large proportion of Americans too', the *Royalauto* observed in 1954.[49] When market researchers asked prospective buyers to say what factors influenced their choice of a car, 'appearance' (5 per cent) came a long way behind more practical considerations such as 'reliability' (32 per cent), 'price' (22 per cent) and 'performance' (15 per cent).[50] Local motoring writers looked on with bemusement as the American manufacturers sought to outdo each other with ever bigger engines, tailfins, headlights and chromium grilles. From the mid-1950s cars became more colourful, with two-tone speed flashes and decorative strips. 'The lady buyer purchased a car with a colour scheme closely matching her clothes', an American survey had allegedly shown. While dad peered under the bonnet and enquired about miles per gallon, mum tried out the seats for comfort and looked for 'better trim and pleasing colours'. But glamour always had a price, and economy and practicality, rather than style, were generally the determining considerations for most Australian car buyers.[51]

Only a handful of left-wing intellectuals and disenchanted suburb-anites challenged the seemingly relentless advance of automobilism. Albert Walker, a 31-year-old engineering draftsman, had emigrated to Melbourne from Britain in 1946. He worked in a city engineering firm, a go-ahead concern run by a man he did not respect, and commuted by train to Glen Iris, a middle-class suburb about 13 kilometres out, where he lived with his wife Margery and their two Australian-born children. His work gave him an appreciation of things mechanical, but he did not share the modernists' confidence in the civilising power of machines. He was an independent-minded, peace-loving man, drawn towards Quakerism and apprehensive that the world might yet erupt into nuclear catastrophe. Like the English socialist, William Morris, he was inclined to feel 'that the machine is in many ways a menace'.

One winter evening in 1955 he accepted a ride home in a friend's car.

> The subject of cars was brought up and I mentioned that wherever I had been, the car question had caused a lot of trouble. It seems to be the cause of petty jealousies and if someone has a car provided by the firm he is looked on as being outstandingly privileged. As far as I am concerned it is altogether silly and I am . . . pleased that I haven't got one and can't even drive. It saves a lot of trouble and bad feeling. On the other hand it gets more difficult to travel in Melbourne without a car. Bus fares are high and trams are chaotic. Trains are in many instances sadly out-of-date and altogether travelling by public trans-port is very wearing. The only consolation is that I am able to read more than if I had a car, although this doesn't console me on hot days in summer when it would make it so much easier to go to the beach with the family, and street corners can be awfully cold in winter, waiting for buses and trams.[52]

Accustomed to the good train and bus services in more compact English cities, Walker continued to hanker for them in the midst of Melbourne's sprawling suburbs. He considered the average suburban garden extravagantly large, and the average suburbanite's obsession with gardening and home improvement excessive. On a salary of £25 a week (more than twice the basic wage) he could better afford a car than most, but still he hesitated. 'All the people in Ashburton Road [his own street] have a car, and some of them have two and we are the exception in this respect, even though we have a double garage', he observed. Conscious, and even a little proud, of his unorthodoxy, he was tempted by gestures of open defiance. 'Tonight Margery and I wondered whether we could get a horse and buggy cheaply. We could then all go out into the country in style, even if a little unorthodox. It would certainly cause a stir in Glen Iris where everyone (except the Walkers) seems to have car, even two.' When he did take the family on a train excursion to the Dandenongs, he acknowledged the inconvenience—'a major undertaking as we have no car'—but consoled himself that it was 'more exciting as an expedition'. Besides, he could see that if the cars multiplied and the suburban sprawl continued, there would be little bush left for them to visit.

By the accumulation of small frustrations—missed trains, hours shivering on tramstops, late-night taxis home from the Friends Meeting House on the other side of town—he was inching closer to the moment of surrender. He toyed with the idea of buying a motorcycle, but dismissed it as 'of no use to the family'. His diary stopped for two years yet when it resumed he still had not taken the plunge. Gradually the truth emerged—the prospect of driving actually frightened him. It was only in 1958 when he finally left his old employer and took a new job at the State Electricity Commission that he was obliged to confront the problem. 'One snag which has arisen is that I must be able to drive a car, and having seen the city at its busiest I didn't altogether look forward to it', he admitted. 'I can't drive at all, and this is rather rare in Australia, especially amongst men of my age.' His employer arranged for lessons at the Modern Motor School, and through January and February, he slowly began to conquer his fears. 'I'll be glad when I've got it over and am able to be more calm about it', he confessed.

Albert Walker was a reluctant convert to the motor age. We may admire his determination not to be drawn into the suburbanite's pursuit of status and his recognition of the way in which the rising tide of traffic was polluting the streets and impinging on the city's precious rim of bushland. We may even share some of his scepticism about the real benefits of a mechanised society. Yet it was fear, as much as high principle, that held him back, just as it was the freedoms conferred by the car—the ability to travel more quickly, more comfortably and more conveniently—that finally persuaded him to surrender.

1960–1975: THE STATION WAGON, THE TWO-CAR FAMILY AND THE GROWTH OF THE SUBURBS

The postwar years had witnessed a great national contest between ideals of liberty and equality. Would Australians create a society based on ostentatious wealth for the few or decent prosperity for the many? By the early 1960s rising affluence had softened that choice. When everyone, seemingly, was acquiring new status symbols—houses, cars, washing machines and televisions—it was possible to believe that everyone was also rising in the world, even though their relative positions remained the same, or even declined. The new suburbs were the material expression of a society still fundamentally unequal in economic and political power, but strikingly uniform in style and manners.

The evolution of the Australian suburban house, from the boxy austerity of the first postwar plans to the sprawling luxuriance of the triple-fronted cream brick veneer is one illustration of this transition.[53] The emergence in the late 1950s of the Holden station wagon was another. 'The station wagon has become a definite part of our Australian way of life', a motoring journalist remarked in 1959.[54] An all-purpose family vehicle suitable for shopping, camping, picking up children from school or transporting household refuse to the tip, the station wagon was a mobile embodiment of a middling-class suburban family life. In 1955 *Australian Motor Manual* had pondered the reasons behind the growing popularity of the station wagon in the United States. 'Two of the biggest factors attested to the phenomenal demand are dispersed shopping centres, which have been cropping up all over the country, and the increasing number of families with young children. The accelerated increase in suburban living has also been credited with the spurt in station wagon demand.'[55] As Australia followed in America's path so, the motoring papers forecast, would automobile fashions follow.

The only station wagons available in 1955 were imported English ones like the boxy little Hillman Husky or the Austin A40 Countryman.

Pictures of the more capacious American Ford Ranchwagons and
Ramblers appeared in the motoring papers but they were unavailable
on the local market. The motoring press was 'beseiged' with readers
asking 'why a reasonably priced station wagon has not been available in
Australia' and a few enterprising local businessmen even offered
improvised substitutes. Ted Bailey, a 'Brunswick motoring enthusiast',
created more than 3000 station wagons by inserting doors and windows into panel vans, while a Port Melbourne firm offered a patented
metal hood, the 'Stationette', for converting utility trucks.[56] In 1957
Holden at last introduced its own Station Sedan, which soon dominated the rapidly growing market. Ford dealers enquired anxiously
about the company's plans to meet the competition but its only
response—the more expensive English-designed Zephyr—made little
impression on the market. It was only in 1960 when Ford launched its
Falcon station wagon that Holden's market share began to decline, and
then only slowly.[57]

From the first, motoring writers emphasised the Holden station
wagon's ideal combination of looks, economy, practicality and reliability.
'The "mostest" motor car for the money available today', declared
Wheels. 'A capable, agile six-seater with ample room for carriage of light
goods, a moderate thirst, unassuming good looks, and uncanny capacity
for hard work.' Capable, agile, hardworking, temperate and ruggedly
good-looking—in describing the ideal car, the journalist might almost
have been describing the ideal Australian family man himself.[58]

It was not until the early 1960s that a clear majority of Melbourne
households had their own car and even in 1964 more than one-third of
households were carless. Melbourne was still largely laid out in accordance with the 'concentric-zonal' pattern familiar to geographers and
sociologists since the 1920s. While the working classes clustered in
congested inner city neighbourhoods, within walking distance of the
port, transport terminals and factories, the middle classes retreated to
leafy suburbs on the fringe, especially to the hillier, more picturesque
country to the south and east. As we might expect, owning a car was
largely an economic matter: while two-thirds of low-income households
were still carless, scarcely one-tenth of high-income earners—the 18 per
cent of households earning over $5000—had no car and 43 per cent
had two or more. In working-class Collingwood, Fitzroy and Richmond
half the households earned less than $2500 per annum and less than
30 per cent owned cars, while in middle-class Camberwell, Box Hill

In the 1960s the station wagon met the need of growing families for a vehicle but offered both workaday transport and holiday pleasure. (FORD DISCOVERY CENTRE)

and Doncaster scarcely a quarter of households earned less than $2500 per annum and more than 75 per cent owned cars.

It was along the cream-brick frontier of new middle-class suburbs that the car-owning habit advanced farthest and fastest. The biggest concentrations of car-owning families were in four wedges lodged between the old growth corridors established by the railways and tramways. One extended from Essendon towards Strathmore, Niddrie and Keilor. A second followed the upper Yarra valley through North Balwyn, Ivanhoe, Doncaster, Bulleen and Templestowe. The third and largest lay in the wide corridor of rolling hills between the Box Hill and Oakleigh lines in such suburbs as Nunawading, Mount Waverley and Vermont. And the smallest lay between the Oakleigh and Sandringham lines in Bentleigh and Moorabbin. In Doncaster and Waverley, the prototypical new executive suburbs, the suburban frontier had advanced hand-in-hand with the rise of the two-car household.

Between 1964 and 1971 the number of households in these suburbs had doubled and the proportion of households with two or more cars had also doubled from 19 to 41 per cent in Waverley and from 24 to 50 per cent—or almost twice the metropolitan average—in Doncaster.[59]

'The growth in multiple car ownership is a reflection of the increasing number of families living in the suburbs and forecasts show that this trend to suburban living will continue to rise in the years ahead with a corresponding increase in the level of multi-car ownership', the *Royalauto* had observed in 1964. 'The second car is becoming more and more a necessity for a family, especially when sons and daughters start work and increasingly the tendency is for them to work in suburban industrial areas rather than in the centre of the city.'[60]

In the mid-1960s the suburban housewife at last began to win the right to drive. 'The "hand that rocks the cradle" has a firm grip on the steering wheel', the RACV *Royalauto* observed in 1968.[61] Between 1968 and 1972 new female licence-holders, many of them probably wives and mothers, almost equalled males.[62] Manufacturers recognised the growing influence of the woman driver. 'Once the man chose the car and the woman the colour', the *Royalauto* had observed in 1964. But now, it claimed, 'many women drive the family car more often than their husbands'. Women used the car in different ways—'for short, around-town journeys, taking their husband to the station, the children to school, to do the shopping'.[63] They looked for different things in a car: more storage space for gloves and shopping bags, safe childproof door catches, light steering and pedals that were easy to reach. A 1972 survey by the Ford Motor Company found that while women were named as the owners of only 11 per cent of their new cars, many more were apparently bought by or for women but registered in men's names. The company estimated that women had a 'fairly strong deciding influence' in nearly half of all new car purchases. Contrary to the stereotype current among motoring drivers in the early postwar years, women were much more interested in a car's convenient size and economical operation than its high fashion colours or interior fabrics. 'They want a car they can handle in the congested streets, rather than something flashy and decorative. They want a car they can run within their budget.'[64]

Mum may have had more use for the family station wagon than dad, but hers was often a smaller, second-hand saloon, perhaps a Volkswagen, Morris Minor or Hillman Imp rather than dad's Holden or Falcon.

At the Motor Show. He looks enviously at the new sports car while her eye is trained on a sensible family car. (ROYALAUTO, 1955)

In 1955 Volkswagen had begun assembling cars at a new plant at Clayton in south-east Melbourne from parts manufactured in the very same German plant that Laurence Hartnett had almost brought to Australia eight years earlier. By 1960 almost 75 per cent of the

Australian Volkswagen was locally made and the 'beetle', as it was affec-
tionately known, had eclipsed the British makes in the Australian market.
Ironically, it was not as a people's car, a cheap family car for the workingman, but as a ladies' runabout and a young people's car that the VW
found its niche in the Australian market.

By the early 1970s, as the children of the postwar baby boom reached
their late teens, the growth in numbers of older female drivers was
eclipsed by the surge of younger male drivers. No sooner, it seemed,
had mum got her hands on the wheel of the family car than she was
having to compete with her growing sons and daughters. The only
answer, it seemed, was for the family to double up. From the early
1970s the ratio of cars to drivers, which had plateaued in the late 1960s,
began a steady upward rise. An increasing number of families were able
to afford two vehicles, typically a six-cylinder 'family car' for dad and a
smaller four-cylinder car for his wife or daughter. The buoyant sales of
the cheap and reliable Japanese-made Toyota Corollas and Mazda 323s
in the 1970s reflected the strength of this 'second car' market. A survey
in 1980 found that more than two-thirds of new small cars were sold to
family members other than the husband, and over half to women,
mainly wives and daughters. Driving to work or school remained the
most important single use of the small car, but shopping, leisure and
holiday travel were also becoming important.[65]

In the three decades since World War II, Melbourne had undergone
perhaps the most dramatic social transformation in its history. The
1850s had certainly witnessed faster population growth. And during
the 1880s Melbourne had built one of the most extensive public transport systems in the world. But no previous era had seen such a radical
change in the relationships between work and home, and between public
and private space. In 1951 scarcely one Melburnian in ten had jour-
neyed to work by car. By 1964 nearly one-third (31 per cent) were
driving or riding in a car. In 1974 the proportion had more than doubled
again to almost two-thirds (66 per cent) and by 1996 it was more than
three-quarters.[66]

Cities all over the world were undergoing a similar transformation,
and some Australian cities—Adelaide and Brisbane, for example—had
reached even higher levels of automobile dependence than Melbourne.
With hindsight, the automobilisation of postwar Melbourne might
almost seem inevitable. But it did not seem so to the returned soldiers
and their families who dreamed of their ideal car in 1944. Over the

following 30 years their 'dream machines' had changed in response to changing economic, social and political circumstances. The American firms that largely controlled the Australian motor industry had sought to cultivate an Australian image for their products, but in the long debate about the ideal Australian car, motorists and their passengers may also have exerted some influence.

The world actually created by the car was far removed from the blueprints of Detroit's 'visioneers'. Even before the oil price crisis of 1974 visitors to the annual motor shows had lost their first eager flush of enthusiasm. Visitors were now more interested in economy and performance than power or looks. Female prospective car purchasers rated the convenience and economy of new cars above their colour-coordinated accessories. 'To most Australians life without a car would be almost unthinkable', another motor show visitor noted in 1976.[67] But the more indispensable the car became, the less powerful was its hold on the imagination. The 'dream machine' had been a figment of that brief moment of postwar innocence when the car was still a chromium glint in the owner's eye, the first instalments had yet to be paid, and the road—soon to be filled by the roar of engines and the stench of petrol fumes—lay beckoning.

2

Women Take
the Wheel

Margery McKenna was furious. She had been surveying the glistening array of motor power in a Melbourne used car yard when a sign on the windscreen of a small car, the tiniest in the yard, caught her eye. 'ONE FOR MUM' it said. 'So much for the emancipation of women!' she retorted. 'To think the suffragettes chained themselves to the railings for this little beat-up bomb!'[1]

In the dream world of postwar consumerism the car was not only a symbol of male power and mastery. It also symbolised women's incomplete emancipation. Cars were gendered objects, conventionally dubbed 'she', and often designed in the voluptuous shapes of male desire. But cars had never been exclusively a male possession. In 1968, the year of Margery McKenna's annoyed outburst in the car yard, women for the first time outnumbered men among new applicants for Victorian driver's licences, although they remained a small minority of car owners. The liberated journalist had bridled at the insult of that condescending sign but to many Melbourne mums even a 'little beat-up bomb' could become the passport to a new sense of personal freedom.

Over a century earlier Victorian moralists had declared that 'a woman's place is in the home'. Men belonged to the workaday world of the city, with its money and materialism, its storm and stress. Women represented the domestic virtues and inhabited the tranquil and secluded world of the home and garden. Men, by implication, were mobile: they ventured out of the home each day, going wherever ambition and the market took them. Women, as the stable centre of domestic life, were more stationary: their expeditions for shopping or sociability were conventionally short and localised.[2]

This symbolism did not mirror life exactly, of course, and even in the Victorian era significant breaches were made in the wall between the two spheres. From the 1870s department stores sought to attract women customers by constructing ferneries, arcades and ladies' lounges designed to create a feminised semi-public zone in the midst of the city.[3] In the 1890s women cyclists made a daring foray into the streets, drawing the jocular disapproval of males. (Mockery would later also become the defensive male's favourite weapon against the female motorist.) The automobile promised a new era of female independence, although for twenty years or more, the costs and hazards of motoring restricted it to a minority of well-to-do lady adventurers. The *motoriste*, as she sometimes called herself, was a figure of self-conscious emancipation, whose mechanical enthusiasm, zest for speed and power, and sometimes mannish dress, set her apart from her more conventional sisters.[4] Male motorists hesitated to welcome women to their ranks. The Royal Automobile Club, unlike its New South Wales counterpart, had admitted female members from 1909, but closed its ladies' lounge in 1918, a move that precipitated the formation of a separate ladies' automobile club. The breach was not healed until 1928 when women were readmitted to the club.[5]

In times of national peril men voluntarily lowered the barriers to female mobility. During both World War I and World War II hundreds of women were recruited into the armed forces to drive and maintain delivery vans, buses and taxis on the home front. In the late 1940s many women also drove for voluntary civilian services or as private company employees. Under stringent wartime regulations, women had become better drivers than men, some observers believed.[6] In 1943 the RACV had predicted that, come peacetime, 'old jokes about the woman at the wheel would have to be revised'.[7] But a volunteer dressed in a glamorous uniform was more easily accepted than a female private motorist dressed in 'civvies' and by the 1950s, as servicemen were demobbed and women returned to their domestic role, the old tiresome jokes were still in vogue.

In the 1950s the female driver was still a lonely figure in a public world of men. Only about 43 per cent of Victorian adults held a licence but among women the proportion was fewer than one in ten.[8] The proportion of women among car owners surveyed by market researchers was lower still, about 8 per cent in 1952, 10 per cent in 1957, although many cars owned by men were probably regularly driven by women.[9] By 1961, however, one licence-holder in three was a woman and by the end of the decade the proportion had risen to 40 per cent.[10] Car ownership was more common among the middle aged and middle class, both male and female, than among either the old or the young. Country women were probably quicker than their sisters in the city to become automobilised.

The 'woman driver'—a term coined in 1920s, and often used pejoratively—was still a target for patronising advice, ridicule and outright hostility. She appeared as a stock figure of low humour in daily newspapers, the new locally published motor magazines and 'barber-shop magazines' like *Man, Pix, People, Smith's Weekly* and the *Sporting Globe*.[11] While the male reader was addressed, man-to-man, in technical articles on new car models or do-it-yourself car maintenance, the surrounding pages were sprinkled with cartoons, jokes and photographs lampooning the mechanical ineptitude of women drivers.

"One has to be prepared for all emergencies these days . . . that's why I always drive with my handbrake on."

The dotty, mechanically ignorant woman motorist remained a staple theme of cartoons in motoring magazines into the 1960s. (ROYALAUTO, 1965)

In the pages of the 1950s motoring magazines, women appear in three stereotypical roles. Buxom blondes sit next to the male driver, or recline languidly across the bonnet of his dream car, their curvaceous bodies reinforcing the sexual symbolism of the car. The stereotypical woman driver, on the other hand, is middle-aged, clumsy and confused. 'It's not the parking I dislike', says a woman motorist in one cartoon. 'It's the crunch while I'm doing it.' In another, a husband opens the garage door to find his car parked upside down. The one-word caption is 'Agnes!' If men patronised the woman driver, they were even more contemptuous of the third stereotypical figure: the hatchet-faced back-seat driver. In cartoonist's shorthand, the blonde on the bonnet is the motorist's lover, the dotty woman driver is his wife and the back-seat driver his nagging mother-in-law.[12] Forty years later, it is the obsessive repetition, as much as the offensiveness, of these stereotypes that strikes us. Designed to reinforce the authority of the man at the wheel, the misogynous humour of the motoring press also hints at the unacknowledged, even unconscious, fears and fantasies aroused by female drivers in some men's minds.

From the early 1950s female drivers began, quietly but firmly, to answer back. In feature items and letters, they asked, 'Who said we can't drive?' and pleaded with men to 'give the women a fair go'. Women contributed articles telling men what women thought of *their* driving and advising them to 'Lay off women drivers!' In 1959, a correspondent scolded the editor of the *Royalauto* for continuing to publish those 'funny sketches' depicting 'women drivers as nincompoops'.[13] Ann Clifford, the RACV's female motoring journalist, noted the male reaction to the new-found sense of power and freedom felt by many of her peers:

> When women drivers were fewer, men treated them with more courtesy . . . Nowadays we girls are brazenly hi-jacked out of parking spaces, bullied out of our right of way, abused, glared at and shouted down by so-called 'courteous' men . . . Maybe we have asked for it, daring to swarm into a male field like car driving. Still, my guess is that women drivers are here to stay.[14]

The RACV itself had come to see the wisdom of changing its tune. Already its allies and advertisers, the automobile manufacturers and retailers, had recognised the female driver as a market to be cultivated rather than a minority to be stigmatised. Once every dad had a car, business logic dictated that mum would eventually also get her chance.

LIBERTY AND UTILITY

From the first, women had recognised the liberating potential of the car. In the intimate politics of the suburban household, however, the freedom to drive was won only slowly, and often begrudgingly, from the 'man of the house'. The first tactical advances came as women demonstrated the utility of the car as a kind of household appliance, enhancing her traditional role as homemaker; only later did people recognise its effect in widening women's horizons and challenging their traditional role.

In 1947 an article in the RACV's journal *The Radiator* entitled 'Car as Blessing to Housewives' showed how driving helped the housewife. 'It is a toy, a necessity or an incomparable amenity, which lends colour and movement to her rather monotonous existence as a home-keeping body.' For a few well-to-do women it was a toy—'indispensable for prestige, and for fulfilling an intricate programme of social engagements'. But for the majority whose lives were devoted to 'home duties' it was 'almost a necessity'.

> Not only does it take her places, but it takes her away from 'the place'—that little plot with its house and garden, its clothes line, telephone and neighbours. All are very dear and necessary but they are not enough to fill the horizon from year's end to year's end . . . Most women these days find that the married state is no sinecure. There is plenty of work all day, every day, and even such labors of love for husband and offspring do weary even the most well-disposed wives and mothers, so that a car, once a luxury, is now almost a necessity.

It turned shopping from a chore to a pleasure, and helped to reconcile the physical and economic demands of the housewife's role. 'It is after all rather too much even for feminine versatility to play two roles so opposed as pack-horse and more or less glamorous wife and mother full of understanding for husband and children.' With a car at her disposal, she could take a neighbour along for company. Or she could take the children on a picnic, or her elderly parents on a trip 'to see the things that they read about in the papers—the new houses and bridges, the crowds at the sports meetings, the city streets and shops'. In 1947, as the context makes plain, the car was only '*almost* a necessity'. The writer assumes a world of limited mobility in which the lucky motoring housewife plays lady bountiful by expanding the horizons of parents, neighbours and children as well as her own.[15]

Of the housewifely roles described here, none was enhanced by the car as much as shopping. In 1947 Maie Casey, pioneer motorist and pilot, and wife of Liberal politician R. G. Casey, gave a stirring Mother's Day address. 'The women of Australia are not nearly well enough looked after', she claimed. A 'flood' of supportive letters poured into the *Argus*, mainly from middle-class readers from the eastern suburbs. Seventy-five per cent of women and 60 per cent of men identified household shopping as the most exhausting responsibility of the Melbourne 'housewife'.[16] Rationing was still in force, and few families had refrigerators or motor cars, so many women shopped almost every day.[17] Women judged each other largely by their success as economical and discerning shoppers.[18]

Depression austerity and wartime rationing had revived an older tradition of domestic self-sufficiency, reinforcing women's identification with home. Housewives sewed clothes for the family and soft furnishings for the house, baked cakes, ran 'chooks' and grew vegetables in the backyard, and made jams and preserves.[19] Many essentials such as milk, bread, ice, firewood and pharmaceutical prescriptions were delivered to the door by local tradesmen, riding bicycles or driving horse-drawn carts. But by the 1950s this localised system of home delivery was under challenge. Door-to-door deliveries of meat, vegetables and groceries were already in decline. The family grocer was being undercut by the 'cash-and-carry' and soon the neighbourhood shopping centre would be under pressure from the supermarket chains. Housewives in the new outer suburbs were poorly served by local tradesmen. For essentials she might go to a general store or milk bar but for fresh meat and vegetables, haberdashery and phamaceuticals she was obliged to look farther afield. Pioneer housewives in Mount Waverley and Clayton, on the city's south-east frontier, took advantage of trips to visit relatives in the inner suburbs, or occasional rail journeys to the city, to stock up on essential items.[20]

Shopping was hard work, especially for young mothers pushing prams over unmade roads with one or two crying children in tow.[21] The incentive to buy—or at least borrow—a car was correspondingly strong. 'With a car, even the most humdrum shopping expedition is a comparative pleasure', the *Radiator*'s correspondent had cheerfully observed. 'This is, of course, specially true when young children are to be considered.'[22] Unhappily, the new suburbs beyond the reach of tram and train were often the very places where husbands were also heavily dependent

'It is on the housewife that falls most of the burden of shopping', the Melbourne Metropolitan Planning Scheme observed in 1954. (MMBW PHOTO)

on the car, and young families most heavily mortgaged. In these hard-pressed households the car could easily become a bone of domestic contention, rather than a symbol of liberty.

THE WOMAN BEHIND THE MAN BEHIND THE WHEEL

In the sexual politics of the postwar years, it was common to distinguish between the exercise of authority, which conventionally belonged to men, and the arts of persuasion, in which women excelled. Dad traditionally took the driver's wheel but, as retailers and market researchers soon discovered, mum was more than a passenger when it came to the business of buying and selling cars.

'Women-appeal Boosts Car Sales', the Victorian Automobile Chamber of Commerce advised Melbourne's car dealers in 1950.[23] Garage proprietors were exhorted to transform their drab, greasy premises into 'gleaming' American-style service stations. Cleanliness, glamour and 'customer-appeal' were the keywords in a consumer revolution sustained, if not led, by women.[24] As the family shoppers, women were regarded as more proficient in the arts of buying than their menfolk. In feminising their premises and products, the motor trade was attempting, not only to win over women customers, but to make them allies in winning over men.[25] In 1956 Ampol, the first oil company to establish single-brand service stations in Victoria, made its marketing rationale explicit when it told its female customers: 'Ampol builds them—you design them.'[26]

Women made their appearance in advertisements for car accessories well before advertisements for new cars were pitched to female customers. In the 1920s American car manufacturers had anticipated this approach when they promoted cars with the new electric starters to women, who did not deign, or could not manage, to crank the engine.[27] Similarly, from the late 1940s Australian advertisements for tyres, motor oil and reliable spare parts were often directed at female drivers of ageing prewar models. In 1952 the new 'Vesta Triangle Safety Jack' was promoted as 'ideal for women drivers and well-dressed motorists'.[28] Sometimes the advertiser seems to have worked on the premise that if a new car accessory or feature made motoring easier—softer and cleaner—it should first be marketed to women and soft-handed gentlemen, in the expectation that other men, contemptuous of such refinements, would eventually follow.

The car industry had long attempted to woo the female consumer but from the mid-1950s she became an increasingly visible target of car advertising.[29] At first she was a discreet presence—a gloved hand on the wheel, an elegantly shod foot resting on the accelerator—but by the 1970s the motoring housewife had emerged as an advertising construct in her own right. A careful reading of advertisements suggests that a kind of dialogue was taking place. The marketing agents of the international motor industry were speaking, sometimes to women through men, sometimes to men through women, and eventually, by the late 1960s, directly to women as motorists in their own right.[30]

In the late 1950s, scientific market research was in its infancy in Australia.[31] Cars were commonly presented to potential buyers in images of power and beauty suggestive of a subliminal sexual appeal. Yet, as contemporary market researchers recognised, 'know[ing] quite what does in fact sell a motor-car' remained a challenging question.[32] More than two decades after the emergence of the market research profession in Australia understandings of consumer behaviour were still ridden with gratuitous gender stereotypes and assumptions.

At first, as 'wife and mother', the housewife was merely invited, as a potential passenger, to act as her husband's helpmeet when choosing the new family car. Women were believed to be more susceptible to the considerations of looks and status, although contemporary market surveys, which seldom analysed female buying attitudes, offered little evidence on the point. Advertisements for imported and Australian-made American cars were crafted, not to attract the housewife, but to reassure her husband that that he could safely select the model of 'style and distinction' which '*she* would like to be seen in' (and for which *he* may have been secretly yearning), knowing that his decision could always be blamed on 'the wife'.[33]

The motoring housewife emerged only slowly from her husband's shadow, but she was a stock figure in advertising long before her actual appearance on the road. At first she shared the family car with her husband, but by the early 1950s the 'little woman' of the household was depicted with a small car of her own. In July 1952 she made her first coy appearance in the homely, conservative *Australian Women's Weekly* in an advertisement for the Morris Minor family saloon. In one panel a dainty woman's hand reaches from the driver's seat to the glove box; in another, the housewife herself assists her husband in choosing the new car. A few months later she appears again, this time at the wheel of the new Morris, with her husband and another couple as passengers. Soon, casually dressed, ordinary mums appeared in advertisements at the wheel of Ford Consuls and Zephyrs with their children or female friends as passengers.[34] By December 1954, an advertisement in the RACV's revamped magazine *Royalauto* shows a confident young suburban mother at the wheel.[35]

In autopia—the imaginary world of the car advertisers—each model had its own feminine or masculine aura. The Holden, already becoming a national icon, was coded unambiguously male. While the 1952 French Peugeot was 'A Man's Car: that a woman loves to drive', the 'New Look' Holden sedan was still 'The Man's Car that Women Love' (but do not drive). Demand for the Holden far outstripped supply, with waiting lists as long as three years; so GMH had less incentive than other manufacturers to cultivate the female driver. But by late 1953 advertisements for the 1954 'New Look' Holden Special feature several fashionably dressed 'New Look' women admiring the car from outside

Now at the wheel of her own small car, the housewife had become a visible presence on the road. (Australian Women's Weekly, 1953, Monash Library Collection)

while another sits at the wheel. By February 1955, even GMH was marketing directly to women as drivers.[36]

Most of this advertising was based on hunches more than quantitative market research. In 1968, in one of the first surveys of women as car buyers published in Melbourne, the RACV invited their 'lady' members to 'have your say' by allocating 100 points to the ten qualities they might seek in a vehicle. Reporting the results, the *Royalauto* expressed surprise that 'you come down overwhelmingly on the side of safety features while you emphatically attach no importance to [the] "social accessory" value or smart appearance of your vehicles'. Of the women who responded: 'Seventy-seven per cent gave less than 10 marks to the importance of colour, line and upholstery in cars. It was pleasant if the car looked attractive, but safety factors would be considered first.' Furthermore, about 12 per cent placed 'emphasis on reliability, even though the point was not listed in the questionnaire'.[37] The female readers' priorities were actually very close to those consistently chosen by Australian men in similar surveys.

A Ticket to Drive

The right of women to drive was won, not in parliament or the public press, but privately, in the daily give-and-take of domestic life. It was in discussing the family budget, deciding who would pick up the kids, and negotiating the complex logistics of everyday suburban life that women gradually asserted their claim to the car. The family car, like the family home, was regarded as joint property, although control effectively belonged to the man of the house. From the 1940s to the 1970s most families could afford o ly one car, and the right of women to drive became one of the fiercest struggles in the contemporary battle of the sexes. This struggle, like all such battles, was fought out in many ways and settings; but it was crystallised, first of all, in the woman's decision to obtain a driver's licence.

Sometimes the right was won almost without a struggle. The sight of the family car standing uselessly in the driveway, while her husband rode to work by train or tram, was enough to spur some wives into action. The Hurleys had lived in Clayton for ten years before Brian began a new job with a taxi-truck firm, leaving the family's 'second-hand', and only, vehicle at home. 'The car was just sitting there', Diane recalled, 'and I thought, "This is ridiculous! I'm struggling around with two children and I could be driving everywhere." So I went out and got lessons.'[38]

The Drapers lived nearby in a cottage Ron had built himself on a block given to his wife Ursula by her aunt. As a panel beater, Ron 'knew cars', and their first vehicles were old prewar models, with 'plastic windows . . . holes and draughty bits', purchased at used car auctions. 'You always had to have a scarf round your neck, and a hat on, and wrap the kids up', Ursula recalled. Persuading Ron that she should return to

WHY CHOOSING A CAR IS A JOB FOR TWO

I looked for . . .

—a car that I could rely on for long-term high performance and comfort; but without expensive upkeep bills.

—a powerful engine with ample · reserve power—an engine that would never need a cylinder rebore, and would give a sparkling performance. A really strong and firm chassis for safety and body life is a "must" for me.

—a completely equipped car—when we bought a car we didn't want to buy extras and attachments.

—a well-finished car—inside, outside and under the bonnet, too. I looked for a car that has a good appearance, and one that will wear gracefully.

I wanted . . .

—to choose the colour that I liked best, and the upholstery and trimming that went with my colour choice.

—roomy, relaxing comfort for six grown-up passengers. I wanted our friends to enjoy riding in our car.

—a car that will have style and distinction over the long time that we will have it. I wanted a car that I would like to be seen in.

—lots of luggage room in the car boot, to carry all the clothes I may need when we're touring.

—a car that's easy to drive—a car with an adjustable seat that just glides into place. A car that I have confidence in—a car that's not hard to park.

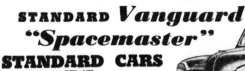

. . . WE FOUND THEM ALL IN THE

STANDARD *Vanguard* *"Spacemaster"*

STANDARD CARS
PTY. LTD.

559-573 ELIZABETH STREET, MELBOURNE.
PHONE FJ 1181

Branch Showrooms :
CNR. RUSSELL & LITTLE COLLINS STREETS.
PHONE CENT. 1722

SOLD AND SERVICED BY STANDARD
CAR DEALERS THROUGHOUT AUSTRALIA

SS/4528

By the 1950s, women as well as men were acknowledged to have a voice in the choice of family car, although their priorities were thought to be different. (ROYALAUTO)

paid work, as a dressmaker in the wardrobe department of the National Theatre in South Yarra, was Ursula's first tentative step away from home. But it was only after their second child was born, and they had purchased a larger car, that she learnt to drive herself.

I'd always wanted to drive. I don't know why I didn't. Perhaps because Ron thought the second car was safer. Either that, or I'd harped at him long enough! 'Cos men were a bit funny about that too, in those days.

She took lessons with 'old Mr Ronnie Mackenzie' who ran a local driving school. Even after passing the test, she would 'drive around the block only doing left-hand turns' until she became accustomed to the larger, but safer and less draughty, family car.[39]

Some women took lessons in secret, defying their disapproving husbands, paying the fees out of 'housekeeping' and slapping the hard-won licence upon the kitchen table as a *fait accompli*.[40] Jessie Reed was marooned on the suburban fringe, with nothing but an unreliable bus service to get her children to kindergarten, and 'going mad' trying to cope. At last she told her husband: 'I don't care if we don't have carpets for years, I have got to have a car, and I've got to have it now.'[41]

It took nearly a decade for some housewives to make the break. When Clem and Nina Harris first settled in Mount Waverley in 1956 they had only one car, an old prewar Oldsmobile. Clem, who had been taught to drive by his father, had always been interested in cars. Occasionally he had gone to hill climbs and motor shows, not to compete or buy but 'just for interest'. On weekdays he took the train from Glen Waverley station to his city office. But it was not until their third child arrived in 1964 that Nina took lessons from a local driving school and began to drive the family car, an Austin A40. Even then she seldom ventured far from home. For shopping trips to Oakleigh or to her mother-in-law in Camberwell she still used the bus and train. The car was reserved for longer trips away from the public transport system, to Dandenong or to her mother's house. Whenever they went out together Clem naturally took the wheel ('He enjoys his driving', Nina explains) and it was only years later that the family car was registered in joint names.[42]

The Harrises' story was often repeated among suburban pioneers of the 1950s and 1960s. Don and Shirley Knights had lived in Mount Waverley for six years, making do with a motorcycle and sidecar, until they bought their first car, a Holden, in 1959. Twelve months later, while pregnant with her second child, Shirley got her licence, mainly so that she could visit her mother in Burwood. She was admittedly a cautious driver but gradually she began to spread her wings. Now she could get to the newly opened Chadstone shopping centre or even to the city to have the children's photos taken. Suddenly her world had stretched.

'Hop in the car and that's it. It does give you a lot more confidence in your own freedom', she reflected.[43]

Most suburban women saw the car as a new means of fulfilling traditional family roles—shopping, transporting children, visiting parents and in-laws.[44] But the freedom and confidence it brought were real enough. 'Nancy's little car is Women's Lib on wheels', a market researcher declared in 1972. 'With the car, comes a broadening of her horizons. The world becomes her oyster.'[45] Sometimes the new freedom came at a cost. The Elliots had first settled in Mount Waverley in the late 1940s. Bill, a spec builder, was a motoring enthusiast—'one of those men that had to have the biggest, the best and the first'. Over the following decade Bill and Edna built three new homes, each bigger and better than the last. They had both worked hard but by the 1950s they were living in 'comparative luxury', had begun a family and were even building a beach house. Edna got her licence in 1956 and sometimes borrowed her husband's car, also the workhorse of his building business. A few years later she got a car of her own, an old Volkswagen 'done up' by her husband. By now, however, the marriage was in trouble. Bill had given her the car as an incentive to go back to work because, she now believes, 'he wanted me off his hands'. Never a confident person, Edna nevertheless found that the car became her passport into a new, independent life. It was not perhaps the life she and her husband had first dreamed of. But in a mobile suburban society it was better to be cast adrift with your own wheels than without.[46]

In 1953 Betty and Les Edmonds married and moved into a 'spec-built' weatherboard bungalow in the frontier suburb of Glen Waverley. Les established the suburb's first modern butcher's shop, while Betty had two babies and transformed their sparse shell of a house into a home.

> I used to go and see my mother in Prahran every Tuesday and I'd have the baby in the pram and the older one with the little seat on the pram. I'd get onto the train and go to Gardiner and get onto the tram and go down to my mother's, and come home the same way . . . I'd leave here at 9 o'clock in the morning and I'd have to be on the 4 o'clock train.[47]

It was difficult to manoeuvre the pram onto one of the high-stepped trams, or from the station platform onto one of the city's notorious 'red rattler' trains. And missing the last off-peak train meant banishment to the guard's van on the home-bound journey.

In the late 1950s the family got its first car, a 1949 Vanguard, purchased for £300. Les had 'always had a licence' but this was Betty's first opportunity to drive. After a few tense sessions with Les she visited a local driving school, and passed the test after only six lessons 'with flying colours'. Driving gave Betty greater confidence, but more important, in her own eyes, was the increased 'convenience' it brought to her role as wife and mother. No longer did she need to don her gumboots and push the heavily laden pram through the mud to the Glen Waverley railway station.[48] Now she could spend the whole day visiting and shopping with her mother in Prahran. Les could join them for the evening meal, then drive the family home.

As her family grew, the housewife's travel patterns became increasingly complex. Her daily journeys between work, shops, school, friends and relations were ever more elaborately choreographed. In the far-flung outer suburbs even the most reliable and punctual bus service running from front door to local shopping centre could not compete with the flexibility of the car. In 1954 the Barkers and their two small sons moved into a sparsely furnished weatherboard cottage on a new estate at the western edge of the future Monash University campus. Olive took an off-peak 'pram bus' to Oakleigh to do her weekly shopping, but gave up when the driver insisted that the prams were no longer to be allowed on board. Baby, bedding and bags had all to be unpacked so that the folded prams could be hung on hooks behind the bus. Already Olive was working part time at the nearby Oakleigh Motel. The combined demands of housework, employment, child-minding and shopping at last prompted her to commit the family's £1000 nest egg to the cash purchase of a new Austin A40.

> I could see we would need a car, and I wanted a car. And if there was going to be a car, we *both* had to learn to drive because my mother never drove, and this was very distressing to her.

Olive was determined not to repeat her mother's mistake by remaining dependent on the 'whim' of her husband for essential car-borne trips. When her sons commenced school, the car allowed Olive to seek better-paid employment at a factory further from home. And with her savings from this new job, she bought a new Volkswagen—'for myself'.[49]

The new suburbs, with their drive-ins and regional shopping centres were built for the cars many young wives still did not have. Until the late 1960s many, perhaps most, Melbourne housewives remained unlicensed and carless. A household survey carried out by the Melbourne Transportation Study in 1964 revealed that of the 50 per cent of the adult population without licences, 85 per cent were females. Sixty per cent of these were housewives. Even in households with one or more vehicle, 60 per cent of females over seventeen years of age remained 'unlicensed'.[50]

There was a clear territorial divide between the inner and middle suburbs, which contained 63 per cent of 'no-car' households and 39 per cent of car-owning households, and the outer suburbs where the proportions were almost reversed (61 per cent of car-owning households and 37 per cent of no-vehicle households).[51] While families in the new suburbs were more likely to own a car, however, they were also much more dependent upon it.[52] Most working-class families could afford only one car, which was driven to work by the male head of the household, leaving his wife and children to negotiate their way between the far-flung nodes of activity—shops, schools, friends—as best they could. In a perceptive analysis of the Transportation Study data, sociologist Ruth Bence demonstrated the considerable 'latent demand' for transportation, especially for multipurpose, cross-city journeys, among the non-driving, largely female, population of the new suburbs.[53] Contemporary transport planning, which gave priority to the journey to work, discriminated against this large and increasingly important group of city-dwellers.

> The Melbourne Transportation Committee's proposals to upgrade the public transport system would benefit non-drivers to a very limited extent . . . [P]eople without [the] use of private transport would become more and more disadvantaged relative to the mobile members of the community . . . It is likely that the trends towards decentralisation of employment and activities generally will result in non-drivers becoming more and more disadvantaged relative to drivers . . . The same trends are likely also to reduce, increasingly, the choice between owning or not owning a car.

The answer, Bence argued, was the development of a more flexible form of public transport that would cater for the complex cross-city travel patterns characteristic of the outer suburbs. But most families had no time to wait for the arrival of a dial-a-bus service or an automated people-mover to solve their transport needs. The second car had already become a necessity.[54]

Younger mothers in far-flung suburbs had a strong incentive to drive, although the prized second car was often beyond their reach. Older women, whose children were off their hands, could often afford a car but were sometimes too nervous, or too caught in a web of dependency, to take the plunge.[55] Motoring writers encouraged the faint-hearted with appeals to their sense of duty as well as their desire for independence. In an emergency, they argued, the older woman driver could take the wheel or relieve her husband if he grew tired.[56] But the opportunity had seemingly come too late for some women. Heeding the appeal to 'be a helpmate', one older woman convinced her husband, 'after much begging and pleading', to give her driving lessons. After one tense lesson he handed her over to a driving school. Eventually she passed the licence test. 'And ladies', she ruefully admitted, 'as I see it now, that was the worst day's work I ever did'. But for the heavy investment she had made in learning to drive, she would gladly have gone back to walking. 'I'm a jangly mass of nerves.' Out on the road, there seemed to be one rule for men and another for women. 'If a man makes a mistake, he is allowed a tolerant chuckle, but if a lady does the same thing, the roof falls in.'[57]

Her confession drew spirited replies from other female drivers. 'It is temperament rather than age, and general commonsense rather than sex' that made for successful driving, one of her middle-aged sisters insisted.[58] But 'temperament' was a product of socialisation as well as nature, and the legions of older women who continued to haul their shopping jeeps around suburban supermarkets testified to a wide gap between inherited gender roles and the often frightening new freedom of the road.[59]

GOD'S MOBILE POLICE

When older women retired, nerve-racked, from the road, they were defeated, one might argue, not only by their own timid 'temperament', but by the aggressive and antisocial behaviour of the males with whom they competed for road space. Stigmatised as 'timid', female drivers could justifiably claim to be the saner, rather than the weaker, sex. Instead of being held up to ridicule, road safety experts began to suggest, they should be held up for admiration.

The evidence was indisputable: women were safer drivers than men. In June 1960 motoring writer Ann Clifford observed that in the previous twelve months, among the 518 men and 180 women killed on Victorian roads, 210 were male drivers and only eleven were female drivers. While men drove more miles than women, these were 'highly significant' figures.[60] Careful interdisciplinary studies by two researchers of the Australian Road Research Board, Ruth Bence and Anne Raymond, confirmed what had been suspected for decades: that excessive speed and high alcohol consumption primarily among male drivers, were the major causes of road trauma. Further studies showed that 'inexperience' was also an important factor in accidents caused by young men, and to a much lesser extent, by older women. (There were as yet too few young female drivers to assess.)[61]

These findings began to force a change in the image of the woman at the wheel. The silly, overcautious, 'crawling' nuisance driver was becoming the 'good girl' of the road—a kind of 'God's Police' on wheels.[62] Like her predecessors—the temperance reformers and child rescuers of the Victorian era—the ideal female driver was devoted to the wellbeing of others, especially children. She cared for other children as well as her own, whether they were passengers in the family car, cyclists or pedestrians, particularly on the new school crossings. By the late 1960s, the public ridicule of 'women drivers' had all but ceased, although they continued to be the subject of patronising advice on such matters as how to dress when driving, the latest in child restraints, the need to look out for child pedestrians and cyclists when backing out of the driveway, or why toddlers should not be left in sealed parked cars, especially in hot weather.[63]

Women exerted a benign influence, not only by their own example as safe drivers, but by their indirect influence on the behaviour of men. Women had once sought the franchise in order to curb male drunkenness. Now, it seemed, they sought the driving licence in order to curb male aggression on the roads. 'The husband is the head of the household, and I would not disagree with this', declared Lady Chesham, wife of a visiting British motoring official. 'But the woman is the heart of the home, and it is through her influence that she can and often does instil road safety training in her family.'[64] It took guile and tact for the back-seat driver to win over the man at the wheel. She should not irritate him with incessant chatter, distract him with food, insist that he take in the glorious view or 'arouse his competitive instinct by urging him to pass the car ahead'.[65] As the dangerous Christmas holidays approached, the RACV's women's correspondent Rosalie Stephenson recognised that 'we women will need to be on the alert with some wily manoeuvres'. 'Perhaps I *am* over-anxious', she might disingenuously admit before entreating her man to take a taxi home from the office party.[66]

By the late 1960s the female driver was increasingly held up as a role model for men. The supposed faults of the 'woman driver'—excessive caution, dithering, slowness and poor sense of direction—were either fictions or unrecognised virtues. Women, according to police and safety officials, were 'more genuinely interested in learning to drive correctly . . . more receptive to teaching, more conscientious and more sensitive to the handling of the car'. Their shortcomings, such as they were, derived more from inexperience than inability.[67] 'Where is equality on the roads?', asked journalist Diane Jarvis in 1971. 'To a man a car is all part of the male thing. It is an extension of his ego. He drives as if to prove his masculinity. Most women drive as if they are murmuring to themselves. "I must be careful. I am in charge of a lethal weapon." ' It was high time, she decided, that the Women's Liberation movement took a look at this 'intolerable road situation'.[68]

TOWARDS EQUALITY

The early 1970s mark a watershed in the history of relations between Australian men and women. The adoption of the contraceptive pill, the attainment of equal pay, the increasing participation of women in higher education and the advent of the Women's Liberation movement combined to generate the most significant progress towards women's emancipation in more than a century. Alongside these sexual and economic changes, winning the right to drive may seem a small advance. In a standard history of Australian feminism the quiet struggle of thousands of Australian women to win the right to drive passes unnoticed alongside the more boisterous minority campaign to win the right to drink in the public bars of hotels.[69] The swiftness with which the right to drive was won may have obscured the passions it once aroused. While families had only one car, and men asserted an exclusive right to drive it, the conflict was intense; but it swiftly dissipated as soon as the second car, the despised 'little beat-up bomb', appeared in the double carport.

Critics of the car, and of the new suburban landscape it created, often doubted the emancipating effects of automobility, especially for women who were increasingly assigned the role of family chauffeurs, couriers and caretakers. Twentieth-century housewives, it sometimes seems, have been shackled to the steering wheel as surely as their nineteenth-century sisters were shackled to the washtub and the mangle. Yet, as the preceding pages show, most women were in no doubt of the liberating potential of the car and regarded a driver's licence as a kind of domestic franchise. By the 1970s the language of politics, like every other facet of modern life, was suffused with the imagery of the road. Women, no longer content to shout from the back seat, or whisper confidentially in the male driver's ear, were increasingly 'taking the wheel' in national as well as domestic life. 'You've got to let go of the steering wheel', a feminist politician, Kay Setches, exhorted her male colleagues in 1993. She was drawing upon the legacy of a time when the car was arguably as important a battleground of the sexes as the kitchen and the bedroom.

3
Sex, Speed and Power

No sooner had the first motor car appeared on city streets than moralists became alarmed about its effects on the city's youth. A young person behind the wheel of a car, especially a young man driving a fast car, conjured up unsettling possibilities in the minds of his elders. Roaring motors, klaxon horns, screeching brakes and the spectre of shattered glass and bleeding bodies haunted their sleep. But these dangers of injury and sudden death seemed no greater than the moral dangers of the car. The car was a new source of social power, opening up fresh possibilities of independence, mobility, sexual opportunity, excitement and self-expression. To drive when and wherever you wished, to feel the surge of power and acceleration as your foot was pushed to the floor, to be admired for your glorious apparel of chrome and duco, and to share the delicious intimacy of the darkened cabin, with its glow of instruments and blaring radio—what prospect could be more inviting to the young, or more troubling to the old?

Until the late nineteenth century, young people usually grew up under the gaze of their elders, working, playing and often finding their marriage partners within walking distance of their own homes. 'Walkin' my baby back home' from the town hall dance, the church tennis court, or the corner pub, was how boys and girls first got to know each other intimately. The appearance, in the 1890s, of that seemingly innocuous device, the safety bicycle, had brought the first real breach in this localised youth culture. 'The bicycle has brought a socially undeveloped multitude of young persons, chiefly of the male sex, into situations in which they are free from the control which can be exercised over them in ordinary circumstances', the *Australasian* warned in 1897.[1] Not many Melbourne girls imitated 'Daisy', the heroine of the popular song, by joining her beau on a 'bicycle built for two'. But some had bicycles of their own and many others walked home with a bike-riding boyfriend from an adjoining suburb.

Not until the 1920s did cars come within reach of most middle class Melburnians, and even then, it was the wealthy middle aged, rather than their sons or daughters, who enjoyed the full freedom of the road. In the nineteenth century a suitor was said to be 'calling' upon a young woman, but from the 1920s young couples were increasingly said to be 'going out' together. For Graham McInnes, a Scotch collegian and Melbourne University student in the late 1920s and early 1930s, 'going out' was largely a matter of access to the means of mobility. From cyclist to passenger in a friend's car to driver of a hired or borrowed car to owner of his own motorcycle, McInnes's social horizons gradually expanded from his own suburb, Malvern, through Ashburton and St Kilda to the homes of the delightful 'Brighton girls'. The car not only extended his range of acquaintance but the possibilities of sexual intimacy. Parked outside a ballroom or dance hall, it served, as he observed, as 'a convenient parking place or outdoor couch'.[2] An outraged correspondent to the *Argus*, writing under the pseudonym 'Dad', deplored the youthful immorality fostered by the car. 'A Peter the Hermit is needed to preach a crusade against the unseemly uses to which motor cars are put at balls and dances in the city and in the country also. At a recent ball in a fashionable suburb nearly every motor-car was a miniature bar; all know with what result. These practices should be stopped in order to save our fine young women.'[3] But it was much easier to bemoan the moral consequences of the car than to suggest how they might be prevented.

It was only after World War II that automobility came within reach of most young Melburnians, and then only gradually. For a generation, from the late 1940s to the late 1960s, possession of a car—and even more, the *kind* of car one possessed—were perhaps the single most defining aspects of identity among young people, especially young males. 'Having wheels', to use the contemporary vernacular, was to be a man; to be carless, in many circles, was to be a nobody. 'How did you feel when you first put the car into gear and moved off?', a young driver was asked. 'Free', was his response. 'It felt like I was in another world, you know? A newborn freedom. Your own set of wheels.'[4] For young women, possessing a car may have been less important than having a boyfriend who owned one. Cars were a significant factor in the rating and dating game; in turn, the looks of the girlfriend contributed, like a beautiful trophy, to the power and prestige of the car and its owner.

The growth of youthful car ownership is hard to estimate precisely— no Australian state published official age-specific statistics of licences or car ownership. In 1951 a Gallup poll showed that possession of a driver's licence rose with age from 40 per cent of people in their twenties, to 50 per cent of those in their thirties, but declined again to 40 per cent of those in their fifties and 30 per cent of those over 60. Eighteen- to twenty-year-olds were evidently not polled and age-specific data on driver's licences was not published by Gallup in later years.[5] In the late 1940s and early 1950s the numbers of young men arriving at driving age—those born in the later Depression and war years—were few, and in the early 1950s they were actually declining relative to the population as a whole. It was only in the late 1950s and early 1960s, as the first baby boomers entered their late teens, that the numbers of prospective young drivers began to increase. Yet while the numbers of Victorian males between fifteen and nineteen increased by 84 per cent between 1954 and 1966, the numbers of male drivers acquiring new licences in the following five years grew by only 27 per cent. From the mid-1960s the numbers of prospective new male drivers fell (only 4.8 per cent increase in the 15–19 age group between 1966–71), but the numbers of new male licence-holders leapt by a staggering 186 per cent. While the data is imperfect it seems likely that the rapid growth in new licence-holders after the mid-1960s represents, in considerable part, the delayed acquisition of the right to drive among the baby boomer generation. It was particularly from the mid-1960s that advertisers, writers, politicians and road safety experts began to focus a more intense gaze on the driving habits and interests of the young.

Owning, or even borrowing, a car radically extended a young person's geographical and social horizons. In the 1950s the teenager's world was still largely bounded by his or her own suburb. The local school, the local church with its youth club and tennis courts, and the local dance were the places where boys and girls usually met. Since the 1920s, the era of the big bands, dance entrepreneurs had begun to build large commercial ballrooms, such as Leggatt's (Prahran), the Trocadero

(St Kilda Road) and the Palais de Danse (St Kilda Esplanade), usually locating them close to train or tram routes. Local dance 'academies' sometimes ran smaller operations from suburban town halls or RSL clubs. The 'Gaiety' dances at the Moonee Ponds Town Hall ('Where romantic tunes lead to honeymoons') ran for more than two decades. But although young people travelled across town for big occasions, geography remained a strong determinant of courtship patterns. Boys would say, sadly, of a pretty girl from a remote suburb that she was 'GI'—'geographically impossible'.

Even before young Melburnians acquired cars of their own, there were signs that the local church and family-based youth culture was breaking down. One telling indicator was the rise and dramatic fall of the Protestant Sunday school. During the postwar baby boom as ex-servicemen pioneered the new suburbs, the Sunday schools also boomed. Enrolments in Presbyterian Sunday schools in Victoria grew from 28 000 in 1956 to 57 000 in 1966; Methodists from 41 000 to 75 000. By the mid-1960s, as the birthrate began to decline, Sunday school attendances also slumped. The pleasures of the Sunday

The Arab Coffee Bar at Lorne was a mecca for the MGs and Triumphs favoured by the sons of Melbourne's elite. (LORNE HISTORICAL SOCIETY)

afternoon drive were proving more attractive to most families than hymn-singing and Bible study. Unable to compete, many Sunday schools changed their meeting times from afternoon to morning. By the mid-1970s enrolments had more than halved and by the 1980s a once-powerful institution was all but extinct.[6]

For many young Melburnians the family Sunday afternoon drive was but the prelude to wider adventures. In 1950, 58 per cent of Melbourne couples getting engaged were from the same or an immediately adjoining suburb. They probably lived within walking or biking distance of each other. But in the course of the 1950s and 1960s courtship was automobilised. Instead of the localised network of 'modern and oldtime' ballroom dances, there sprang up a new metropolitan-wide but class-segregated network of teenage dances. Middle-class youths drove their MGs and Triumphs to jazz dances, such as 'Q Club' and 'Powerhouse', located mainly in the eastern and southern suburbs. Working-class lads drove their customised Ford Mercurys and FJ Holdens to rock dances in the west and the north. In summer the tribes gathered at their own favourite beach resorts—'Jazzers' at Lorne and Portsea, 'Rockers' at Rosebud and Dromana. Music and motor cars were the totems by which strangers from across the metropolis learnt to recognise and avoid, rate and date each other.[7] By the 1970s the bounds of the 'geographically possible' had been greatly widened. More than 60 per cent of couples getting engaged now came from suburbs well beyond walking or biking distance while the proportion coming from the same suburb had halved from 24 per cent to 12 per cent since 1950.[8]

SEX AND THE CAR

The car changed sex in more obvious ways as well. The car became an essential prop to a young man's ego. Girls—so many men believed—were dazzled by cars, and the young man's prospects of sexual conquest depended as much upon the glistening chrome of the car's grille and mascot as the driver's Brylcreemed hair and Pepsodent smile. Car manufacturers soon began to exploit the sexual attractions of the car in their marketing campaigns. In 1956 songwriters Norma Hall and Don Bennett responded to a commission from GMH with the romantic ballad, 'Holdin' you in my Holden'.

Holdin' you in my Holden
Life is simply divine
All the world is fair
I'm a millionaire.

On the road ahead there's a happy sign.
Holdin' you in my Holden
You were meant to be mine
We will have a wedding, no regretting,

Baby ain't that fine
Now we can't expect all sunny weather,
Troubles come my dear.
But as long as we two travel together,
We'll take them in top gear.

Holdin' you in my Holden
Life is simply sublime
I'll be holdin' you all life through
When you're mine, all mine.[9]

When we get the car
A complete short story
By JEAN E. TURNLEY
ILLUSTRATED BY BROADHURST

As Mr. and Mrs. Bowman gazed admiringly at the car the salesman, Bill Hunter, kept his eyes just as admiringly on their
daughter, Mary.

In women's fiction, buying a car could become a courtship ritual, invested with
romantic possibilities for passengers, salesman and driver.
(AUSTRALIAN WOMEN'S WEEKLY, MONASH UNIVERSITY LIBRARY COLLECTION)

Not everyone who was holdin' his baby in his Holden was heading for a wedding—at least not without regretting. The car was a new zone of intimacy for young people, the more attractive because of its mobility. A team of contemporary American sociologists solemnly noted that: 'Freedom to drive the family car *alone* assumes even greater importance for the male adolescent since the privilege carries with it at least the possibility of sexual expression uncontrolled by direct adult super-vision.'[10] From kissing in the back stalls of the local picture theatre, they graduated to petting on the front seats of parked cars. From petting on the front seat they moved to copulating on the back seat. Along the darkened sections of the Yarra Boulevard, amidst the ti-tree at Black Rock and Seaford, and in a hundred quiet cul-de-sacs, a new generation of automobilised youth was experiencing the first tremors of a sexual revolution. The young businessman's two-seater sports car, with its bucket seats and floor shift, was a powerful lure but a less explicit instrument of seduction than the working-class boy's black-painted panel van, with its curtained rear windows and lay-back seats.

Did the car change adolescent morals, or merely accelerate changes that were already under way? The number of exnuptial births, which might stand as an index of unwanted pregnancies, rose steadily throughout this period, though the biggest jump occurred between the mid-1960s and the mid-1970s, the period when car ownership among young men was also rising sharply.[11] As yet few young women had cars of their own. It is hard to separate the effects of automobilisation from other forces changing sexual behaviour, most notably, perhaps, the advent of the contraceptive pill. But it seems likely that in sex, as in safety, young women were often exposed to the high risks of being passengers in cars controlled by impulsive young men.

In the male talk of the time, the car was often personalised as female and driving was regarded as a skill analogous to seduction. Jack Hibberd's 1967 play *White with Wire Wheels* dramatises the interplay between cars and sex through the reactions of two young Melbourne men, Simon and Rod, to their friend Mal's decision to purchase a new car, a white Valiant with wire wheels. In the first scene the friends are recovering from a hard night on the town. Rod has bought a newspaper and some magazines. '*Man Junior* or *Synchro-Mesh?*' he asks, proffering a girlie magazine and a motoring journal. Their conversation swings back and forth from girls to cars to girls again, as both are ruthlessly appraised for their styling, handling qualities and performance. In talking about their ideal car, the boys are establishing their social and sexual identity. Mal, self-made and hardworking, wants a big flashy car, painted white, the colour of cool. Simon, the ambitious company man, prefers 'something more conservative, solid, a touch of class'; a 1962 Rover perhaps. The sexually predatory Rod wants something fast and powerful; he chooses a red Mustang sports car. As the boys talk about their cars the language of sex and the language of automobility become fused. 'What do you think of the new Cortina?', Mal asks. 'Not bad, not bad at all', Rod replies. 'Nice lines?' 'Very classy', agrees the status-conscious Simon. 'Still there are other jobs I'd prefer', Mal confides. 'Such as this little job here. Get a geek at those lines gentlemen', says Rod, displaying a photograph from *Man Junior*. 'What a set!', exclaims Mal. In their boys' talk the car—'she'—becomes invested with female qualities while girls are rated, sometimes statistically, in the manner of a road test report. In this auto-erotic world, it is naturally the car, not the girl, who is the true and lasting object of desire. As Mal is contemplating the delivery of his adored Valiant he is about to dump his girlfriend Sue. 'I'm sure I won't get a moment's sleep tonight', he confides to her. 'I'll be outside those rooms at eight o'clock, flashing the big cheque book. I'm going to crawl over that bloody car . . .' 'Kiss the carburettor and tickle the tyres', she jokes, aware how pale, by comparison, is his ardour for her.[12]

In his novel *My Love Had A Black Speed Stripe* (1973), Henry Williams carries the Australian male's love affair with his car to new heights of satirical absurdity. His hero, Ron, lives with his 'missus' Rose in a brand-new heavily mortgaged house in the suburbs, but the great love of his life is his Holden Monaro. Ron's philosophy of life is simple:

> They talk about love at first sight with sheilas, but with sheilas I don't think it ever lasts like that. A sheila can knock you for six the first time you see her, hair, eyes, chassis, the lot, but it doesn't stay like that if you start seeing her a lot . . . But I've never had that sort of let-down with a car. Any car I've had has always stayed looking beaut in my eyes right to the day I've parted with her.

For Ron, the car is more than an object of desire; he cares for 'her' more lovingly, anticipates 'her' needs for oil and water, gasoline and tyre rubber more attentively than the most ardent suitor. As his love for his missus grows colder, and his infatuation with his car grows stronger,

When you own your own Monaro the ball never ends.

Monaro is as good to drive as it is to be seen with. And as easy.
It may look commanding but it does what it's told when a lady stamps her foot. Gearchanging can be manual or automatic. And with a choice of five engines you can pick just the power and economy you want. On the inside, comfort comes first. With deep-pleated bucket seats up front. And room for a handful of children in the rear. So put on your soft shoes and see your Holden Dealer. The ball starts rolling at $2,575.

CINDERELLA'S GOWN BY TULLO THE PALACE LE CHATEAU MELBOURNE

Holden's young body. Monaro

*Mimicking the voluptuous shapes of male desire, the Holden Monaro was 'as good to drive as to be seen with'. (*AUSTRALIAN WOMEN'S WEEKLY, *1969, MONASH UNIVERSITY LIBRARY COLLECTION)*

Ron actually moves out of the bedroom and makes his bed beside his beloved Monaro in the carport.

Ron's love for his car is blind. It is left to his neighbour, the carless immigrant and would-be intellectual Michael, to articulate what Ron refuses to acknowledge himself. 'The car is modern man's virility symbol', says Michael.

> Many psychologists have remarked on the obvious undertones of sexuality in the motoring mystique. They [cars] are sold as objects possessing power, speed, thrust, stamina, strength. The tiger in the tank. The brute beneath the bonnet. Their names are loaded with suggestions of male sexual aggression. The Mustang, the Falcon, the Stallion, the Corsair, the Jaguar . . . The bright colours of these motor cars suggest the male bird displaying his finery and plumage: the roar of the exhaust echoes the cry of the jungle male in the mating season: this obsession with speed is an expression of the need for reassurance of one's virility.

'What are you trying to make out?', Ron retorts. 'Anybody with a driving licence is some kind of sex maniac?'[13]

Of course neither Michael, nor the novelist Henry Williams, was suggesting anything quite so simple. Cars were more than trophies, more than symbols of sexual aggression; they were instruments of social power, offering access to opportunities, pleasures and perceptions beyond the reach of the carless. They were also works of art. Cars were the biggest, most complicated and most fascinating machines ever to appear in the average household. Watches, clocks, pianos, even radios and refrigerators, seemed primitive by comparison. For many young people, men especially, the appeal of the car was largely mechanical: what could compare with the sweet rhythm of its engine, its response to the driver's touch, or the fascinating array of lights, dials and flickering needles along its dashboard? For many young men the car was a mechanical toy—something rather like a grown-up meccano set—to be pulled apart, modified, improved, rebuilt. Taking an old Holden, Hillman or Vanguard, the young enthusiast bored out the cylinders, fitted new valves and fuel injectors, moved the gear change to the floor, lowered the suspension and widened the tyres, rejuvenated its sagging body with fibreglass fins and added a bright new coat of British racing green. The hot rod or customised car become a demonstration of the mechanical and artistic skill of the owner, a mobile work of art. It was also a statement of the owner's individuality. 'You want to make it a bit different', one driver remarked, 'so you start off. Maybe you put on heavier shock absorbers or you try to make it go faster or something like that. And then you think "well I'd like to make it look different".'[14]

CHAMPIONS OF SPEED

Urban youth took pride in their skill with cars just as their forefathers had once taken pride in their horsemanship. Melburnians had once worshipped the champions of the turf and the men who rode them. Thousands had crowded the city streets for the funeral of a leading jockey in 1894.[15] Now they cheered a new breed of heroes, the champions of the motor racing track.

In the 1930s car racing had been a minority sport, largely confined to a handful of enthusiasts who conducted hill climbs or open-wheel races on the Fisherman's Bend airstrip or on the road circuit at Phillip Island. In 1947, 30 000 people gathered on an old RAAF airstrip at Ballarat to watch Victoria's first car-racing meeting since the war. Some of the drivers were ex-servicemen, usually in their twenties or early thirties, and their cars—MGs, Alfa Romeos and Ferraris—were mainly rejuvenated 1930s 'specials'. Some of the leading drivers, like Lex Davison, heir to a footwear fortune, Bill Patterson, son of a former Wimbledon tennis champion, and John Youl, a young Tasmanian grazier, were wealthy young sportsmen, with the nonchalant style of the playboy. 'Urbane', 'smooth' and 'affable' was how journalists often described them.[16]

The poor man's version of grand prix racing, a modern counterpart of the old pony track, was the 'dirt track' or speedway. On tight little circuits on the wrong side of town, at Maribyrnong and Baxter Park, amidst clouds of dust and the deafening screech of engines, working-class lads on motorbikes, in midget cars or behind the wheels of 'stock cars', biffed and buffeted their opponents in a more gladiatorial form of motor sport. Not for them the coolness and finesse of the open-wheel racing driver; the champions of the speedway were bare-knuckle fighters on wheels.[17]

In the 1950s the old class-based pattern of motor racing began to be transformed. A new breed of professionals, often motor engineers or motor retailers by trade, had begun to enter the sport. From Melbourne, the acknowledged national centre of motor sport, came the Ford retailer Bib Stillwell, the Holden retailer Reg Hunt and the used car dealer Stan Jones; from Sydney the ex-RAAF mechanic and midget car driver Jack Brabham and the car dealer and finance company director Arnold Glass; from Canberra the Chevrolet agent Alex Mildren. In 1956, Melbourne's Olympic Year, permission was granted to stage a special

grand prix race on a road circuit around Albert Park Lake. While
Betty Cuthbert thrilled the Olympic crowds at the Melbourne Cricket
Ground more than 100 000 car racing enthusiasts watched the British
ace Stirling Moss and the Frenchman Jean Behra defeat local heroes like
Davison, Jones, Whiteford and Hunt in the Australian Grand Prix.[18]

Among the crowd at Albert Park was a 26-year-old Brunswick leather
tradesman and bike racer, Bob Jane. Jane's parents had split up during
the war years and his mother had moved to Brunswick where she ran a
milk bar. Bob left school at thirteen to be apprenticed to his uncle
Denzil Don, manufacturer of a popular brand of football. Small,
nuggety and aggressive, he quickly graduated in the school of hard
knocks. 'In Brunswick I was beaten up regularly by the local gangs', he
later recalled. He decided to confront the bullies, and one night outside
the local picture theatre, he trounced a local gang leader. 'This became
widely known and life in Brunswick became easier for me.' In his
late teens he took up bike racing and for a time alternated work as a

Motor racing driver Bob Jane with his white Jaguar.
(PHOTO COURTESY EXXON MOBIL AND MUSEUM VICTORIA)

woodcutter with races at the Essendon board track. He bought his first car, a 1934 Chev, and raced his friend Norm Beechey along the back streets of Brunswick. In his late teens he started his own seat cover business and at 21 was already a used car dealer in Sydney Road.[19]

Bob Jane was a young man in love with cars. They were a mechanical extension of his raw power, independence and aggression. Henry Ford, the father of modern motoring, became his hero. He admired Ford's combination of technical ingenuity, organisational genius and fierce competitive instinct, qualities he would demonstrate himself as he later built up a formidable business empire of motor car and retail tyre outlets. Like Ford, he knew instinctively that fear is a greater motivator than love. Racing cars were an ideal vehicle for his competitive instincts. When he saw Stirling Moss and Jean Behra throwing their cars around the track at Albert Park, he knew—as certainly as Ginger Mick had once heard 'The Call of Stoush'—that he had to join them. He began driving modified early-model Holdens in stock-car races at the Baxter Park Speedway in Preston, competing against his old mate Norm Beechey, now also a Sydney Road used car dealer. The short, intense and ascetic Jane driving his white Jaguar was a natural foil for the burly, hard-drinking, devil-may-care Beechey in his pitch-black Chevrolet Impala. The symbolic dimensions of their rivalry—quiet little guy vs big loud guy, Britain vs America, black vs white—demonstrated the way in which the racetrack was becoming a new kind of outdoor theatre. By the mid-1960s Jane and Beechey had attracted their own bands of devoted teenage fans and their rivalry had spread to the new car-racing tracks recently opened at Sandown and Calder. 'Most men like to be heroes and out there on the circuit I am a bit of a hero', Beechey admitted. 'I'd be a liar if I didn't say I loved it.'[20]

On the fringes of the metropolis, there had emerged a fantasy world in which the young drivers' dreams of speed, sexual conquest and mastery came true. Calder Raceway, on the city's north-west fringe, and Sandown Park, to the south-east, opened within a few months of each other in 1962. Calder was the brainchild of Clayton service station proprietor and part-time racing driver Pat Hawthorn and Keilor builder and landowner Pat Houlahan. With tighter curves and better visibility for spectators, and its proximity to the working-class suburbs of the north-west, it became the favourite venue for production car and drag racing.[21] Bob Jane later purchased the circuit and added a new track, 'Thunderdome', as a circuit for Amcar racing. Sandown, 'a magnificent circuit . . . surpassed by few others in the world'—was strategically located in the main corridor of middle-class suburban expansion to the city's south-east. Its long straight and greater variation of terrain were better suited to the faster and more glamorous open-wheel and grand touring cars. Its opening in March 1962 was a glittering event with several of the big international names including Australia's former world champion Jack Brabham, and the British aces Stirling Moss, John Surtees and Jim Clark competing in the 120-mile Sandown International Cup. This time it was the Australian, Brabham, who won.

Within the closed arena of the racetrack, the everyday restraints on speed and youthful bravado were suspended. The heroes of the production car race were local lads, with only a bit more skill, daring and mechanical flair than those whose 'souped up' Falcons and Holdens rent the midnight air in many a quiet suburb. As earlier generations of bush-reared Australians had demonstrated their manhood by breaking horses or killing Germans, so the racing drivers and the youths who emulated them proved their mettle by driving their machines, and themselves, to the mechanical and physical limit. In the closed arena of the racing circuit or the stunt-car show, the element of danger was part of the spectators' pleasure. Bob Jane had sustained serious injuries four or five times in his racing career. Daredevil driving took its place alongside knife-swallowing and tightrope-walking as an entertainment in circuses and country fairs. The crowds stood breathless, hearts in their mouths, as Crash Kavanagh, leader of the Hell-drivers stunt team, gunned his supercharged Ford Falcon to a roar, sped across the showgrounds arena towards an 8-foot ramp then soared through a ring of fire before crash-landing just a few metres clear of the line of brand-new Falcons lined up below.[22]

By the late 1960s motor manufacturers were beginning to cater specifically to the young Australian male's obsession with speed. 'Sporty two-door cars are becoming more popular, especially with young people', the *Royalauto* observed in 1969. New models were becoming lower, sleeker and more powerful. In 1968 Holden had released its Monaro GTS and Ford had followed with its Falcon GT, both limited production, high performance cars capable of more than 140–160 mph (220 kph). Ordinary motorists could now emulate the heroes of Calder and Sandown by purchasing cars identical in looks, and only marginally inferior in performance, to theirs. Ford advertised its new sedan as the 'Mustang-bred Falcon'. Few young drivers could probably have afforded these limited production models, but, as the manufacturer well knew, the ' "performance image" which attaches itself to the name of the winning car . . . sits well on the self-esteem of the buyer of the least powerful, most basic model'. Sitting in his Monaro or Falcon the young driver could imagine himself as a Norm Beechey or a Bob Jane and, his elders worried, he might seek to act out his delusions on the city streets.[23]

DRIVING INTO DANGER

Older Australians responded to the rise of car-use and car ownership among the young with mingled fear, anxiety, envy and mistrust. Behind the contemporary headlines about road safety, drink-driving, unroadworthy 'old bombs', 'joy-riding' and teenage pregnancy lurked a fear—a reasonable one, at least in part—about the new freedom of movement, self-expression and moral behaviour symbolised, and made possible, by the car.

During the 1950s and 1960s adult anxieties about the nation's youth were focused on a seemingly new phenomenon, the 'teenager'. Manifestations of a culture of rebellion, such as 'bodgies' and 'widgies', rock music and the film *The Blackboard Jungle*, led some people to fear a wider breakdown of society.[24] In 1956 the Victorian Government had established an advisory committee under the judge and criminologist J. V. Barry to investigate the allegedly increasing problem of juvenile delinquency. It reviewed the statistics of juvenile offences (which showed, at worst, a modest increase) and rehearsed a variety of explanations for them. In common with other authorities in Britain and the United States, Barry and his colleagues saw juvenile crime as a response to the breakdown of traditional institutions, especially the family. 'Changes in traditional forms of social organisation and in the structure of communities and their habits and customs have altered the character of family life of a considerable and increasing section, and there has been a general lessening of respect for authority in its various forms.'[25] Crime, according to the authorities the committee consulted, was a manifestation of 'acquisitive, aggressive, sexual and escape tendencies'. Within a normal range such tendencies might be harmless; it was only when the controlling influence of the family or local institutions was removed that the young person became a menace to himself or society. Within such a

In the era of the mini-skirt, the tiny, boxy Mini-Minor became an improbable symbol of sexual liberation. (AUSTRALIAN WOMEN'S WEEKLY, MONASH UNIVERSITY LIBRARY COLLECTION)

framework of interpretation, the motor car, with its enormous potential for the expression of these primal 'tendencies', and for enabling the young person to break the restraints of family and neighbourhood, appeared as a mighty disruptive force.

'Should teenagers drive?' the motoring magazine *Wheels* asked in 1967. Most Australians thought that eighteen was soon enough for a young man to get wheels, although a significant minority, mainly women and wowsers, thought they should wait until 21. A decade earlier it had noted the appearance of a new word—'teenicide'. 'Teenicide, in popular parlance, means the destruction of teenage life by a deadly weapon, the automobile.' Young people had always been prone to risky behaviour but now they had access to more powerful means of destruction. Australian teenagers, according to some observers, were imitating the dangerous pastimes of their American cousins—'joy-riding', 'playing chicken', drinking while driving. Young drivers had better eyes and faster reflexes than their elders. The trouble was not their physical fitness or alertness but their psychological volatility. 'Youngsters', a psychologist declared,

> are subjected to mental stresses far beyond those found in normal adults. This can make a highly strung youth go temporarily insane, and, if he happens to be at the wheel of a car, drive to a point of recklessness—all because of some real or imagined grievance. Alternatively, an eighteen-years-old can become so absorbed in the prospect of meeting his evening's 'date', that he loses concentration altogether and drives as if in a 'dream'.[26]

From the mid-1950s the number of deaths and injuries among teenage drivers and passengers began to rise alarmingly. A 1960 federal parliamentary inquiry into road safety found that young people between the ages of seventeen and twenty comprised 5.5 per cent of the national population but were involved in 15 per cent of road casualties and 12 per cent of fatalities. 'Being youthful and exuberant, full of confidence and in many instances irritated by restraints imposed upon them', teenage motorists were more accident-prone than their elders, although, as the inquiry admitted, their high accident rate was partially explicable by their relatively high rate of car usage.[27] What the inquiry did not say, but was obvious from a closer scrutiny of the road accident statistics, was that in the 1950s and early 1960s problem drivers were not young people in general, but specifically young *men*. In 1982 male drivers were still about four times more likely to be killed than female drivers, but in 1963, when female drivers were still a minority, male drivers were about fourteen times more likely to be killed than female drivers. And in the 17–20 age group, the ratio was about 36 to one. When young women died on the road, it was mainly as pedestrians, or as passengers in cars driven by men.[28]

Conservatives often yearned to stop reckless young people from driving, either by raising the minimum driving age, introducing a stiffer driving test or imposing long periods of suspension on youthful offenders. The right to drive, they believed, must be balanced by the moral capacity of the driver to avoid harm to others. If the young driver was unable to drive safely he (less likely, she) should simply forfeit that right. Liberal-minded commentators, including the leaders of most motoring organisations, were reluctant to prohibit young drivers. They reminded older drivers of their own youthful enthusiasm.

> Let's face it, you want to drive when you are young. It's the thing you really want to do, and in most instances, do well. When you sit at the wheel with your girlfriend beside you, a long road ahead and a swim and a picnic to go to, you feel free and you feel good. There's nothing quite like it, and you will never believe that someday you won't find driving so thrilling.[29]

Older drivers, especially parents, had an obligation to educate the younger. 'Teenagers *should* drive and, further, should learn from sympathetic, young-minded people the kind of good manners and consideration for other road-users that goes to make really good drivers. It can be done, and everybody with any kind of influence at all over a youngster can help.'[30]

A motoring journalist, Charles Stamp, summarised the feelings of many anxious parents in a letter addressed to his 'dear son' on the day he passed his licence test. 'Your Mum and I haven't really looked forward to this day', he admitted. 'I suppose for a long time [we] will lay [sic] awake listening for the return of your car when you've been out to a drive-in or a party.' Stamp remembered only too well his own youthful recklessness, his boundless confidence, and the exhilarating sense of power enjoyed by the young man behind the wheel. 'The engine was an extension of our desires. We thought of it as part of ourselves, but it never was. It didn't have a brain sitting on top of those 20-odd horses.' For all their recklessness, the older generation had been lucky. The roads had been less crowded, and cars usually less powerful and lethal. Now he was pleading with his own son to do as he said, rather than to do as he used to do. 'We don't want you to do the stupid things we did; nevertheless, you may do them; it seems to be the way of things . . . Sorry if I ear-bashed you a bit', he added, as though aware of how narrow was the scope of parental authority. In the end, it seemed, all an anxious parent could do was to hope and pray: 'May God protect you', he concluded.[31]

A few weeks later, Stamp returned to offer a second homily, this time to his 'dear daughter'. The scenario he addressed was significantly different: the daughter was not about to become a driver herself, but had just met her first boyfriend, Peter. 'When Peter takes you out', the anxious father observed, 'he will often do so in a car'. Peter, he reminded her, was also crossing those other thresholds of adulthood, drinking and 'partying'—a euphemism for sex. 'Three individual pleasures of adult life drop in to your lap at the same time. You mix them too heavily and they become an entangled mess in more ways than one.' A good girl, Stamp suggests, would prevent her boyfriend going too fast as well as too far.

> No matter how much driving you do, you'll probably spend most of your days in a car sitting beside a male driver . . . in the 'suicide seat.' Are you going to spend much of your life sitting there . . . saying nothing when the needle climbs too high; curling your toes slightly when the traffic lights change to red, saying prayers when you are rushed across the intersection without any slackening of pace?

Young men, he knew from his own youthful experience, resented the 'backseat driver', but experience also had taught him that a woman's timely word could save lives. 'Don't go so fast', his old girlfriend had warned, as the needle crept above 50. Only because he heeded her did he live to have this 'dear daughter' of his own. According to the older generation, endangering a young woman's life, like getting her drunk or taking her virginity, was to deny her proper 'respect'. A new dimension was being added to the old code of respectability. A suitable young man would control his car, as well as his thirst, his cheque book and his libido, and a good girl would firmly insist that he did so.[32]

But was the moral influence of the devoted parent and the 'good girl' enough to stem the rising slaughter of young lives? In 'Modern Times', some verses contributed to the *Royalauto* in 1969, the reckless young driver is portrayed as a reincarnation of the bushranger:

> *He was just a carefree youngster, his parents' pride and joy,*
> *A mixture of the jet set and the 'Wild Colonial Boy',*

He'd had it pretty easy, though his parents wouldn't dare
To suggest in any language, that he hadn't done his share.

The spoilt youngster, short of money but 'keen to be the owner of a car with lots of pace', buys a car on hire-purchase.

So the lad became a victim of the hire-purchase 'mob',
Who'll gladly charge their 10 per cent and garnishee your job.
They'll fit all the safety gadgets, say the car's got tons of power,
And proudly mention that it tops a hundred miles an hour.

The poem ends with a lament for the wastage of young lives because of the failure of the older generation, politicians especially, to curb the recklessness, and perhaps limit the horsepower available to the young.[33]

As the teenage road toll rose through the 1960s, road safety experts intensified and widened the scope of driver education among the young. It was no longer sufficient to rely on the moral sway of parents or other 'sympathetic, young-minded people' to stop the young people killing themselves. 'It is becoming increasingly difficult for the home or the church to train young folk to understand the problems of car control, traffic regulations, the need for trained enforcement and proper behaviour and attitudes', the general manager of the RACV observed in 1967.[34] In 1957 the Victoria Police, assisted by local service clubs, had opened the first Children's Traffic School at Kew. Eight- and nine-year-olds were taught the rudiments of road safety by negotiating their bikes and pedal cars through the traffic lights and stop signs of a miniature road system. But would the small children who obeyed the police officer in the playground setting of the Traffic School grow into teenagers who drove safely on the highway? Prompted by the Police and the Education Department, the RACV began in 1967 to offer road safety summer schools for teenagers and twelve-week courses of 'pre-driver education' to senior pupils in state high schools, beginning in the outlying car-based suburbs of Karingal, near Frankston, Noble Park and Glen Waverley.[35]

The motor lobby had relied on education to turn the reckless and rebellious teenager into a safe driver. There was little evidence of its effectiveness. Yet it was not until 1969 that the government finally, and reluctantly, moved to curb the liberty of the young driver by introducing a probationary licence system requiring new drivers to display 'P-plates' and to observe a 50 miles an hour speed limit for the first three years on the road.

The lure of the car was often stronger than the buying power or the moral inhibitions of the young would-be motorist. In the mid-1950s Melbourne witnessed an epidemic of 'joy-riding'. Young men would break into parked cars, start them up and go for a 'burn' before dumping them a few hours later, usually miles from where they had been stolen. Between 1953 and 1963 the number of vehicles 'illegally used' in Victoria almost doubled. Joy-riding was more common in Melbourne than in the country and, judging by the ages of convicted offenders, it was especially prevalent among the young, including those under the legal driving age.

As early as 1948 the RACV was complaining of the light penalties dispensed by magistrates to youthful joy-riders, and insisted that they should be treated as criminals rather than pranksters. The law had traditionally distinguished between 'illegal use'—the temporary use of a car—and theft—its conversion to another's use. 'A boy may steal a ride without stealing the donkey', according to an old legal adage. The apparent leniency of the courts provoked outrage among the victims of joy-riding. In the late 1940s cars were still very expensive and in short supply; a motorist might have to wait months to replace his car if it was lost or damaged beyond repair. 'Car thieves', the RACV believed, were 'notoriously reckless drivers, having no more respect for the lives of others than they have for their property'. They should there-fore be punished as criminals. 'The time has come for the Courts to realise that the theft of a car can no longer be regarded as a temporary borrowing of the vehicle to have a joy ride. It should be treated as a major crime and severely punished.'[36] The RACV consistently main-tained this view, and in the mid-1950s, as the numbers of stolen cars continued to increase, it almost won over the government of the day. In February 1955 the Opposition Leader Henry Bolte promised that an incoming Liberal administration would abolish the outmoded charge of 'illegal use' and ensure that car thieves were gaoled.[37] When they came to power, however, the Liberals were more circumspect. They increased the penalties for both theft and illegal use, but, probably on legal advice, retained the distinction between them. Car thieves could be forced to pay for any damage they caused. Yet, since 80 per cent of stolen cars were recovered undamaged, the new penalty had little effect on the numbers of joy-riders, which continued to increase.[38] In the late 1950s Labor's Clive Stoneham questioned whether this 'serious social prob-lem' could be reversed by simply imposing stiffer penalties. If car-stealing

MAKE THE PUNISHMENT FIT THE CRIME!

Motoring organisations like the RACV campaigned to have the 'joy-rider' treated as a car-thief rather than simply the 'illegal user' of a motor vehicle. (RADIATOR)

was a 'social problem', then public officials needed greater insight into the social influences that produced it.[39]

In the words of an expert committee appointed to investigate the problem in 1963, joy-riding was 'a highly infectious disease among certain types of young people'. The committee was acutely conscious of the status-enhancing qualities of the car.

The motor vehicle has become a status symbol with both adults and young people. From early adolescence onwards the urge to drive and to be seen driving a motor vehicle becomes irresistible to some youths. Among them are some who are prepared to use other people's motor vehicles illegally to achieve this satisfaction . . . Today status depends on materialism . . . Driving a motor car is indispensable to status. Many youths embark on hire purchase of a car, frequently an old car, as soon as they reach 18 years. Others take one from the street to satisfy this urge to drive even before they reach 18 years.[40]

While the numbers of cars illegally used had grown rapidly, so, the committee pointed out, had the numbers of cars on the road, and the numbers of young men able to steal them.

Car-stealing, it found, was usually a spontaneous rather than a planned activity. In the early 1960s, when most suburban houses were still without garages and carports, motorists often parked their cars in the street. More than half the cars illegally used were Holdens, usually the early FX and FJ models, which were notoriously easy to steal. It required only a bent coathanger inserted through the front louvre window and the door was unlocked. A ball of 'silver paper' pushed between the points of the ignition and the motor was started. A police report based on interviews with offenders put 'cruising' at the head of the list of motives, followed by the desire to make a specific journey, for example, to the beach or the hills, or to a dance in a distant suburb. Sometimes the destinations were even less adventurous: one car thief was apprehended conveying his wife to a maternity hospital. The desire to get somewhere and the status of being able to drive there were more important than the thrill of speed or the desire for rebellion. 'Most lads', the experts concluded, 'get pleasure from driving a motor car without speeding'. They suspected that some joy-rides were provoked by a family row or the rider's desire to get away from his home or parents. If so, they hypothesised, the children of cruel, neglectful or 'incompetent' parents might seek psychic compensation in the thrills of car-stealing. But the evidence presented by the committee in support of this theory—the somewhat higher proportion of offenders from families in which the parent was divorced or in which both parents worked—was less than compelling.

The experts attempted to draw a collective portrait of the joy-rider—his age, social status, educational background and residence. The incidence of joy-riding was greatest among young men just under legal driving age (14–18). Their fathers were more likely to come from a skilled working-class background than either an unskilled or a white-collar occupation, although young offenders themselves were often labourers or other unskilled workers. A striking number of offenders were actually in the motor business as apprentices, mechanics, panel beaters, spraypainters, garage attendants, drivers or other automobile tradesmen. One young offender admitted that he just 'loved machinery'. Among the youngest teenagers, those who were legally as well as financially debarred from driving, joy-riders seemed to come from all social classes. They came as much from average or well-to-do suburbs as from poor ones, although disproportionately, it seems, from new, outer working-class suburbs poorly served by public transport, such as Braybrook, Reservoir, Noble Park, Dandenong, Sunshine, Broadmeadows, St Albans, and Altona. Perhaps significantly, more cars were also abandoned in, than stolen from, such suburbs. Melbourne, we must remind ourselves, was a city where the pleasures and liberties of driving were still very unequally distributed, especially among the young, and where being without wheels was more of a liability if you lived in some suburbs than in others. On the lonely fringes of the sprawling metropolis, nothing symbolised a young man's dreams of independence and sexual conquest as powerfully as possession, legal or otherwise, of a motor car.[41]

As car ownership gradually increased among the city's youth, that symbolism underwent a slow mutation. In the early 1970s a young doctor, George Miller, was completing his residency in the casualty ward at Sydney's St Vincent's Hospital. Every night the ambulances arrived, sirens wailing, and unloaded the bodies—crushed, bleeding, sometimes ominously inert—of young people maimed in the city's escalating road toll. The young doctors did their best to revive them, staunch the bleeding, patch them up. But on the talented Miller, this nightly trauma produced a powerful imaginative effect. As writer-director of the film *Mad Max* (1978), he turned the lethal battle for road mastery among the city's car-crazy young men into a compelling urban myth, perhaps the most extraordinary creative response to Australia's motor age.

Miller and his producer Byron Kennedy shot their film on Melbourne's western industrial fringe. It opens 'a few years from now' on the road to Anarchie, named with obvious symbolic intent after Anakie, an actual township at the foot of the You-Yangs. The hero, Max (Mel Gibson), and his companion 'The Goose' are members of the Main Force Patrol, a demoralised band of highway warriors, locked in mortal conflict with the demonic Night Rider and his lawless retinue of hoons and bikies. The rivals drive painted war-chariots along deserted back roads, through a bleak landscape of truckies' cafes and oil refineries, chemical dumps and wreckers' yards. Their contest is a kind of tournament, a test of mechanical strength and personal

courage. As knights once faced each other in the joust, so young
drivers now challenge each other to the deadly game of 'chicken'.

Mad Max is striking among modern road films for its grimly realistic portrayal of injury and death. When cars crash or incinerate, we see
the arrival of the 'meat truck' (ambulance), enter the hospital wards and
see the torn limbs and the burnt flesh. Of course Miller did not intend
his film to be anything as literal as a tract on road safety. But in turning
the car-crazy youths of Melbourne's urban frontier into tribal warriors,
he hinted at the deadly potential hidden within the promise of mass
motorisation. 'I am the Chosen One, the mighty hand of vengeance',
yells the Night Rider as he charges down the 'road to freedom'. It takes
Mad Max, a man of peace driven to vengeance, to bring this outbreak
of cosmic road rage to an end.

The apocalyptic violence of *Mad Max* recalls a moment when
Melbourne's roads were truly killing fields. Other Australian films of the
1970s demonstrate a similar preoccupation with the violence and social
dislocation of a car-based society. In Peter Weir's gothic fantasy *The
Cars That Ate Paris* (1974) an outback town, Paris, conducts a canni-
balistic trade in car parts, a grotesque metaphor for the dehumanising
effects of the car. Michael Thornhill's *The FJ Holden* (1977) is a grimly
realistic portrait of the car-based youth culture of Sydney's west. The
film's hero Kevin, an apprentice motor mechanic, cruises the mean
streets of Bankstown in his FJ Holden, looking out for pretty girls. He
meets Ann at the local pub and takes her out to a restaurant, but like
Ron in Henry Williams's *My Love Had a Black Speed Stripe*, he seems
unable to find sexual fulfilment, and the film ends with his violent
ejection from her house. The young Australian male's love affair with
his car was symptomatic, Thornhill implies, of an impoverished sense
of manhood, as much as a disadvantaged place.

Over the following two decades, as car ownership spread across the
city, and among women as well as men, the symbolic link between automobility and manhood was subtly transformed. Nadia Tass and David
Parker's *The Big Steal* (1990) is also a story of a young working-class
man's coming of age, set in Melbourne's western suburbs. Like the
heroes of earlier road movies, Danny Clark has two great desires in
life—a stylish Jaguar car and a girl, the spirited Joanna Johnson. But the
gently ironic mood of *The Big Steal* is a world away from the manic
violence of *Mad Max* or the mindless sex of *The FJ Holden*. Danny gets
his way, with the crooked car salesmen Gordon Farkas as well as with

the lovely Joanna, by a combination of wit and daggy charm rather than brute violence. In the *The Big Steal* the car has not ceased to be a youthful status symbol, but its meaning has changed to reflect new ideals of manhood.[42]

The most recent of Melbourne's road movies, Geoffrey Wright's *Metal Skin* (1994), however, offers a much bleaker vision of adolescent motor mania. Like *Mad Max* it is set on the city's western fringe, but Wright's main protagonist, Psycho-Joe, a petrol head from Altona, though named in obvious homage to Miller's hero, has none of the heroic and redemptive qualities of the Mad Max character. His drag racing exploits reflect a deadly syndrome of nihilism and self-destruction.

For almost a century moralists have feared the heady mix of sex, speed and power presented to the nation's young, especially its young men, in the glamorous form of the automobile. In the 1960s, when cars were still relatively scarce, sexual morals strict, and the risks of injury and death high, it became perhaps the most potent symbol of independence among young Australian males. As ownership has become more widely diffused, among young women as well as men, as sexual morals have relaxed, and as new ideals of manhood (the 'sensitive new age guy') gained currency, the symbolic power of the car declined, though it is far from spent.

4

The New Landscape

In 1945 Melbourne was still a recognisable child of that epoch of self-delusion and greed, the land boom of the 1880s. Seen from the air, it looked like a giant hand, the palm representing the central business district and the core of closely settled industrial suburbs, and the fingers, the web of railway and tramway suburbs. So extravagant had been the expectations of 'Marvellous Melbourne' that real estate agents and builders were still selling land and building houses in streets subdivided by the land boomers half a century before. At the end of the war most Melburnians lived within walking distance of a train or tram, or along a short bus route that connected with the rail. In the middle and outer suburbs, the fingers of development ran along the higher ground and were interspersed by wedges of open country defined by the creek valleys of the Yarra, Maribyrnong and their tributaries. Growing up in Essendon, only eight kilometres from the GPO, I could easily walk to open countryside to the east, along the Moonee Ponds Creek, to the west, in the Maribyrnong valley, and to the north, beyond Essendon airport, where the flat basalt of the Keilor plains began.

Within a decade of the great crash of the 1890s the first motor cars had made their appearance, yet at the end of World War II only about one family in four owned a car and the landscape of the suburbs was still largely formed by older patterns of foot, horse and rail transport. From the railway stations, with their clusters of Victorian shops and terraces, development had extended in concentric bands, Edwardian cottages giving way to 1920s Californian bungalows and the occasional 1930s moderne until, at last, the ragged suburban frontier of dirt roads, empty building lots and sales hoardings was reached. The outlines of the rail and tram network had hardly altered since the 1890s, but electrification, which enabled trains to run faster and more frequently, had greatly increased railway and tramway patronage. Between 1900 and 1945 the traffic on Melbourne's suburban trains and trams had multiplied more than fourfold.[1] In 1945 almost as many Melburnians walked or cycled to work as drove, yet walkers and drivers together were barely half the number of rail and tram commuters.

Essendon, a lower middle class enclave on the city's north-western side, had fewer motorists than the leafier suburbs to the east, although more than its working-class neighbours. Of the twenty or so families in our street only three or four had cars at the end of the war, though one or two more had access to the boss's car or truck. Essendon's main street, Mount Alexander Road, had once carried thousands of prospectors hurrying to the Castlemaine and Bendigo fields. Now electric trams ran between palm trees down a central plantation while cars and

Corner Shop, Richmond, 1970. A relic of a fast-changing pedestrian society.
(PHOTO MARK STRIZIC)

buses bound for Essendon airport flowed along its dual carriageway. The North Essendon shopping centre ('Mount Road' as the locals called it) clustered near the Bulla Road tram terminus, the natural transfer point for commuters and, until the extension of the service to Niddrie in the 1950s, the effective frontier between the metropolis and urban–rural fringe.

The horses tethered outside Mr West's farrier's shop and the squawks of live poultry in the pens at Kirk's Bazaar were reminders of how close we were, in space and time, to the horse-and-buggy era. Suburbia was still almost as dependent on shoe leather and bike tyres as on petrol. North Essendon had one shoe retailer, three shoe repair shops, and a bicycle shop but only three motor garages or service stations. Boot repairers, like the SOS ('Save Our Soles') Boot Repairers, were located strategically at tram stops or near railway stations, the point where riding ended and walking began. Morning and evening we saw their customers—serious workingmen in gabardine overcoats, Gladstone bags in hand, the *Sun* or the *Herald* tucked under their arms—striding to and from the tram stop.

In the days before cars and refrigerators, shopping was a frequent, local and predominantly female activity. This was the era of the wicker basket, the string bag and the shopping jeep rather than the trolley and the hatchback. Most of the things we consumed were carried home, or delivered by tradesmen from horse-drawn carts and vans. Among shopkeepers there was a clear gender division. Ironmongers, butchers, fishmongers, bakers, watchmakers, barbers, chemists, grocers, delicatessens and motor garage proprietors were nearly always men. Confectioners, haberdashers, ladies drapers, ladies hairdressers, pastrycooks, florists and dressmakers were usually women. Some shops, like Cafarella's and Lazarello's fruiterers and Tighe's Dairy were family affairs, with mum and dad sharing the work through the week and the children helping out at weekends.

There was not much a suburban family needed that could not be bought in Mount Road. Our food was almost entirely unprocessed and unpackaged—meat was cut from the carcase as we watched, butter and cheese were sliced from the block and wrapped in greaseproof paper, milk was ladled into a billycan brought from home, biscuits scooped from a large tin into brown paper bags, and boiled sweets tipped from glass jars into paper cones. There were no supermarkets, no delicatessens, no milk bars and no restaurants in our shopping centre. Our only takeaway was Winter's Fish Shop. What entertainment we did not provide ourselves, or get from the radio, we obtained locally. We had our own picture theatre, the Circle, with nightly showings for adults and popular Saturday matinees for kids. Two privately run lending libraries dispensed cheap fiction, mainly to housebound wives.[2]

Shopping centres like Mount Road were found all over the suburbs. Only every month or two did mum need to put on her hat and gloves, and board the tram for 'town'—the central business district of Melbourne—perhaps to buy clothes or shoes, or to search for a special length of fabric, or a pattern out of stock at Miss Lewis's ladies drapers. Looking back, I am surprised at how simple, yet how complete, was the suburban society that shaped, and fed upon, the shops in Mount Road. It was, in every sense of the word, a pedestrian society. Bounded, especially for women and children, by the mental and geographical horizons of the walking city, it was as yet untouched by the new tyrannies of fast food, parking meters and traffic congestion.

In the following twenty years this landscape would be utterly transformed. Many new influences would touch it—TV, the electric cash register, rising wages, forklift trucks, telephones. But none was as formative as the automobile. The new suburban landscape, as the poet Bruce Dawe bleakly prophesied, was an automobilised landscape:

In the new landscape there will be only cars
and drivers of cars and signs saying
FREE SWAP CARDS HERE
and exhaust-fumes drifting over the countryside
and sounds of acceleration instead of birdsong.[3]

The car brought a new sense of time and space to the city. It reinforced the suburban sprawl that had been a feature of Australian cities since colonial times. It reshaped the suburbs, pushing their perimeter out beyond the rim of mountains and far along the coastline, filling in the gaps between the rail and tram lines, transforming the regular oscillation of commuters from city to suburb into a more complex web of movements across the metropolis. It created a new engineering, a new architecture, a new aesthetic.

This new landscape is an 'ordinary landscape'—ordinary, that is, in the sense that it is now so familiar, so omnipresent, that we scarcely notice it. So far from making these landscapes unimportant, however, their ubiquity is perhaps the most powerful reason for trying to understand them. 'In trying to unravel the meaning of contemporary landscapes and what they have to say to say about us as Americans, history matters', an American writer, Peirce Lewis, advises.[4] So too with ordinary Australian landscapes. Because of their very familiarity, it is often hard for us to see these mundane features of the landscape as their creators saw them, to recover the moment when they were new, problematical, open to rejection. Aesthetic snobbery may also stand in the way of understanding: a suburban motel or a drive-in theatre may tell us as much about the culture of the era as the ICI Building or the Olympic swimming stadium.

In the minds of many Australians the cultural influence of the car was almost inseparable from that of the first car society, the United States. In the postwar era, America embraced what historian Kenneth Jackson has described as a 'drive-in culture'.[5] The landscape, especially the suburban landscape, was systematically remodelled to accommodate the car. In the process, America invented, and then exported, a repertoire of novel urban forms: the interstate highway, the roadside diner, the garage and carport, the parking meter and the multi-level parking station, the motel, the drive-in theatre, the service station, the automobile-based shopping centre, and the mobile home. The Americanisation of the Australian city often seemed to be most vividly expressed in the changing roadside, as these new forms of urban life reproduced themselves.

One of the most acute observers of Los Angeles, Reyner Banham, coined the word 'autopia' to describe the new landscape brought in to being by the motor car, and most strikingly realised in Los Angeles.[6] His Australian counterpart, Robin Boyd, coined his own word for the mean, local version of the style—'Austerica'.

> Austerica [Boyd wrote] is on no map. It is, as an Austerican advertisement would say, not a place but a way of life. It is found in any country, including parts of America, where an austerity version of the American dream overtakes the indigenous culture. As its name also implies, it is slightly hysterical and it flourishes best of all in Australia, which is already half overtaken by the hysteria. Austerica's chief industry is the imitation of the froth on the top of the American soda-fountain drink. Its religion is 'glamor' and the devotees are psychologically displaced persons who picture heaven as the pool terrace of a Las Vegas hotel. Its high priests are expense account men who judge the USA on a two-weeks hop between various Hilton and

Architect Robin Boyd became the most acute observer and critic of 'Austerica', the debased version of American architectural style that flourished along Melbourne's highways in the 1950s and 1960s. (ILLUSTRATION FROM ROBIN BOYD, *THE AUSTRALIAN UGLINESS*, PENGUIN BOOKS, 1960; WITH PERMISSION FROM PATRICIA DAVIES)

Statler hotels and return home intoxicated with conceptions of American willingness to labour (judged by the attitude of martini-waiters), the average American's standard of living (judged by a week-end at the managing director's house on Long Island), and

American godliness (judged by a copy of 'Guideposts . . . an inspirational publication', which is left by the bedside for every one of the hotel guests of Mr Conrad Hilton).[7]

In coining the word 'Austerica', Boyd performed not a double, but a triple, word play. 'Austerica' was not just a hybrid American-Australianism, but a frenetic (hysterical) pursuit of what was cheapest and nastiest in American culture (the austerity version). Australian cities in the 1940s and 1950s were eager, if distant, seekers of 'autopia', confident—at least until the mid-1960s, when the freeways began to clog—that America's present was Australia's future.[8]

Many elements of the new landscape were created during America's first automobile age in the 1920s and 1930s. The first self-proclaimed 'motel' had appeared in San Luis Obispo, California, in 1926, the first drive-in theatre in Camden, New Jersey, in 1933, the first drive-in shopping centre in Kansas City in 1923, the first drive-in restaurant in Dallas, Texas, in 1921.[9] Already, by 1948, there were 26 000 self-styled motels in the United States. By 1958, there were more than 4000 drive-in cinemas. Only in the postwar era did the drive-in principle become ubiquitous, first in North America, and later throughout the rest of the world. Europeans often made their own distinctive accommodations to the car—the German autobahn, the British roundabout, the Italian autostrada—each reflected something of their national character and local engineering traditions. The hypermarché gave a distinctively Gallic twist to the American supermarket, just as the European campervan was a local variation on the American trailer. Some American inventions such as the motel and the drive-in theatre generally failed to take hold in Europe, where they had to overcome climatic and geographical constraints.

In this international context, Australians stand out as early, enthusiastic and relatively uncritical followers of American fashions and expertise. In 1950 the *Australian Automobile Trade Journal* noted 'an increasing tendency on the part of the people of the USA to organise their lives around the car' and 'a spectacular growth of drive-in businesses since the end of World War II'. 'Shops, markets, banks, theatres, post offices, hotels and even churches now cater for the "anti-walkers" through provision of drive-in services, and all these businesses are prospering and booming.'[10] Australians were eager to follow their lead. Perhaps it was because the two countries had similar geography, and were less inhibited by institutional precedents. But the drive-in culture also flourished precisely because, as an American invention, it had the imprimatur of modernity.

In Essendon the imposition of the new forms produced a kind of visual cancer. An old cinema palace and a blacksmith's shop came down to make way for drive-in filling stations. Drive-in bottle shops in cream brick and tubular steel were tacked onto Victorian hotels, now shorn of their iron-lace verandahs. Front gardens were stripped of foliage to make way for concrete driveways and carports. Plantations of ancient trees were ripped up to widen roadways. In the newer suburbs farther out the drive-in culture was built in from the beginning. In Doncaster, Vermont and Dandenong the carport merged with the house, new drive-in service stations sheltered under cantilevered wings like those on the cars they serviced, gardens extended to the kerb in a smooth sward of lawn without the interposition of fences and footpaths, and roads meandered in elegant curves since no-one worried any more about how long it might take to walk. Social habits were changing too. Out went the shopping jeep, the corner shop, the horse-drawn milk float, the winter overcoat and (temporarily, as it turned out) the Akubra hat. In came the station wagon, the supermarket, the takeaway restaurant and the 'car coat'.

Cars were everywhere in the new landscape, but some parts of the postwar city were virtually created by the car. From the windows of my office in Monash University's Menzies Building, about 20 kilometres from Melbourne's centre, I look out on a tapestry of cream brick walls, terracotta roofs and dark green foliage that stretches all the way to the mountains and the sea. Founded in 1961, Monash became the country's first drive-in university. Our students now park on the abandoned site of Australia's largest drive-in theatre. A mile or so to the north is the extension of the South-Eastern Freeway, Melbourne's first, and nearby is the Pinewood shopping centre (1957), built by the biggest of Australia's project builders, A. V. Jennings. From the top floor of the Menzies Building you can glimpse the sawtooth roofs of Holden's Dandenong plant and, closer by, the now-abandoned Nissan factory. Drive back along Dandenong Road towards the city and you pass Melbourne's first motel before you come to Chadstone, its first regional drive-in shopping centre. This is Austerica's heartland, a world made possible by the car but shaped, unmistakeably, by American style, organisation and know-how.

The World According to Ford

The new landscape of suburbia was made, not only by those who drove cars, but even more fundamentally, by those who designed, made and sold them. Melbourne was Australia's leading centre of car manufacture and the influence of the car on the city began even before it left the assembly line and arrived in the showroom. In encouraging the growth of the car industry Melburnians were building on a long local tradition of tariff protection, regulated wages, fixed working hours and stable employment. Car production encouraged the creation of a skilled work-force, with strong traditions of unionism and expectations of steady material advancement. Car makers were also among the most eager car buyers.

In 1945, when the Chifley Government's plans to develop the auto-mobile industry became known, state governments, conscious of the multiplier effects of such substantial investments on local employment, began to jostle for a share of the action. The British Nuffield company was lured to Sydney while the Rootes group, manufacturers of Standard cars, investigated sites in Victoria. Labor premier John Cain, committed to policies of decentralisation, at first attempted to attract the company to Bendigo. But as the company's local representative explained, only a capital city location would do.

> Our purpose here is to manufacture. We can only do that by a close association with all the subsidiary manufacturers who are established here. We must be in daily touch with them . . . Lord Nuffield has taken a place in Sydney—we feel that we want to go one better and estab-lish ourselves in Melbourne.

A flat, extensive site close to transport, markets, labour and subsidiary manufacturers was the ideal place for a car plant. Eventually the company plumped for a site at Fisherman's Bend, a tract of reclaimed swampland on the lower Yarra, next door to the plant established eight years earlier by Holden.[11]

Soon Holden had outgrown the Fisherman's Bend site. In 1951 the company acquired a new 61-hectare site at Dandenong, about 30 kilo-metres from the city, and began to contruct the biggest and most modern assembly plant in Australia. Located on the main Gippsland railway, Dandenong offered cheap land and good transport. In 1955 when the 7-hectare plant opened, a new public housing estate, designed to provide workers for the new factory, was under construction at nearby Doveton. Four-fifths of the company's employees still commuted from elsewhere in the metropolis (it set the new starting time at 7.50 to allow its Fisherman's Bend workers an extra 20 minutes' travelling time) but by the mid-1960s most of the factory workforce were new immigrants resident in the adjoining suburbs. More than 4000 other manufacturers supplied Holden with subsidiary products—radiators, upholstery, electrical products, duco, tyres.

Over the next decade the strip of flat land between the Princes Highway and the Gippsland railway line from Clayton to Doveton became the largest industrial area in the metropolis.[12] In 1952 the agricultural implement maker International Harvester selected a site next door to Holden. The spare parts firm Kirkall-Repco, the electrical component manufacturer Robert Bosch, the German motor car manufacturer Volkswagen and the British paint manufacturer BALM built plants in nearby Clayton.[13] By 1960 over half the workforce of Clayton was employed in manufacturing, much of it in small back-street engineering shops, foundries and factories producing parts and spares for the big firms.[14] The rail link had helped to draw the new factories away from the waterfront and the CBD, but even more important to their survival were the new technologies of rapid and decentralised movement represented by the semitrailer, the container and the forklift truck.[15]

While Holden anchored the development of the industrial south-east, its main rival, Ford, built its main plant at Campbellfield on the city's northern perimeter. In 1956 Premier Henry Bolte announced the sale of 400 acres of land on Sydney Road to the Ford Motor Company for a new £15 million assembly plant. Ford was eager to establish a base in the metropolis, not only because the Geelong plant was reaching capacity, but, as one of its chief engineers, Brian Inglis, explained, because it saw the city as a ready source of labour. 'We decided to look to the north of Melbourne to where the migrants were settling. They were coming off their boats in their tens of thousands and here was a labour pool suited to our needs.'[16] Ford paid £200 000 for the Campbellfield site which the government had originally acquired by compulsory purchase for the Housing Commission. A special act of parliament was required to authorise the sale of the site, originally intended for working-class housing, to the car manufacturer who, it was said, would 'provide opportunities of employment for at least a proportion of the residents' on the nearby estate. As a further sweetener, the government undertook to reopen and electrify the nearby Fawkner to Somerton railway and to widen local roads for heavy transport.[17]

The suburbs that grew up around the new auto plants became, as historian Mark Peel has shown, the distinctive locale of a new suburban working class.[18] Doveton, Norlane, Broadmeadows, Fisherman's Bend— like their interstate counterparts, Elizabeth, Green Valley and Inala— were the product of a unique conjunction of economic and political circumstances. High levels of public and private investment, heavy government subsidies in the form of cheap land, tariff protection, public housing and assisted immigration had undergirt the booming car industry. Relatively high wages and low unemployment had enabled working-class people, including those who assembled the cars, to attain car ownership themselves. (Poor public transport in the new suburbs may have helped.) For a quarter of a century, from the end of World

Ford's Geelong factory. Cars, assembled by Ford Australia, and houses, prefabricated by the Victorian Government Housing Commission, were indispensable features of the new Fordist landscape of the 1950s. (PHOTO WOLFGANG SIEVERS, 1951)

War II to the oil price hike of the early 1970s, this was the regime that pushed Melbourne's suburban growth and shaped its landscape.

The car factories were not only powerhouses of economic growth; they were also a paradigm of flow technology, streamlined efficiency and synchronised activity that soon set the standard for the whole of modern life. Along the assembly lines at Dandenong and Broadmeadows every worker had a special repetitive job to do and just enough time to do it. The entire manufacturing process was broken down into a sequence of discrete operations. As the chassis moved along the assembly line, one component after another was added until the entire vehicle was complete. Analysing the process of manufacturing, breaking it down into discrete tasks, arranging them in strict sequence, timing each operation to the second, smoothing the flow from one stage to the next: these were the secret of a mode of production that has aptly been dubbed 'Fordist'.[19] When Ford invented the automobile assembly line he hit on a principle that would ultimately be applied to a host of other activities: from supermarket shelves and highway interchanges to drive-in theatres, fast-food outlets and bottle shops, even suburban housing estates.

When Robin Boyd inveighed against 'Austerica', it was the style or look of the borrowed American culture that he most objected to. But Americanisation went deeper than aesthetics: it influenced the engine as well as the fins, the plan of the house as well as the colour scheme, the soda as well as the froth on top. Postwar Australian suburbia was the product of a new cultural logic, the logic of Fordism, as well as a new aesthetic. Reading the new landscape is to recognise how many and pervasive were its applications.

THE CAR, THE HOUSE AND THE STREET

Possibly the subtlest manifestation of the ways in which the car changed the landscape was in that most familiar of environments, the local street and neighbourhood. For almost a century Melbourne had followed its colonial masters in reproducing the rectilinear grid of Robert Hoddle's first surveys. The grid was an efficient way of dividing and selling land and its wide straight streets provided a legible map and an efficient pattern of movement. It was considered a democratic form of town planning.[20] It required almost everyone to move along the vertical

Flow technology in action. Photographer Wolfgang Sievers captured the spirit of the new regime in this study of the production line at General Motors Holden.

and horizontal sides of squares; there are no diagonal short-cuts, no meandering curves to interfere with the travellers' crab-like movement, north–south, east–west, towards their destinations. In the mid-nineteeenth century, when it was first adopted by Australian town surveyors, the hierarchy of roads accorded with the contemporary status system. Arterial roads, with their wide carriageways and high visibility, were also the most prestigious places to live: the grand mansions along St Kilda Road and Royal Parade are a legacy of that era. Narrow back streets, by contrast, were regarded as sinister precisely because they were secluded from the gaze of respectable society. Many councils used powers conferred under the 1914 Local Government Act to prevent the creation of blind alleys and cul-de-sacs.[21]

The car changed all this. Traffic made main streets noisy and dangerous. The long straight street created by the grid encouraged the motorist to speed and the pattern of four-way intersections was a recipe for collisions. Already in the 1920s American town planners had begun to discern the outlines of an alternative street plan that would correct the defects of the grid. Streets would now follow the contours of the land, with curves and narrow carriageways that forced the motorist to slow down and cul-de-sacs that secluded houses from through traffic. Pedestrian movement should be separated as far as possible from motor traffic. If long straight streets could not be avoided they should be broken up with circles and ovals that slowed the movement of traffic.[22] The new street plan would reverse the social hierarchy of the old: now it was the secluded courts and cul-de-sacs rather than the crowded arterial roads that became the most favoured residential locations. Segregated from traffic, they were safer, friendlier, quieter places to live.

The rectilinear grid had taken such firm root in the minds of Australian surveyors, developers and municipal officials, however, that alternative principles of street design made only halting progress. Occasionally, as in the Windsor Park Estate in Surrey Hills, a nineteenth-century developer chose to vary the grid with serpentine curves, and in the 1920s the American innovator Walter Burley Griffin introduced cul-de-sacs and curving streets on his housing estates at Castlecrag overlooking Sydney's Middle Harbour and Eaglemont on the upper Yarra.[23] In the late 1930s, the Melbourne builder Albert ('A. V.') Jennings incorporated cul-de-sacs in his middle-class residential estates, Beauville, Beaumont and Beauview, in Murrumbeena and Ivanhoe.

Such experiments were rare, however, until the mid-1950s when several forces combined to reshape the suburbs. Much of postwar Melbourne was settled within the grid subdivisions drawn up in the pre-automobile era. With the ending of postwar austerity, developers and builders began to move back into private house building. Some, like A. V. Jennings, set out to apply the techniques of mass production and mass marketing to the housing business.[24] Following the example of the motor car industry, they sought to integrate all phases of the business— subdivision, manufacture, construction, town planning, marketing and finance—into a single, efficient operation.

The new housing estate was shaped by similar principles, with streets designed to direct the movement of people and vehicles in accordance with a clear hierarchy of functions and activities. Because of the scale of their operations, project developers like Jennings were better able to secure the large tracts of outer suburban land that permitted a more

comprehensive approach to street planning. In 1960 Jennings outlined
the thinking behind the creation of his new estates:

> Safety factors require attention by the elimination of all cross traffic
> and the introduction of a number of cul-de-sacs. These provide quiet
> sections to the community and are particularly safe for children, who
> unfortunately will always tend to play in the street rather than their
> own backyard.
>
> Uninteresting 'grid' subdivisions are never considered in a properly
> planned neighbourhood unit, an area such as Trentwood Estate offi-
> cially coming within this category.
>
> Gentle curving of streets in the general road pattern slows down
> traffic to internal streets, and gives added interest to the frontages of
> rows of houses because they can be readily seen and appreciated from
> a distance, in any direction. This also tends to aid the aspect of indi-
> vidualism to each house, which is almost a prerequisite for the
> Australian home builder.[25]

Safety, quiet and individuality rather than a concern for neighbourhood
interaction seem to have been the underlying motives for the Jennings
experiment. In 1955 the Local Government Act was amended to
require housing estates to be serviced with streets and drains in advance
of development, and henceforth Jennings incorporated cul-de-sacs and
narrow carriageways in most of his new estates. By the 1970s road
and traffic engineers had demonstrated the safety of the new road
plans and had distilled the underlying principles into codes and standards widely followed throughout Australia.[26]

Drive towards the Dandenongs through Melbourne's eastern
suburbs and you eventually cross Springvale Road, the longest of the
city's north–south arterial roads. To the east the land becomes more
undulating, the tree cover more dense and random. The oatmeal brick
and terracotta tiles of the 1950s and 1960s give way to the mud-browns
and white painted brick of the 1970s. Only here, about 20 kilometres
from the CBD, does suburbia begin to shake off the linear monotony of
the grid. Between 1956 and 1965, A. V. Jennings carried out six major
subdivisions along this frontier within the former City of Waverley: the
company's mark on the landscape, with its sinuous curves, walkways,
hierarchy of circulation and distribution roads, is unmistakeable.[27]
A few miles back most of the houses had garages and improvised
carports; now most of the carports are built into the houses themselves,
many with accommodation for two or even three vehicles. Suddenly,

it seems, we are in a new territory, one in which the car is no longer a stranger but a familiar and indispensable element in everyday life.

Take a turn off Burwood Highway, just as you cross Springvale Road, and along one of the side streets of Vermont you come to Pin Oak Court, the cul-de-sac made famous in television's *Neighbours* as 'Ramsay Street'. Here, in soap opera if not in life, the automobile suburb acquires the gossipy intimacy of a village. Vermont is a suburb created by the car but in the television world of *Neighbours*, the car is all but invisible. Fiction has filtered out the traffic noise, the pollution, the visual clutter of autopia.

Suburbanites were often ambivalent about whether the car belonged at home. Suburbia was traditionally conceived as a place of refuge from the mechanised workaday world, a zone of peace and quiet where city-dwellers were restored to Nature. In the 1920s when the automobile first appeared in numbers in Australian cities, car owners puzzled about how these new residents of suburbia should be housed. Often the car was housed in a public garage away from the home or secreted in a shed located, stable-like, at the rear of the property. Increasingly, however, experts advocated the construction of a purpose-built 'motor-house' attached to the house itself. 'It doubles the usefulness and pleasure of owning a car to be able to accommodate it on the premises, it is always near at hand, and it is likely to receive better attention from the owner.'[28] In the early days of motoring, when cars were unreliable and motorists often had to carry out running repairs, the favoured 'motor-house' was a combined garage and workshop, sometimes equipped with a pit and workbench.[29] Suburban subdivisions increasingly made provision for a driveway and garage, even if the garage was not built at once, or even occupied by a car when it was. Americans had already invented a cheap and simple form of motor-house, the carport, but in Australia, as Robin Boyd observed in 1952, it was 'seldom used by a nation which paid a lot for its cars and valued them highly'.[30]

By the late 1950s, however, cars were becoming relatively cheaper and the problem of housing them more pressing. The carport, a simple roof deck supported by brick pillars, timber posts or steel frame, housed the motor car with less dignity than a garage but it was enough to protect its duco, and the self-respect of the owner. 'The cars which are garaged and well cared for can be easily distinguished from those which are always in the open exposed to sunshine and rain', an RACV official advised.[31] Cheap to buy and quick to construct, the prefabricated carport was also, its makers claimed, 'smartly designed to enhance any home'.[32] It soon became ubiquitous, tacked on the side of houses, standing free in the middle of the backyard, even, where no other space was available, rudely planted in front of the house itself. The carport was the cuckoo of suburban landscape, a cheeky intruder that soon began to rule the roost. By the 1960s project builders had begun to domesticate the carport, acknowledging the car as an intimate member of the family by bringing it under the same roof.[33] A. V. Jennings incorporated carports as a standard feature of its designs from 1961, at first by simply extending the roof-line to create a room without walls at one end of a low-slung ranchhouse. By the 1970s the house itself was sometimes hoisted into the air to enable the carport to take pride of place beside the front entrance.[34]

THE SERVICE STATION

To the passer-by, there was no more evident symbol of mass motoring than the decline of the old motor garage and the rise of the 'service station'. The first motor garages were simple barn-like buildings, sometimes actually converted from the coachhouses or stables of the preceding horse-and-buggy era. The customer approached the garage through a front office, often decorated with oil company posters and girlie calendars. In the adjoining garage, mechanics bent over the bonnets, or descended into pits dug in the floor to carry out repairs. Outside, a row of colourful hand-operated pumps lined the kerb. Motorists pulled up and selected their favourite brand—Shell, Plume, Golden Fleece or Ampol—and the proprietor, wiping the grease from his hands, emerged from the dark interior of the garage to serve them. He pushed and pulled the lever on the side of the pump until the golden fluid filled the glass reservoir to the appropriate level, then placed the nozzle of the hose in the tank and released the outlet valve. He checked the oil and water, and perhaps the battery too. A few modern service stations had a double row of pumps set back from the road under a kind of verandah, but most were still independent family businesses, about half on their own freeholds, earning as much from repairs and motor spares as by selling petrol.

In barely a decade, between the late 1940s and the late 1950s, Melbourne—like almost every other city in the developed world—

Proprietor Frank Smith, holding son Barry, stands outside his garage and adjoining home on the corner of Warrigal and Dandenong roads, Oakleigh, in the mid 1930s.
(PHOTO COURTESY PROFESSOR F. B. SMITH)

witnessed the almost total annihilation of the independent motor garage by the American-style one-brand, company-owned leasehold service station. Once petrol rationing had been abolished in 1949, the rival oil companies embarked on an all-out war to increase and consolidate their position in the burgeoning metropolitan gasoline market. Since one brand of petrol is really much like another, the oil companies sought to gain advantage over their rivals, not by differentiating their products— although they sometimes sought to create that mystique through the promotion of patented fuel additives—but by promoting brand loyalty through superior standards of driveway service and a more efficient network of distribution. The old motor garages had been distributed with little regard to metropolitan patterns of traffic flow and the service they offered was as variable as the business acumen of their independent proprietors. Moreover, selling petrol through multi-brand independent garages was an intrinsically inefficient system of distribution. Winning the petrol wars, the oil companies believed, required a more comprehensive and efficient approach to marketing. The key to their strategy was for the oil companies to own the service station sites but to lease the business to self-employed operators under exclusive agreements requiring the stringent observance of standards of service, including such items as the wearing of the company's uniform and politeness to customers, and an undertaking to sell the company's products exclusively. Rather than selling petrol as an adjunct to motor repairs, the service station operator focused his energies on the sale of oil products and the provision of 'service'.[35] An Australian businessman who visited the United States in 1950 observed that, 'Every service station is, in fact, a department store of motorists' supplies and the display of accessories is scientifically laid out, well in view of the motorist who calls for petrol.'[36]

Every service station was designed to be a roadside advertisement for the company's products. In the 1930s the American industrial designer Dorwin Teague created a standardised functional service station for the Texaco company. This soon became the prototype for other companies around the world. A simple box-like building with full-length glass windows stood behind a broad concrete forecourt covered with a wide, cantilevered roof. The petrol pumps stood on islands, designed to smooth the flow of customers through the several driveways. Thus, as Teague boasted, 'a simple utilitarian construction becomes beautiful through careful organisation and efficiency'. Each company added its distinctive architectural gestures, colours and logos: Mobil's starkly painted red and white, Shell's gold and red, BP's cream brick with green and gold trim, Ampol's brown brick offset by the company's red, white and blue and distinctive cylindrical brushed aluminium pumps.[37]

The bright, modern appearance of the new service station, with its smartly dressed attendants and prompt driveway service, made a stark contrast with the grubby overalls and offhand demeanour of the old-time motor garage proprietor. A survey by the Shell Oil Company in 1950 found that while 70 per cent of garage proprietors were opposed to the introduction of the 'one-brand' petrol station, their customers were keenly interested in the improved standards of driveway cleanliness and efficiency.[38] 'Today, tyre-pumping, windscreen wiping, showers, toilets, restaurants are what the motorist expects and demands from the service station. If one doesn't offer these things, he will drive to the next one.'[39] Old-timers were sometimes contemptuous of the way in which the modern motorist was wooed with give-aways and free services. 'The way things are going these days, with service stations cum garages, . . . I won't be surprised to find some of 'em sporting swimming pools to be used by customers as they wait for services', one contemporary wryly observed. The 'Service Station De Luxe', he suggested, might even include a children's nursery or a coffee shop, camp stretchers for resting lorry drivers, telephone booths for commercial travellers to call their clients and a 'comfy theatrette for the screening of appropriate films'. He was joking of course, but over the following decades many of his satirical suggestions would come to be adopted. By recognising the petrol stop as a new marketing opportunity, the service station had taken the first step on the road to the 24-hour convenience shop.[40]

The soft-sell approach encountered by the motorist had its ugly side in the harsh internal reorganisation of petrol retailing. 'In recent years the Americanisation of our industry has been complete, thorough and ruthless', *Wheels* observed in 1959. 'In all departments the drive for American efficiency and American style-selling has gone on apace.'

Opening Day 1969 at the Esso service station in Doncaster, Melbourne's most automobilised suburb. (PHOTO COURTESY EXXON MOBIL AND RICHARDS COLLECTION, MUSEUM VICTORIA)

Some people objected to the uniform adoption of American styles of operation as inconsistent with the more casual Australian outlook. 'I found the whole attitude of the company got on my nerves', one disenchanted service station operator complained. 'I think this excessive drive-way service gets on the motorists' nerves too . . . It's a very American code and it rubs me up the wrong way.' 'Un-Australian, undemocratic . . . and socially immoral' was the way another group of endangered retailers described their adversaries.[41]

By the mid-1950s the oil companies were engaged in a seemingly reckless war of attrition to command the best selling points. Along the main arterial roads, hundreds of houses, shops, picture theatres, and even churches were razed to make way for the broad concrete driveways with their cantilevered awnings, rows of brightly coloured electric pumps, and space-age lubritoriums.[42] No sooner had one company staked out a new site than its rivals moved in next door or across the road. In July 1954, Mr T. J. Francis, a long-established independent operator in Camberwell, explained his decision to close the business by pointing to the appearance of three new company-owned stations in the neighbourhood. 'Napoleon called the English a nation of shopkeepers', he recalled. 'If he'd been alive today, he would have called Australians a nation of garage attendants.'[43] The shrinking remnant of independent garage proprietors, supported by residents affronted by the wanton destruction of local landmarks, called upon the government to intervene, perhaps by introducing a system of petrol station licensing, like the systems governing the distribution of hotels and newsagents. But the Liberal Party, which came to power in June 1955, was hostile to any attempt on the part of the petrol retailers to curb free competition by restrictions on the number of new service stations or limitations on their trading hours. Since the 1940s the RACV had been pressing for extended trading hours. 'As a commodity for which there is no substitute, petrol must be available at least daily', it declared.[44] In January 1956, in spite of a vigorous campaign by service station operators, the government extended the hours of opening from 61 to 77 hours, including Saturdays and Sunday mornings.

For the small one-man business, extended hours were a recipe for domestic misery, financial ruin, or both. Between 1948 and 1958 the number of service stations in Australia increased from 11 071 to 17 974, or 62 per cent. The oil companies argued that this was not excessive, considering the 183 per cent growth in the number of motor cars. But

From grease-stained overalls to neatly pressed uniforms, the single-brand service station announced the arrival of an American-style drive-in society.
(PHOTOS COURTESY OF EXXON MOBIL, SHELL AUSTRALIA AND RICHARDS COLLECTION, MUSEUM VICTORIA)

to the hard-pressed garage proprietor, operating on low margins and obliged by his new masters to offer higher standards of service, the statistics told only a part of the story. Little by little the oil companies were squeezing the independent operator out, and tying their own lease-holders into ever-more stringent operating agreements.

With its wide apron of concrete driveway, its illuminated company logos, massive advertising hoardings and roadside sandwich boards announcing 'free offers' of everything from glass tumblers to Gold Coast holidays, the service station constituted a rude assault on the conventional boundary between neighbourhood and street. For centuries, shops and houses had been implicitly designed for pedestrians, who moved slowly along the street, sometimes pausing to chat or to gaze into a shop window. But the service station was the prototype of a new and more intrusive form of urban architecture, designed to catch the eye, and temporarily slow the progress, of the fleeting motorist. When Jason moved faster, the roadside sirens had to call louder. The roadside soon became a jumble of clashing colours, flashing lights and catchy slogans. 'Australian businessmen are rapidly following the lead of their American counterparts by making use of the facades of their premises—especially when they are prominently situated—for displaying large, eye-catching models of their particular products for advertising purposes', *Australian Motor Manual* reported in 1955.[45] One Sydney service station announced itself with a tower of 67 used car tyres while motorists passing through Liverpool on the Hume Highway encountered a gigantic bottle of Sunnybrook Port—the progenitor, perhaps, of that prolific Australian breed of roadside giants—'The Big Merino', 'The Big Pineapple', 'The Big Banana' and 'The Big Tomato'.

'Wherever there are cars, you are likely to find Austerica unalloyed', observed its arch-enemy, Robin Boyd.[46] Along the outer sections of Melbourne's main arterial roads, the station-wagon trails of the suburban frontier, there appeared a relentlessly Austerican landscape of service stations, car showrooms, used car yards, spare parts and tyre distributors, discount houses, brake and suspension specialists, windscreen repairers and wrecking yards. Drive along the Nepean Highway between Brighton and Moorabbin, the Maroondah Highway between Blackburn and Ringwood, Dandenong Road between Oakleigh and Clayton, and Sydney Road between Fawkner and Broadmeadows and you can see it still. Here the car is king. Autoland has its own tribal language and its own male hierarchy of sales executives, floor salesman, mechanics and detailers. But it is a kingdom that lives, almost predatorially, on the passing trade of motorists. Behind the plate-glass windows of the showroom or office, keen-eyed men in shiny suits survey the acres of spotless duco, ever on the lookout for the tiny clues that mark out the real sales prospect from the 'just-looker'.

THE MOTEL

Mass motoring not only changed the internal geography of the city; it transformed the relationship between city and country. For more than 100 years most Melburnians had taken their holidays, if they had holidays at all, at guesthouses or campsites, or with country cousins, within reach of the city by rail. Occasionally they might travel by steamer to Sydney or Launceston, or take a motor coach along the newly opened Great Ocean Road; but most of coastal or inland Victoria still lay beyond their reach. Yet within a generation, the family car changed all that: suddenly there was hardly a beach or valley where the camper and caravanner had not penetrated.

In the days of the hotel and guesthouse, holidays were almost as

Austerica Rampant. Swan Street, Richmond, 1967. (PHOTO MARK STRIZIC)

regimented as the rest of life. Family life was subordinated to the timetable of the camp or guesthouse, with its dinner gongs and organised games.[47] But the car offered the promise of a more relaxed kind of family holiday, less regimented by the timetables of the railway and the guesthouse, more responsive to the desire of the suburban family to do things together and in their own way. The caravan, the bayside campsite and the motel each represented a kind of home-away-from-home.

In 1950, when petrol rationing had barely been abolished, a Sydney company announced plans to build 'modern roadside accommodation on American lines' up the east coast from Melbourne to Brisbane. '"Motels" are very popular in the United States, and if run on the same lines, and not hedged about with too many Government restrictions, should be just as popular here', a motoring magazine forecast.[48] In the postwar period the American motel had been reborn. The first motels, established on the outskirts of big cities in the 1920s and 30s, had a sleazy image and were often nothing more than motorised assignation houses. The establishment of the Holiday Inn chain in 1952 began the process of rehabilitation, and it was the respectable family tourist motel, rather than a venue for what Americans called the 'hot pillow trade', that the first Australian motel operators aimed to introduce. They capitalised on 'the growing discontent' with ordinary hotels which, as one contemporary complained, were 'really only drinking houses'. 'I feel that motels, built on American lines, will gradually cater for the travelling public to the near exclusion of the present so-called hotels.'[49] By 1954 there were still fewer than a dozen motels in Australia, all privately owned. But the American correspondents of Australian magazines were already describing the latest developments in the motel business in the confident expectation that 'as the business becomes more competitive, motel keepers are sure to dip into the tried and true American bag of tricks' such as flashy neon signs and palm-fringed swimming pools.[50] Some motel operators underlined the American connection by choosing names like 'The Niagara', 'The Atlantic', 'The Bel Air', 'The California' or simply 'The American'.[51]

In fact, although Australian motel operators sometimes dipped in to the American bag of tricks, they picked and chose what they borrowed. An American motel expert, W. L. Edmundson, who visited Australia in 1955, believed that Australian motels might become a model for the rest of the world 'because all the mistakes of the American motel industry would be avoided'. With a modern motel chain Australia might enjoy what had hitherto failed to materialise—a bonanza of American tourists. Edmundson shrewdly identified the points on which motels beat hotels and anticipated the tastes of an affluent leisured society. 'Americans like motels because of the informal, pleasant atmosphere, without elevators, hotel foyers and parking difficulties. Motels provide good friendly service and there is no tipping.'[52] If anything, Australians excelled even Americans in their informality, their preference for self-catering, and especially their aversion to tipping. The typical Australian motel of the 1950s was a low-slung ensemble of single-storey or box-like rooms, grouped around a courtyard and entered by a small reception office and breakfast room. All rooms were equipped with electric jugs, toasters, irons and sometimes a stove. Unlike the grand hotels of an earlier generation which had created an aura of the exotic and the opulent, the motel impressed by its familiarity, by being simply a home, albeit an up-to-date home, away from home. Unlike the guest-houses and camping grounds, which had been the favourite holiday resorts of the 1920s and 1930s, the motel carried the privacy of travel established by the motor car into an essentially self-contained, cellular form of accommodation. Guests could arrive, pay their tariff, sleep undisturbed, have their breakfast delivered through a hatch in the wall and depart without so much as a goodbye.[53]

The Oakleigh Motel, Melbourne's first, opened in 1957 on the Princes Highway at the city's eastern gateway, just opposite the spot where the Olympic marathon runners had turned back towards the MCG a few months before. It was the brainchild of Cyril Lewis, 'formerly well-known in the car-selling game', who had toured the United States, inspecting and living in motels all the way, as he gathered ideas for a motel that he boasted was 'equal to America's best'. 'Australia shows America' was the headline of one advertisement. 'Your car in your bedroom' read another, perhaps inviting the thought that the Australian male's love affair with his car was to be physically consummated.

Victorians had been slower than their northern neighbours to embrace the motel. Australia's first, the American Motel at Bathurst, had opened in 1954 and by 1958, when the Australian Motel Feder-ation was formed, there were 24 in New South Wales and nine in Queensland, but only four in all Victoria.[54] Cyril Lewis had struggled to secure finance for his Oakleigh Motel, even appealing to Premier Henry Bolte to give government assistance to enable it to open in time for the Olympics. Bolte refused but wrote on his behalf to the federal Treasurer Arthur Fadden in support of a loan (Fadden refused).[55]

Modernity, luxury, comfort, convenience and individuality—the values associated with the car itself—were also those built into the motel. From its sleek signage and hangar-like entrance to its air-conditioning and sound-proofing, the Oakleigh Motel was a model of modernity. But it was in the modernity of its private spaces rather than the opulence of its public spaces that the qualities of the motel were most clearly revealed: 'Every room is air-conditioned; every room has its own shower recess and toilet; every room is tastefully furnished with the most modern fittings, and every room is sound-proofed for slumber comfort.'[56] Only a few cosmetic details of Cyril Lewis's motel, like the waratah flowers in the dining room carpets, could be described as

Oakleigh Motel, Melbourne's first, opened on Dandenong Road on Melbourne's eastern fringe in 1957. (PHOTO COURTESY OAKLEIGH MOTEL)

authentically Australian; what, if anything, was novel, was the way in which the elements of the American prototype were adapted, recombined and sometimes omitted.

In the eyes of its most astringent critic, the typical motel was a textbook example of the 'Australian Ugliness'. 'In its approach to the public, in social and aesthetic values, in style, the motel often turned out to be a substantial offspring of the merry-go-round or the juke-box', said the fastidious Robin Boyd. He poured contempt on 'the raw colours, the checker-board painting of fibro panels, the jaunty skillion roof and the angled props to the eaves, the autumnal stone veneering and the rest of the catchpenny style'.[57] The indignation of Boyd the critic of 'Austerica' was the greater, perhaps, because Boyd the modernist architect recognised the possibility of creating motels in a less gimmicky and more authentically Australian idiom. In 1960, the year he published *The Australian Ugliness*, Boyd had met a 30-year-old businessman, David Yencken. Yencken, the son of an Australian-born British diplomat, had grown up in Europe and had been educated at Cambridge. In the late 1950s the young graduate returned to Australia by way of the United States where he observed the new fashion for motels and became

Proprietor Cyril Lewis presides behind the counter in the dining room of the Oakleigh Motel. (PHOTO COURTESY OAKLEIGH MOTEL)

interested in the possibility of importing the idea to Australia. At first he encountered considerable scepticism, especially about the potential for high-class, well-designed motels. 'They won't be appreciated or treated properly', he was warned. 'Australians are born thieves.' But Yencken persevered. He began looking for suitable land on the Hume Highway, but couldn't find anything that fitted the requirements as set out in American literature on the subject. He purchased some land at Warrnambool, but later sold it in order to acquire a more promising site in Bairnsdale where, in 1957, with the architect John Mockridge, he built the Mitchell Valley Motel. In 1960 he was approached by a group of Melbourne residents about the prospect of building a motel further around the coast at Merimbula. Boyd, who had admired the Bairnsdale motel, had already approached Yencken about other possible motel projects and was the natural choice to design the new motel, which Yencken called The Black Dolphin. With its simple construction, use of unpainted rough-sawn timber, and splendid views of bush and sea, the Black Dolphin sought to show how a true, environmentally sensitive modernism might humanise the new functional forms of the motor age. In his advertisements in the fortnightly magazine, *Nation*, Yencken cleverly appealed to an intelligentsia newly awakened, largely thanks to Boyd, to the aesthetic sins of 'Austerica'. 'At the Black Dolphin you will not find—Palm trees—Pretentious menus—A war of primary colours—Second-rate imported wines—The latest American gimmicks', a typical advertisement read. 'Even our architect, Mr Robin Boyd, assures us that we are not featurists.'[58]

The advertisement highlights a contradiction between Yencken's and Boyd's commercial and educative purposes. They had sought to elevate the general standard of architectural taste, but they had concluded by reinforcing a division between elite and popular standards. Meanwhile the craze for motel building continued unabated. 'The age of the motel has definitely arrived', *Wheels* observed in 1959.[59] A year later Australia had over 80 motels and a further 80 were under construction. Some were little more than upgraded hotels or tourist cabins. 'The motel means vastly different things in different places', one journalist warned.[60] The first motels had been located on interstate highways or, like the Oakleigh Motel, on the fringes of cities, but increasingly motels were becoming a part of the suburban landscape; Melbourne had motels in Parkville, Kew and West St Kilda as well as Braybrook, Oakleigh, Clayton and Chadstone.[61] Most of them were as glitzy and tacky as the first; their proprietors were inclined to see progress in terms of the addition of new gimmicks rather than better style. 'The American motel of the future will be even flashier and more gadget conscious', an American observer noted in 1963. 'Guests will find color television in all rooms, two baths, vista vision phone, pneumatic tube message service direct to their rooms, complete hot meals from vending machines, and parking once more beside their door—even in multi-level motels.'[62] Australian drivers were probably less gimmick-prone than their American cousins, but if the Australian motel was generally a less pretentious, low-slung building than the American, it was not aesthetically much superior.

THE DRIVE-IN THEATRE

Like the motel, the drive-in theatre was heralded long before its arrival in Australia. As early as 1950 Australians were reading that American drive-ins were growing at a rate of almost a thousand a year. 'The drive-in', it was reported, 'appeals to a different audience from that of the indoor theatres. Many of its customers are elderly people, cripples, and "shut-ins". They also attract people who dislike dressing for the movies, and couples who bring their children and thus save the cost of a baby-sitter.'[63] Like the motel, it represented a step away from the formality and inhibition of personal behaviour in public places. 'You can talk, smoke, chew peanuts, eat sandwiches, and nobody cares a hoot', observed Australian journalist Keith Dunstan from California.[64]

The first Australian drive-in at Burwood, on Melbourne's suburban frontier, opened in July 1954, just two years before the arrival of tele-vision, and a second at Ringwood had opened by Christmas. Hoyts announced plans for drive-ins in Dandenong Road, Moorabbin and Preston, and others were planned for Maribyrnong, Malvern and Geelong. At Bulleen local residents objected to the lease of public land on the river flats for a drive-in. It was better, they argued, to keep the reserve for pony rides ('a healthy outlet for the young people of the district') than to 'ruin' it with a drive-in. But the rush to drive-in was apparently irresistible and the locals' protests were overruled.[65] In 1956 MGM commenced work on Australia's first twin drive-in, the Metro, in Clayton. With space for 1500 cars, double-size driveways, a superior meals service, even a 'nappy nook' for changing babies, it claimed to be the biggest in the Southern Hemisphere.[66]

In their first years of operation, before the little screen began to undercut the appeal of the big one, visiting the drive-in became a popular family outing. Like the motel room, the parked car was a new kind of domestic space, a mobile extension of the family living room. Burwood drive-in claimed to have improved upon the American proto-type by offering a superior standard of service, similar to that of an old-fashioned cinema. As the motorist drove through the entrance gates, he was shown to his parking space by an attendant waving a torch, like a cinema usherette, and as he stopped, another attendant handed him a loudspeaker to hang inside the car. A switch on the top of the speaker enabled the driver to call an attendant for hot refreshments, hot water bottles for the shivering children or to clean the fogged-up windscreen. Raw steaks, hamburgers and hot-dogs could be purchased at a central cafe and barbecued while the family warmed themselves by coke braziers. Below the screen was a special children's playground with swings and toys and a doorkeeper dressed as a frog who welcomed the pyjama-clad youngsters with free sweets as they entered. Ringwood added new attractions—a swimming pool, merry-go-round, open-air dance floor and miniature golf course.[67]

The golden age of the drive-in was short-lived. The competition of television soon forced proprietors to cut the level of services and seek a more specialised audience. By the 1960s, most young families preferred the superior comfort and privacy of the family room and the television screen. Only as they acquired cars of their own, and a need for entertainment of a kind not supplied by the small screen, did the younger members of the family again resort to the drive-in. Soon the playgrounds and family barbecues were shut down, cartoons and musicals gave way to rock-and-roll and horror movies, and, as car-ownership spread among the young, the family playground was turned into the 'passion pit'.

DRIVE-IN SHOPPING

In the 1950s, when only a minority of city-dwellers used cars on a daily basis, the application of the 'drive-in' principle was largely confined to experimental uses in well-to-do car-owning suburbs. In 1954 the E, S and A Bank opened Australia's first drive-in branch at Camberwell in the midst of Melbourne's well-to-do eastern suburbs. Parking had already emerged as a problem in the suburb's congested shopping streets (Sandy Stone, Barry Humphries' archetypical Camberwellian, was wont to complain that he 'had a bit of trouble parking the vehicle' down at the Junction) and the bank boasted that the one and a half minutes it took to carry out a transaction at the glass-fronted drive-in teller's booth was much less than it took a driver to park and lock the car and walk to the bank to do business in the usual way. The bank planned to open more drive-in branches elsewhere in Australia because, as its general manager believed, 'it realised that the car had attained such an important role in the business and social life of the community that it often demanded special facilities. It was rapidly approaching the status in this country which it now held in America, where it was recognised as "king", and where much of the nation's business activity was designed to meet the special needs of the motorist.'[68] Despite the continuing growth of automobile ownership, however, the drive-in bank remained a novelty, and even in the day of the automatic teller machine, few banks offer drive-in facilities.

The drive-in shopping centre, on the other hand, was slower to make its appearance, but has now become so ubiquitous that it threatens the very survival of older-style strip shopping centres.[69] In the new suburbs, where public transport was scarce, shops could sometimes only be reached by car. As early as 1955, the rising popularity of the station wagon was credited to the growth of families with young children, the 'accelerated increase in suburban living' and 'dispersed shopping centres which have been springing up all over the country'.[70] It was not until 1958 that the City of Kew in Melbourne's eastern suburbs opened what claimed to be 'the closest thing in Melbourne to a drive-in shopping centre', a 300-place off-street carpark.[71] Its claim may have been false: at least two other automobilised centres, at Chermside 10 kilometres north of Brisbane and at Pinewood on Melbourne's eastern frontier, had opened a year earlier, the latter as part of a new housing estate created by A. V. Jennings. Also in 1957, the Myer Emporium, Australia's largest department store, announced that it would 'seriously seek to develop its first suburban outlet'.[72]

Chadstone was the creation of Kenneth and Baillieu Myer, the sons of the company's founder Sidney Myer. The Myers had maintained close family and business connections with the United States since the early 1920s when Sidney had lived for a time in California; his sons were educated partly in the United States, and after their discharge from the Australian Navy at the end of World War II, they had both worked and travelled extensively in America.[73] Baillieu, the younger son, had worked for Macy's both in Manhattan and in suburban White Plains and had visited the company's influential Garden Plaza development in New Jersey and Northland in Detroit.[74] Kenneth had been educated partly at Princeton and had visited the United States to observe retailing trends in 1949 and 1953. He was especially influenced by his observations of motorised shopping on the West Coast and on his return alerted his fellow directors to their possible application in a rapidly automobilising Australia. 'Gentlemen, I am convinced of the future development of retail business in areas other than the centre of capital cities. We should be turning our minds to the possibilities of regional centres of the kind making their appearance in America.'[75] Some encouragement had been given to the development of regional shopping centres by the 1954 Melbourne Metropolitan Planning Scheme, a point that Myer would have been quick to grasp. (He was a prominent member of the Town and Country Planning Association and a founder of the City Development Association, a pressure group of civic-minded businessmen, again based on American

Australia's first Kmart, Burwood, Melbourne. (AUTHOR'S PHOTO)

models.) The Myer brothers purchased a large parcel of land on Burwood Highway but were unable to persuade their fellow directors to back their plan for a regional shopping centre; the land was later sold to a rival retailer, G. J. Coles, and became the site of Australia's first Kmart.

Two years later the board was won over and Myer resolved to build its first drive-in shopping centre in Melbourne's rapidly growing eastern suburbs. It engaged the Larry Smith Organisation of Seattle to carry out preliminary research and planning. (Smith and Victor Gruen were co-authors of influential American textbook, *Shoppingtowns USA.*)[76] The location was determined only after a survey of metropolitan traffic patterns and residential development had demonstrated that the largest potential patronage lay in an area centred on the intersection of Warrigal and Dandenong roads, about 20 kilometres from the CBD, at the threshold of the city's main eastern development corridor. More than 400 000 people lived within an 8-kilometre radius, and 66 per cent of those households owned a car.[77]

Premier Henry Bolte opened Chadstone in October 1960. 'Decentralised shopping is vital to a growing city like Melbourne', he declared. The centre, which comprised more than 85 shops arranged

Aerial view of Chadstone shopping centre, Melbourne, 1960.
(Photo courtesy Chadstone shopping centre)

along an outdoor shopping arcade, as well as a large Myer department store, represented a new scale, as well as a new style, of retailing. 'Colossal', 'fabulous', an 'extravaganza', even 'super-colossal' were some epithets that Bolte, inspired perhaps by the spirit of Barnum, applied to the centre. Situated in the grounds of an old convent, only 600 metres from the ideal location determined by the American consultants, the centre had been constructed in less than a year, a feat said to have impressed even the 'go-ahead' Americans.[78]

According to the journalist Graham Perkin who covered the opening, Chadstone embodied 'a new shopping logic. It is not an original logic because it has been adapted from an American pattern, but it is refreshingly new in Australian conditions.'[79] Like Henry Ford's production line, the drive-in was designed to save time: 'one stop and shop'. Some observers were impressed by Chadstone's 'luxurious, expansive atmosphere', but like that other Austerian landmark, the Oakleigh Motel, just a few miles down Dandenong Road, its clean, functional lines seemed to denote more efficiency than luxury.

Myer created Chadstone for a customer who had scarcely yet appeared on the Australian urban scene, the motoring housewife. 'Since women do most of the shopping Chadstone is planned and geared for women's needs', a contemporary observed. 'Mrs Suburbia can drive into the centre after the morning peak hour with her under-age school children and the family dog.'[80] Like the Myer central city store, Chadstone offered a special feminised meeting place for women, the Strawberry Room, and 'entertainment . . . especially for housewives'.[81] Parking spaces were angled at 45 degrees, in order, so it was said, 'that women will be able to park easily. There will be no embarrassing manoeuvres into small spaces.'[82] Child-care facilities, a supervised children's playground, a delivery service from store to car, and a motoring school advertising lessons for would-be drivers were some of the other facilities Chadstone offered its new female clientele.

Like the first drive-in theatres, Chadstone sought to reinforce, and perhaps exploit, contemporary family and community values. Town planners in the 1940s hoped to promote the creation of community centres in the new suburbs, and Chadstone incorporated an auditorium for theatrical productions, reception rooms and a tenpin bowling alley. It is hard to know whether these community facilities were designed as bait for the shoppers or as a gesture of civic idealism. By the late 1960s it had become clear that, with the exception of the Bowl, they were not paying their way, and like the Strawberry Room, they have gradually been absorbed into the retail complex. No similar facilities were incorporated in the company's later drive-in shopping centres at Northland, Southland (1964) and Eastland (1970). While retailers needed to persuade nervous customers that the new shopping centres were compatible with community values, they made strenuous efforts to incorporate community facilities, but once that battle had been won, they allowed market forces to take their course.

THE SPIRIT OF PLACE

It took some time for Australians to recognise the deeper implications of the drive-in logic of their new suburbs. The car had seemingly given a new lease of life to the old suburban dream of space and seclusion. By stretching the communication lines of an already far-flung metropolis it had brought the quarter-acre block within reach of a new generation of postwar settlers. But in stretching and reshaping the suburbs, the car had also transformed their character. The new landscape of suburbia—the drive-in, the motel, the regional shopping centre, service station, the carport and the thousands of acres of bitumen linking them together—was designed to promote the speedy, almost frictionless, movement of individuals and families from place to place. The car promised to give everyone access to their own bit of semi-rural seclusion, to offer Everyman and Everywoman their own little Eden.

In changing the scale of the city, and patterns of movement through it, however, the motor car had changed something else as well. Americans, who had invented the new landscape, were also first to recognise its social consequences. In 1957 the editors of *Fortune* magazine commissioned some of America's leading intellectuals to assess the implications of *The Exploding Metropolis*. 'The motorist is not "strangling" the city', suggested Francis Bello, '—in fact he drives in and out a lot faster than he thinks. But he is changing the fundamental character of the metropolitan area—and, many planners fear, for the worse.' Jane Jacobs, author of a best-selling critique of American life, deplored the corrosive effects of the car on the edgy intimacy of the city streets.[83] Even in the new suburbs, as planning guru Lewis Mumford argued, the car was a destructive force. 'As soon as the motor car became common, the scale of the suburb disappeared, and with it, most of its individuality and charm. The suburb ceased to be a neighbourhood unit; it became a diffused low-density mass, enveloped by the conurbation and then further enveloping it . . . Instead of buildings set in a park, we now have buildings set in a parking lot.'[84]

In the 1950s and 1960s many Australian suburbanites still carried unhappy memories of an old landscape of narrow streets and overcrowded houses. The visual blight and social fragmentation of the new landscape seemed a small price to pay for the delight of their own homes and gardens. Privacy and security ranked higher in their scale of values than urbanity and sociability. Only by degrees, as the tarmac encroached further on the bush, and as the spaces between home and destination grew longer and emptier, did they begin to appreciate the flaws in the Fordist logic that had shaped the new suburbs. By the 1970s social scientists had begun to suspect that not all was well in the land of malls and motels. Restless youth and bored housewives seemed to reflect an emptiness that was more than physical. But it was not until their spoiled children fled the parental nest for the narrow streets of yesterday's slums that the suburban dream began to lose its allure.

5

The Freedom of the Road

On 10 November 1949 Robert Menzies, leader of the revitalised Liberal Opposition, launched his campaign for the forthcoming general election before the electors of Kooyong in Melbourne's leafy eastern suburbs. Expectations were high among Menzies' supporters who filled the Canterbury Soldiers's Memorial Hall to overflowing long before the 7.30 pm starting time. Hundreds of others stood outside the hall listening to his speech on loudspeakers, or sat in cars lining the surrounding streets listening in on their car radios. Many thousands more had tuned into the 40 radio stations broadcasting his message to the nation.

Ever since his humiliating fall from the prime ministership in 1941 Menzies had been preparing for this moment. He had gradually welded the fragmented non-Labor forces into a new disciplined party. In a series of inspiring wartime broadcasts he had summoned 'the Forgotten People'—the thrifty, home-loving, suburban, middle class—to the cause of individual enterprise and social progress. Four years after VJ Day Australians were still enduring the austerity of the war years. Many commodities, including petrol, were still rationed. The shortage of American dollars limited imports of all cars especially the American models most favoured by Australian motorists. Menzies attacked the evils of Socialism, the sinister and gloomy dogma that inspired his Labor opponents' dogged attachment to state enterprise and controls. The Liberals would deliver Australia from the dead hand of Socialism and usher in a new era of freedom and prosperity. Menzies' attack on Labor's plans to nationalise the banks drew enthusiastic applause from the business suits of Canterbury. And his promise to abolish petrol rationing prompted loud and prolonged tooting from the motorists parked in the streets outside. 'Empty out the socialists and fill the bowsers' became the Liberals' catchcry.[1]

As political scientist Judith Brett has suggested, Menzies' political message skilfully blended diverse, and even contradictory, themes: independence and social harmony, enterprise and tradition, dynamism and stability. In appealing to the idea of Home ('Homes Material', 'Homes Human', 'Homes Spiritual') Menzies had stressed the stabilising values of 'sanity and sobriety', 'continuity' and 'health'. But the Liberals also presented themselves as the dynamic party of youthful enterprise and material progress, an impression reinforced by the large number of young ex-servicemen among their candidates. While the home was the figurative representation of stability, the motor car was emerging as the symbol of liberty, movement and change. Emptying out the socialists and their hated state controls was the first step towards getting petrol in the bowsers and cars on the road. When the abolition of rationing was finally announced in February 1950 Menzies hailed it as 'an earnest of the new freedom . . . to which the Commonwealth has pledged its endeavours'.[2] A contemporary cartoon shows Menzies, sitting at the wheel of one of the new Holden sedans, asking young Australia, depicted as a comely girl waiting on the kerb: 'Going my way?'

THE IDEOLOGY OF AUTOMOBILISM

For almost half a century before Menzies' speech, cars had been potent political symbols. In the early days of motoring when it was a rich man's hobby, cars signified social privilege. The Royal Automobile Club of Victoria (RACV) began as a sporting club for a small band of well-to-do motoring enthusiasts united in a knightly code of high adventure and gentlemanly honour. In the 1940s the gentleman-motorists still dominated the club and its policies. As full members, with access to the club's handsome lounge and dining rooms, they paid a higher subscription and elected most members of the RACV Council. City businessmen, many with offices within walking distance of the club's Queen Street headquarters, were the major office-holders. In 1955 only the two most recently elected councillors had joined the club since the war, and even a decade later over one-third of the council had been in office for over

"GOING MY WAY — ON A FULL PETROL TANK?"

In 1949 Robert Menzies's Liberals, rather than Ben Chifley's socialists, best captured the aspirations of an Australia tired of wartime controls and eager to embrace the freedom of the road. (BULLETIN, 1949)

twenty years.[3] The mass of 'service members', who joined to take advantage of the club's emergency roadside service, had only two representatives on the club's twenty-member council. Only occasionally, as in the early 1970s, when public transport activists challenged for positions on the council, was this gentlemanly oligarchy threatened.

Cars were also symbols of modernity, an embodiment of the speed and technological efficiency often admired by new authoritarian regimes. They had injected an attractive sense of momentum to the political resurgence of Fascists and Nazis, and their Australian imitators such as the New Guard. Speeding across the city in the dead of night, carrying bands of excited patriots to secret rendezvous, cars also became valuable organisational tools of the militant Right.[4] Some Australian intellectuals, such as the architects and planners George and Florence Taylor, imagined future cities in which the muddle of 'horse-and-buggy' democracy would be supplanted by the rule of scientific experts using new forms of communication, such as radios, telephones, aeroplanes and cars.[5] The coming of the car strengthened the power of the technological expert, even among the majority of Australians who resisted the lure of doctrinaire fascism.

To most people, however, the car was a symbol, not of privilege or authority, but of liberty. Since the 1910s, when motorists first began to organise themselves politically, the ideological affinities between political liberalism and organised motoring had been strong.[6] The car was a freedom machine, a physical expression of the liberal principles of free movement, free association and free enterprise. Motoring journalists and publicists like the RACV's George Broadbent had distilled a self-conscious philosophy of 'automobilism' that inspires motoring organisations like the RACV and the NRMA even today.

In 1947, when the Royal Automobile Club of Victoria honoured its founders with life memberships, George Broadbent was hailed as the 'Grand Old Man' of Victorian motoring. In his youth, he had been a champion cyclist, in 1889 setting a world record by riding one of the old solid-tyred penny-farthing cycles 204 miles in 24 hours. He turned to motorcycles and motor cars early in the new century, participating in races and reliability trials as both a driver and official. He founded the Good Roads Association to campaign for better Victorian roads and established the RACV's Touring Department to encourage motorists to enjoy them. 'The motor bears us into far fields of unexpected delight and enables us to understand the beauty of our country', he wrote euphorically. His own Broadbent Map Company became Victoria's largest supplier of road maps and touring guides. In 1914 he became the motoring correspondent for the *Argus* and over the following twenty years his weekly column became the most influential voice of 'the man behind the wheel'.[7]

Broadbent's favourite theme, endlessly repeated and elaborated, was 'The Motor as Emancipator'. The freedom conferred by the motor car answered a natural human aspiration. 'From the earliest time extant, mankind in general, and the British race in particular, has been imbued with the spirit of travel and exploration.' The coming of the railways had greatly extended people's horizons, 'but they are too gregarious and limited in scope for the true traveller'. Only with the automobile 'was man really able to gratify his desire for travel and adventure and learn the full flavour of the joy of the open road'.[8] As the historian Wolfgang Sachs observes, the automobile was seen to herald a new era of personal liberty:

> Automobiles promised to resurrect the old independence of self-propelled vehicles, to help individual authority to regain its own, for they offered emancipation from the inconveniences of the railway; the regimentation of the timetable, the compulsion of the unwavering rails, and—not least—the perspiration of the crowd.[9]

The car cut human beings free from the conventional limitations of time and space. It was a mechanical extension of the self, conceived as an autonomous, rational, self-actualising individual. The triumph of automobile was accordingly believed to be as benign, and as inevitable, as the triumph of liberal democracy itself. Automobility, free enterprise and democracy were each dimensions of the same sacred principle of liberty. 'Perhaps', observed Albert Bradley, Vice-President of General Motors, 'the motor car gives physical expression to our love of in-dependence, just as in the economic sphere that love of independence finds expression in free enterprise, and in the political sphere in our democratic form of government'.[10]

It is as a metaphor for freedom—personal as well as national, politi-cal as well as economic—that the motor car has performed conspicuous service in the last half-century. Car talk has become an almost universal metaphor for power. When someone takes charge, they 'slip into the driver's seat'. A political novice is said to be still 'on his P-plates' while a doctrinaire reformer may determine, as Mrs Thatcher did, to make 'no U-turns'. Were Australia to become a republic, one advocate suggested, it would at last have taken the car keys.

As freedom was a natural right, so the automobilisation of society was seemingly ordained by nature. Automobile advocates showed a particular fondness for naturalistic metaphors—cars were often invested with animal, or even human, characteristics. Police and pedestrians labelled the rampaging motorists as 'road hogs', but in the eyes of the motorists themselves they were a superior species, entitled by a kind of natural evolution to dominate their environment. 'The self-propelled vehicle will ultimately become the *dominant form* of land transport of passengers and goods, and it were better that we recognised that inescapable position as soon as possible', predicted Broadbent in 1924. 'In the near future the number of vehicles will be *multiplied* and will assume such immense proportions that there will be little room in the city streets for any other kind of traffic.'[11]

'It is time to encourage conditions that make for a faster flow', Broadbent exhorted.[12] Anything or anyone that impeded or slowed the free flow of motor traffic was both hindering personal liberty and denying a law of nature. Motor advocates thought that nature should be encouraged to hasten its course. Horses should be subject to punitive taxation. Trams should be banned from crowded inner city streets. Pedestrians should be educated and regulated so as not to impede the passage of vehicles. (Too often, the motorists complained, they were made the 'scapegoats' for the errors of foolish pedestrians.) Instead of the pace of the vehicle being set by the conditions of the road or the pace of slower-moving horse-drawn vehicles, roads should be remade or controlled so as to accommodate the speed of the car. Similarly, motorists should not be fettered by heavy taxation or regulation. 'Motor owners largely are drawn from that numerous and respectable and responsible class of successful citizens who realise the value and the need for law and order, and are guided in their actions by humane instincts.' They could be left to simply regulate themselves.[13]

THE VOICE OF THE MAN AT THE WHEEL

The rise of the Liberal Party had paralleled, and occasionally intersected with, the emergence of a newly invigorated motor lobby. Two seemingly unconnected events in the early months of 1943 signalled an important shift in the political landscape. In March, Robert Menzies placed himself at the head of a younger group of Liberal activists, the National Service Group, determined to offer more vigorous opposition to the Curtin Government and to promote an alternative vision of the postwar social and political order. Two months later in May 1943 the president of the RACV, Sir Thomas Nettlefold, proposed that the Australian Automobile Association (AAA), which had been inactive since its last federal conference in 1938, should be revived at a new conference in Melbourne in December 1943. Nettlefold, a prominent industrialist and lord mayor of Melbourne, had been a political supporter of Menzies since the early 1930s, when they had founded the Young Nationalists as a ginger group within the United Australia Party. The objective of the conference, for Nettlefold and his supporters, was to gain the support of the constituent state motoring associations for the reorganisation of the AAA as a professionally administered, aggressive national lobbying organisation. In Australia, as in the United States where the American Road Builders' Association had emerged as a national representative body in the same year, war had heightened public consciousness of the need for national systems of communications and organisations to promote them.[14]

Automobilism, the belief in the motorist's unfettered right to the freedom of the road, was now confronted by a national Labor government invested with large powers for the enforced mobilisation of the population, for the rationing and taxation of resources, and for the planning of a postwar social order. 'In these times when there was so much Government control there was a necessity to speak with one voice', observed RACV councillor A. J. Kennedy. 'Towards the end of the war and probably for a considerable time afterwards there would be a greater necessity for a Federal body representing motorists than at any time in motoring history', agreed F. L. Hayes.[15] In October 1944 the AAA appointed a 36-year-old Scottish-born manager and publicist, T. G. (Tom) Paterson, as its first federal secretary, with headquarters in Melbourne and a directive to strengthen the association's influence in the corridors of power. For Paterson, this was the beginning of a long, and often tempestuous, career as a motoring and road safety publicist. In less than a year he had conducted more than 60 interviews with federal MPs, established a Canberra office, addressed community groups, written numerous reports and policy statements and contributed a regular column to the *Radiator*.[16] Paterson's zeal as a publicist sometimes exceeded his masters' expectations and he was chided more than once for presenting his own views as those of the association.[17]

In May 1945 Paterson outlined the objectives of the revitalised AAA in an article, 'The Voice of the Man at the Wheel'. The organisation was a 'Corporate Consumers' Cooperative' dedicated to protecting the interests of motorists and promoting 'the importance of the motor vehicle to national development'. The AAA was 'entirely non-political, is not representative of any particular stratum of the community, and is entirely devoid of any "trade" interests or affiliations'.[18]

The claim that the AAA was not 'political' was true in almost none of the standard meanings of the word. In seeking to protect and advance the collective interests of motorists it was obviously playing a political role. In lobbying parliamentarians on taxation, road finance, petrol rationing and other questions it was directly involved in formal politics. Even in the narrow sense in which Paterson used the word—the promotion of party, class or sectional politics—the AAA was by no means as neutral as he claimed. Of the delegates at the association's 1948 conference in Adelaide several were, or would soon become, prominent office-holders of the Liberal Party. Besides Nettlefold, they included Dudley Turner, Deputy Chairman of the South Australian Liberal and Country League and Leon Trout, long-serving president of the Queensland Liberal Party. The RACV also maintained close informal connections with Victorian Liberals: premiers Tom Hollway (1947–50), whose brother had headed the club's Ballarat centre, and Henry Bolte (1955–1972) were both members of the RACV.[19] The Voice of the Man behind the Wheel was uncannily like the voice of Robert Menzies' 'Forgotten People'.

In 1945, 50 000 Victorian motorists, about 40 per cent of licensed motorists, were members of the RACV. Over the next twenty years membership increased in proportion to car ownership, reaching 100 000 by 1948, 200 000 by 1958, 300 000 by 1962 and almost 600 000 by 1971. Its monthly magazine, the *Radiator*, later the *Royalauto*, probably reached more households than any other paper, with the possible exception of the *Women's Weekly*, although how many of its recipients read its editorial matter is impossible to estimate. The club promoted itself as the voice of the man (or woman) behind the wheel, but the vast majority of its members were 'service members' whose interest in the club began and ended with its emergency roadside service and other tangible benefits of membership. The policies formulated by the oligarchs of the club's council and trumpeted by the *Royalauto* did not necessarily echo the voice of the ordinary motorist, but the financial, research and lobbying resources of the club still made it a force to be reckoned with.[20]

The motor lobby exerted its growing influence through all three tiers of Australian politics: at the federal level, where its attention was focused especially on issues of taxation and road finance; at the state level, where it defended motorists against restrictive road laws and broke down the remaining defences of public transport; and at the local level, where it lobbied for an ever-growing share of public and private space to be allocated to the needs of the automobile.

THE NATIONAL AGENDA

In their pioneering years, motoring organisations in the 1920s and 1930s had constructed a political ideology around principles of laissez-faire liberalism, asserting the motorist's unfettered right to the freedom of the road against onerous taxation, officious policemen, careless pedestrians and inefficient public transport. Like Menzies' revitalised Liberals, however, postwar motoring organisations had absorbed many of the lessons of the Depression and World War II. While continuing to warn against the threat of socialistic controls, the AAA largely accepted the increased fiscal and regulatory powers of the national government but sought to direct them towards the democratic goal of mass motorisation. They appropriated many of the watchwords of Labor's plans for Postwar Reconstruction—'planning', 'coordination', 'organisation', 'democracy', 'national development'—in order to strengthen the motorist's claims upon the national political agenda.[21] Reducing the costs of cars and petrol, creating a national network of highways, standardising and simplifying road regulations across the Commonwealth would help to realise the democratic dream of 'Cars for the Millions'. 'Lower costs will turn the hopes and desires of thousands of average Australians into golden realisation', Paterson predicted.[22]

One of the lessons which the motor lobby learnt from the war was the need for organisation. In 1945 Paterson foresaw a need to strengthen the organisational links between motoring organisations in the postwar period.

War-time has seen control of practically all forms of transport and its ancillaries passed over rather fully to Commonwealth authorities for purposes of national defence. Due to the pertinent experience gained in these years, the trend towards Commonwealth control is likely to continue during the post war period when plans for the much to be desired nation-wide coordinated transport system are being formulated and implemented.[23]

In the previous year the AAA had revised its constitution to expand its objectives and give it a more aggressive posture. Over the following years it began to develop a more active role in lobbying both federal and state governments, especially on issues concerned with road provision, petrol and automobile sales tax, road safety and tourism.

Long before motoring had become a majority pursuit, the rhetoric of the motor lobby and its Liberal allies had transformed the car from a luxury to a necessity. In 1945 Paterson had attempted, by a somewhat tortuous and unconvincing line of statistical argument, to argue that motoring was no longer a 'luxury' 'alongside, say polo-playing and pig-prodding in Peru' but a 'normal' and 'essential' feature of postwar life.[24] Two years later, in the debate on the Commonwealth Aid Roads Bill, the Liberal member for the North Shore seat of Wentworth and later minister in the Menzies Government, Eric Harrison, echoed this democratic message:

Once a person who could spend several hundreds of pounds in the purchase of a motor car was considered a fairly rich man, but that time has long since passed, for today motor vehicles are as much a necessity to middle class people as are radios, refrigerators and the like.[25]

This dream could not be realised while the Labor government treated cars as a luxury item. 'If the Federal Labor Government desires the worker to enjoy the benefits and pleasures of motoring it will have to reduce taxes that add so materially to the cost of a new car', urged the *Radiator*.[26] In 1946, when these words were written, lowering taxes on imported cars may have benefited a middle-class minority more than it hastened the prospect of mass motoring. But it presaged a new politics in which Labor's concern with fair shares for all would be contested by the Liberals' offer of a bigger cake. It was this democratic objective— '[rendering] the motor car more and more part of the Australian way of life'—that justified the claim of the motor lobby to have transcended class and sectional politics.[27]

Between 1945 and 1949 the AAA and its constituent organisations fought a vigorous national campaign focused on five prime goals: removing wartime restrictions on the supply of petrol and imported motor vehicles; establishing the car as the dominant form of overland transport for both goods and people; directing revenues derived from taxes and charges on motorists to road construction; standardising and simplifying regulations; promoting road safety and research and planning on road issues. These would remain key planks in the RACV's and the AAA's platforms over the next 50 years. Motor car politics were more remarkable for their consistency and tenacity than their novelty. The freedom of the road remained a cardinal principle, but the motor lobby was gradually forced to recognise other concerns with social equity and, increasingly, with physical and environmental health.

Motor lobbyists had long insisted that the revenue contributed by motorists through petrol tax and driver's licences should be spent exclusively on roads. However, the exigencies of the Depression and war had severed the nexus between the levying of these taxes and the purposes for which they had first been raised.[28] Motoring representatives complained of their 'diversion' or 'siphoning off' into general revenue, as though the politicians had put their hands into the till. If all the motorists' contributions through taxation, customs duties and licence fees since the mid-1920s had been devoted to their 'true purpose' Australia would already have 10 000 miles of *autobahnen*, Paterson calculated. The share of petrol tax spent on road construction in Australia (53 per cent) compared unfavourably with both the United Kingdom (78 per cent) and the United States (87 per cent).[29]

Politicians, especially on the Labor side, preferred to treat these taxes as a source of general revenue. Because motorists were predominantly middle class, taxes on motoring were socially progressive in effect, so it was only fair that some went to pay for schools, hospitals and public transport. Cars imposed social costs in the form of accidents, pollution, law enforcement and congestion as well as the direct cost of constructing roads.[30] By the early 1960s motor taxation was contributing almost 20 per cent of state and local revenue, but the more motoring became a mass pursuit, the greater were the political risks of taxing it.

As the number of road vehicles increased, so did the flow of taxes into the coffers of the Commonwealth Government. In 1947 the Chifley

Government proposed a significant increase in the provision of funds for roads. Road construction, it was argued, was an urgent need both for national defence (the Pacific War had highlighted the need for trunk roads especially in the north) and for 'national and economic development'. Neither Labor nor Liberal governments accepted the motor lobby's view of petrol tax as a levy on motorists for the construction of roads. As a vital ingredient within a broadly Keynesian framework of 'national development', however, Commonwealth support for road construction came to enjoy much wider cross-party support.

The Commonwealth Government had made grants for road construction to the states since 1926. The formula used to distribute funds was strongly influenced by the needs of the large 'developing' states like Queensland and Western Australia, and the interests of the Country Party, which traditionally held the portfolio for Transport. It incorporated three factors: population, car ownership and the area of the state, and required that at least 40 per cent of funds were spent on rural roads. Under these arrangements Victoria was estimated to receive back only one-quarter of what its motorists contributed through petrol tax.[31] Within Victoria, Melbourne suffered in comparison with rural areas, since most Commonwealth grants were tied to the construction of rural roads or to main roads outside the metropolitan area. This fiscal imbalance was reinforced institutionally by the division of responsibility between the Country Roads Board (CRB) and the Melbourne and Metropolitan Board of Works (MMBW). While the CRB had responsibility for main roads beyond the metropolis (as defined by the limit of the tramway system) and drew approximately $27 million in Commonwealth Roads assistance in 1965, the MMBW, which had responsibility for main roads within the metropolis, derived less than $5 million from its main source of revenue, the Metropolitan Improvement Rates. By the early 1960s the board believed that the shortage of funds for large road projects in Melbourne had become acute.[32]

In the early 1970s, when oil prices began to rise and awareness of the environmental hazards of 'automobile dependence' increased, one or two state governments toyed with the idea of deterring motoring with more severe taxes, but over the longer term the share of government revenue derived from motoring has steadily decreased. As one recent commentator observed, 'motor taxes are long overdue for a tune up and service'.[33]

The RACV, as voice of the Victorian motorist, was a constant critic of arrangements that 'starved' the state of Commonwealth road funds. (ROYALAUTO, 1954)

PRIVATE VS PUBLIC

In promoting 'the freedom of the road', the motor lobby was consciously challenging the mental habits of a society shaped by the regulated mass movement of the railway and the tram. While motorists regarded transport as a matter of individual choice and provision, public transport authorities, and many of their clients, conceived it as a public service. One began with the individual and thought of the city as an aggregation of individual desires; the other began with the community and thought about how transport might be organised to serve individual needs. The world of the automobilist was a world without limits: of infinite space and boundless resources. The public transport advocate thought of the city as a bounded space in which resources, including the opportunity to move, were limited and had to be shared between competing interests. Each view had its strengths and weaknesses. Motoring advocates were prone to ignore the repercussions of their policies on the rest of the community; public transport advocates to plan for what they thought was in the interests of the community rather than what people actually wanted.

One of the difficulties of thinking about transport as a community resource in a city like Melbourne was that there was simply no appropriate political framework for carrying those thoughts into action. Public transport was a responsibility of the Victorian state government but it was discharged through several, often warring, bureaucracies. The Railways was a state department administered by commissioners with independent statutory powers. The Tramways were administered by a Tramways Board, independently of the Railways. Buses were run, either by the Tramways Board on some inner city routes, or by private operators subject to a state regulatory board. Local roads were maintained by municipalities but major highways, beyond the tramways system, were the responsibility of another state bureaucracy, the Country Roads Board. No single minister had an overall responsibility for the coordination of transport. Melbourne was divided into more than 40 local governments, and there was no elected metropolitan government or legislature. There was no way in which Melburnians, *as Melburnians*, could express their political will on transport policy. The only body vested with planning responsibility for the metropolis, the Melbourne and Metropolitan Board of Works, consisted of commissioners elected by local councils, but it operated remotely and often secretly under a succession of powerful chairmen, the most autocratic of whom, Alan Croxford (1966–82), notoriously summoned state ministers to his Spencer Street office, rather than visiting them in Spring Street.[34] The dispersion and bureaucratisation of power over Melbourne's transport may not have been planned in the interests of the motor lobby, but they greatly inhibited the development of a political constituency for public transport.

The link between automobilism and possessive individualism went only so far, however. For the car and its driver were never, and never could be, fully autonomous agents. The car was inseparable from the road on which it ran. In the 1920s, when licensed drivers comprised no more than 2 or 3 per cent of the Victorian population, claims for the natural dominance of the car were also claims *against* the majority of other road users, such as horse-drawn vehicles, cyclists, tram passengers and pedestrians. In effect, they sought to monopolise a publicly provided asset. Motorists justified this claim on the grounds, either that they soon would become the majority, or that, since they contributed disproportionately through petrol tax and motor licences to the cost of roads, they should have the first priority on how roads were used.

Motorists were a noisy lobby group, never reluctant to blow their own horns. Their opponents were a more diverse and defensive group, steeped in traditional attitudes and institutional loyalties, conscious of their declining patronage and often forced onto the back foot by the aggressive propaganda of the motorists. Transport debates in the 1940s and 1950s took place within a limited framework of economic and social assumptions. Criticisms of the environmental devastation of the car made little impact compared with the social and economic concerns of other transport providers. Public transport drew strong support from state governments which, as the proprietors of publicly owned transport systems, were reluctant to allow cars and motor buses and motor trucks to drive their enterprises out of business. Liberals, as well as socialists, took pride in a strong Victorian tradition of public enterprise. In the 1930s the young Robert Menzies, as state Minister for Railways, had established the Transport Regulation Board in order to defend the railways against the threat of the motor bus and lorry.[35] Militant unions of railway and tramway workers vigorously represented the interests of public transport within the counsels of the Labor Party. In 1947 as many workers were employed by the railways as in all forms of road transportation, and were much more likely to be unionised.[36] In the first postwar Labor government, led by John Cain senior (1952–55), four of the fourteen members of Cabinet had strong railway connections: chief secretary L. W. Galvin was a former railways engineer, Clive Stoneham a former railways clerk, Thomas Hayes an ex-Australian Railways Union official and Joseph Smith a former locomotive engine driver.[37]

The contest between private and public transport was also a class question. Public transport was patronised, as well as owned, by the people. Defending the train and tram against the car meant upholding the interests of the majority who could not yet afford cars against the vociferous minority who could. The motor lobby and Liberal politicians invited Labor to support taxation and pricing policies that would hasten the advent of mass motoring, rather than prop up a faltering public transport system. But at any time before the early 1960s the Melbourne Labor voter was much more likely to be a strap-hanger than a driver. The inner core of working-class suburbs was also the main catchment for the public transport system. Many Labor voters probably aspired to own a car in the near future, but in the meantime, the special pleading of the motor lobby may have inspired more resentment than hope among the carless majority.

Public transport advocates also sometimes alluded to a more subtle dimension of the contest between the car and public transport. As they travelled by train or tram, passengers rubbed shoulders with a wide cross-section of their fellow citizens. They overheard conversations and observed ways of speaking and acting that they were unlikely to encounter in their work or domestic lives. Riding together on the city's crowded trains and trams may have reinforced a sense of common citizenship among Melburnians. This sense of fraternity was qualified, however, by the stratification of the public transport system itself. White-collar workers traditionally travelled First Class, often on a monthly or yearly ticket, while workingmen bought concessional Second Class fares. Gentleman and ladies occupied the padded seats in the enclosed inner compartments on trams, while workingmen and smokers rode in the airier outer compartments. By the 1950s this class division was already breaking down. As car ownership grew among the middle class, the number of First Class rail passengers declined from 44 per cent in 1948 to 28 per cent in 1958, when the Bolte Government abolished the division.[38] It made no sense to keep running half-empty First Class carriages while Second Class passengers were strap-hanging, but in democratising rail travel the railways managers had, perhaps unwittingly, confirmed public transport as the transport mode of second choice.

PUBLIC TRANSPORT UNDER SEIGE

One of the great champions of public transport, Victorian Railways Chief Commissioner Harold Clapp had anticipated the threat posed by the automobile to the state's greatest public service. 'Seeds are being sown to wreck the railways—and everything else must be involved in the wreckage', he warned a meeting of Young Nationalists in 1934. 'Nothing will be safe.' Motor transport, he argued, was a form of 'subsidised piracy' since the motor bus, lorry or car travelled free on the public roads while the railways were obliged to pay for their own track and rolling stock. 'If anyone thinks that this country, with its handful of population and a staggering public debt, can afford two costly systems of transport to do the work that can quite satisfactorily be done by your railways—then I say that person does not recognise the price that is being paid for the wasteful duplication.'[39] Public transport, Clapp insisted, was a communal enterprise: the railways are 'yours', just as the public broadcaster is now said to be 'your ABC'. Victorians did not need to buy cars; they already owned a perfectly good transport system of their own.

While railways ran at a profit, and motorists were outnumbered by other road users, Clapp's was a convincing line of argument. The 1930s and 1940s, when depression and war restricted car travel, were a prosperous time for the railways and tramways. But 1945 was the last year in which the railways ran a profit. Through the 1950s and 1960s, as car ownership soared and public transport usage plummeted, the deficits of public transport increased almost exponentially.[40] People were naturally less interested in owning a losing enterprise than a profitable one. And, as motoring organisations never tired of pointing out, the taxes paid by motorists through petrol duty and licence fees were greater than the funds spent on the construction of roads. Car drivers, they argued, were subsidising an antiquated and unprofitable state enterprise. 'The trend today is toward car travel', observed RACV chairman C. E. Clements in 1959. 'Car numbers will increase tremendously in the next few years and force trams, economically and physically, off the road.'[41] Public transport authorities were now forced on to the defence, making excuses for their losses and appealing for a 'balance' to be struck between the insatiable demands of the car lobby and the needs of those who either did not want, or could not afford, to drive.

Public transport officials often complained that they had been starved of the capital needed to modernise their services and compete with the car. But even if investment in public transport had been less niggardly, it is far from certain that trains, trams and buses could have offered a serious challenge to the car. Public transport operators may not even have spent them in the most effective ways. Two decades of retrenchment, with little investment in new routes or rolling stock, had left railway bureaucrats with filing cabinets full of unfulfilled plans. At the end of the war they dusted them off, hoping that peace might offer new opportunities for expansion.

But times had changed and the needs of the city had changed with them. The dominant pattern of railway traffic from the 1920s to the 1940s was centripetal, from homes in the suburbs to jobs in the central city. Flinders Street Station, the main exit for passengers to the CBD, was said to be the busiest and most congested railway terminal in the world. Railways officials had long hoped to ease movement into and out of the city centre by constructing an underground loop providing several exits around the periphery of the CBD. This plan, hatched in the 1920s, had become the sacred cow of official railway thinking by the 1950s.[42]

As industry and commerce began to migrate to the suburbs, and the employment base of the CBD shrank, the rationale of the underground loop had become largely obsolete. Supporters of the scheme argued that the provision of a modern underground system might itself help to arrest this trend, by stimulating new commercial development in locations remote from the old transport nodes. In a confidential paper presented to the Metropolitan Transportation Committee in 1967 economist Stewart Joy subjected these arguments to a searching cost–benefit analysis. He showed that the likely increases in traffic, efficiencies in operation of the system and beneficial effects on land-use in the CBD were insufficient to pay even a small fraction of the cost of project. 'The Underground would be a very wasteful investment for Melbourne', he concluded.[43] The sacred cow was dry, but railway officials, and their minister Vernon Wilcox were reluctant to kill it. Joy's report was suppressed and the Underground Rail Loop was finally opened in 1981.

Public transport, its friends argued, was also disadvantaged by adverse planning policies. If planners had curbed suburban sprawl and encouraged development around the fixed rail public transport system then public transport would have remained more profitable. As early as 1958 the Tramways Board was complaining that 'the undoubted development and improvement of suburban shopping facilities have contributed in some degree to the Board's loss of passengers during the year'.[44] By the early 1980s the Railways Board observed 'with concern a number of land use policies which adversely affect the efficient operation of the metropolitan services'.[45] These included amendments to the Melbourne Metropolitan Planning Scheme limiting more intensive commercial and residential development in the vicinity of railway stations and facilitating car parking in the CBD.

Between the 1940s and 1970s it is possible to discern a shift in the debate between public and private transport. In the 1940s and 1950s public transport was still a major contributor to the city's transport needs. Its friends sought to show that, under better circumstances— with more capital or better planning, for example—it might carry more passengers and run closer to a profit. Motoring interests argued that they deserved government support because they took pressure off an overstrained public transport system, rather as private school parents later argued that their fees took pressure off the state school system. By the 1970s, the terms of the argument had shifted. Public transport was now justified mainly as a subsidiary service for city-bound commuters and the carless minority of children, women and old people. Its supporters no longer pretended to justify it as a business; the weight of their arguments now shifted to social and environmental issues. Public transport was of benefit, not only to the minority of patrons, who did not wish, or could not afford, to drive, but to the majority of other city-dwellers, including motorists. Their roads would be less congested and less dangerous, their air less polluted, because of the traffic diverted to trains and trams. In the technical language of economists, public transport deserved to be subsidised because it minimised the 'externalities' of full motorisation.[46]

The arguments in support of public transport now relied predominantly on their assumed benefits to the whole community ('externalities') rather than the direct return to the operators and their patrons. Public transport relieved road congestion, and hence benefited other road users. Trams actually increased road congestion too, but because they carried more passengers than cars, it was argued, they were net contributors to maintaining the circulation of the city. The politics of public transport were increasingly connected with a more localised issue, the politics of public space.

THE POLITICS OF PARKING

The politics of automobilism were, at the most local level, a contest for territory, for the right to occupy and control the increasingly crowded spaces of the city. Cars transformed the dynamics of urban space. They were bigger, faster and more dangerous than the humans or horse-drawn vehicles that had previously dominated the city streets. Cars were dangerous when they moved, but they were almost as much of a problem when they were stationary. Nineteenth-century grid cities like Melbourne were designed for the pedestrian and the horse, but they made little provision for the thousands of motorists who now began to insist on their unfettered right, not just to drive, but to park, on the city streets. Every car occupied a space of approximately 150 square feet (14 square metres), or 250 square feet (23.2 square metres) if allowance was made for driveways and backing space. It required garage space, not only at home, but at work, shopping and recreational places.

Thirty years earlier Melbourne's town clerk had invoked council regulations, designed for the horse-and-buggy era, in a vain attempt to 'forbid the indiscriminate use of busy streets as garages for motor cars'.[47] Motorists were officially viewed as inconsiderate trespassers into people's space. But the trespassers were a growing, and always noisy, minority. The businessman who left his car standing outside the stock exchange, or the matron who instructed her driver to wait outside George's Department Store, were important, not only to themselves, but to the city interests with whom they did business. By their spending power, if not their voting power, the motorists claimed special rights, at least to the zone now usually called 'the central business district'. The politics of parking reproduced locally and in miniature many of the ideological and economic issues governing the politics of the car at national and state levels. Here, as there, mass motorisation was gradually forcing an accommodation between the individualist ideology of automobilism and community expectations.

By taking most cars off the road, the war had temporarily alleviated the parking problem, but by the late 1940s inner city congestion had again reached crisis point. Authorities struggled to gauge the dimensions of the problem. In 1948 Melbourne lord mayor James Disney, proprietor of Disney Motors, took to the air in a RAAF helicopter for an aerial survey of the city's traffic problem. This bold experiment yielded no useful information, however, because the appearance of the

By 1955 traffic congestion in central Melbourne had convinced many motorists that the city council was incapable of solving the problem. (ROYALAUTO, 1955)

novel aircraft caused so many sightseers to gather that the streets became impassable.[48]

A more scientific method was the traffic census. In 1925 George Broadbent reflected on the transformation of Melbourne in his own lifetime. 'For more than 45 years it has been my privilege to use the streets of the metropolis, and never during that long period has there been such a rapid change noted as in the last two years. It appears to me that the volume has doubled.' Broadbent's estimate was based, not only on his own memory, but on a traffic census taken the previous year.[49] By 1947 a new census suggested that the overall volume of traffic in the metropolis had doubled yet again. In 1926 motor vehicles had comprised only about half the flow, but by 1947 they were more than 90 per cent. The count of vehicles actually entering the city centre during the day, however, had increased more slowly (35 per cent), a sign, perhaps, that congestion was choking off some of the inward flow.[50]

With nowhere else to go, the irresistible tide of automobilism had engulfed the city streets. Cars and trucks double-parked in Bourke Street, jammed up the little streets and spilt onto every available bit of vacant land. RACV councillors, accustomed to parking conveniently outside their club headquarters in Queen Street, drove endlessly around the block, tummies rumbling, while their lunch guests waited impatiently inside. Furious delivery drivers, unable to load or unload consignments, threatened to strike if parking cars were not cleared from the streets.

Like King Canute, the authorities at first commanded that the angry waves of motorists retreat. In 1947, the Melbourne City Council debated a motion to ban all private vehicles from the city centre between morning and dusk. Labor councillors supported the ban, but city businessmen feared that it would create a 'dead heart' in the centre of the city. Their representatives narrowly carried an amendment to impose the ban only between the hours of 7 am and 12 noon and from 4.30 pm to 6.30 pm.[51] Some planners, like the chairman of the Town and Country Planning Board, J. S. Gawler, considered that 'the complete prohibition of parking in the main streets of Melbourne . . . [was] almost sure to come'.[52] The RACV, on the other hand, regarded a ban of any kind as an 'arbitrary' interference with the motorist's right to drive and park freely on the city streets.[53] Parking spaces were as indispensable to the private motorist as terminals to the busline or railway.[54] Unable to satisfy either side completely, the MCC tightened and relaxed its parking regime according to the fluctuations of congestion and politics.

Prohibition was at best a temporary expedient until the city could devise more comprehensive measures of traffic control. Debate over the parking problem increasingly concentrated on either of two general strategies: boosting the supply of parking space, either on the streets or elsewhere; or restricting the demand either by pricing or rationing. From the early 1950s onwards no-one seriously proposed a total and permanent ban on parking.

Amateurs and experts were eager to contribute their solutions to the parking crisis. Why should the parklands around the Melbourne Cricket Ground remain empty through most of the week when they could provide good parking space? Could the old Western market be turned over to indoor parking? Or should the railway yards or even the Yarra River be roofed to provide additional room for vehicles? Perhaps carparks could be constructed along the north side of the river where a fire in 1951 had destroyed most of the old buildings. Or underground carparks built under the Flagstaff Gardens. Why not narrow the unnecessarily wide footpaths so as to allow cars to angle-park in city streets? Or do away with the city's old-fashioned trams and their fixed lines in favour of the more mobile trolley buses?[55]

The common thread in these proposals was the attempt to boost supply by turning supposedly under-utilised public land or road space into garage space for private motorists. Surprisingly, the economic and political implications of such a transfer of assets were seldom questioned, although their limited practicality was soon apparent. A conference chaired in 1952 by the chief planner of the MMBW, E. F. Borrie, estimated that an additional 4000 parking places could be provided by more intensive use of such sites.[56]

Bolder and more expensive schemes called for a total separation between motor traffic, trams and pedestrians. In 1946 a journalist proposed to build elevated 'footways' above the street, to remove pedestrians from hazardous traffic and expand the space for moving and parked vehicles. Twenty years later the RACV revived the idea, this time with the further refinement of a third underground level for the hated, but indispensable, trams.[57] These fanciful schemes testify both to Melbourne's growing sense of desperation about its parking problem, and to its hope that through science, technology and rational planning an answer would be found.

In the meantime, the only practical course for a city council short of funds and desperate to alleviate congestion was to control the demand

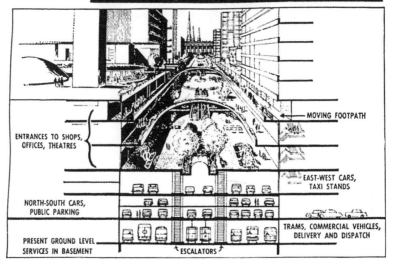

RACV shows plan for split level city

MOVING FOOTPATH

ENTRANCES TO SHOPS, OFFICES, THEATRES

EAST-WEST CARS, TAXI STANDS

NORTH-SOUTH CARS, PUBLIC PARKING

TRAMS, COMMERCIAL VEHICLES, DELIVERY AND DISPATCH

PRESENT GROUND LEVEL
SERVICES IN BASEMENT   ESCALATORS

In the RACV's 1965 plan for a split-level city, trams were relegated to the bottom level. (HERALD, 1965)

for parking space by restriction, rationing or more vigorous policing. Motoring organisations opposed almost all such measures as an unwarranted interference with the freedom of the road. Police and city officials, on the other hand, were constantly frustrated by the difficulties of detecting and prosecuting illegal parking. Many motorists were able to shield themselves from prosecution because the vehicle they parked illegally was not their own. In 1950 the state government legislated the principle of 'owner-onus' under which owners, whose name and address could be traced from their number plates, were obliged to demonstrate that they were not actually 'in charge' of their vehicle when an offence occurred. The RACV, as the voice of the man on the registration papers (if not actually behind the wheel) opposed the new law, as shifting the onus of proof from the police to the downtrodden motorist, but their protests were ignored.

In 1950, Len Frazer, the Deputy City Engineer of Melbourne, claimed that the introduction of the parking meters he had recently observed in American cities would 'work wonders' in Melbourne.[58]

Parking meters on Wellington Parade. (Photo Mark Strizic)

Half slot machine, half policeman, the meter simultaneously charged motorists a rent for occupying parking space and helped to monitor their compliance. Motoring organisations were lukewarm about the new machines. They were reluctant to pay for what they had previously regarded as a right and doubtful whether the machines could solve the parking problem, which they saw as a problem of deficient supply.[59] City officials, on the other hand, were enthusiastic about a device which promised both to swell the city's coffers and cut policing and administration costs. By 1955, when the first meters appeared in Melbourne's streets, the RACV had abandoned its opposition although, in line with its general policy on motoring taxation, it argued that the proceeds of parking fees and fines should be devoted exclusively to the provision of additional parking space, especially on the city fringe.

A New Order

Since the advent of the motor age, traffic in the city had been managed, when it was managed at all, through an informal process of negotiation

between interested groups, drawn together in ad hoc 'traffic conferences' under the city council or state government. The first such
conference in 1914 had been called to discuss the implementation of
the recently passed Motor Car Act. Motorists, police, public transport
operators, state and local governments, public utilities, business organisations and trade unions all had a stake in public streets and roads; the
conferences attempted to reach a consensus about how they should be
regulated.[60] But by the 1950s it was becoming clear that traffic regulation was an issue no longer within the competence of an ad hoc,
inexpert and insufficiently representative body. Conferences called in
1948 and 1952 had debated a wide range of solutions to the traffic
problem, but failed to agree on a credible package of measures.

As congestion increased, and access to the CBD became more difficult, city businessmen grew restive. Retailers like the Myer Emporium
and Patersons Home Furnishings were heavily dependent on the provision of parking space for their customers. At their new suburban
Chadstone regional shopping complex Myer provided the parking
themselves, and in 1954 the company also opened a 300-place off-street
customer carpark near its Lonsdale Street store. But individual retailers
could not solve their parking problems alone. Congestion was a civic as
well as a commercial issue. If the horse-and-buggy city needed to be
replanned and re-engineered for the motor age, then business and
government, which had a mutual interest in the outcome, would have to
share the responsibility, just as their as their American cousins had done.

Since the turn of the century American cities had coordinated the
process of planning and development through a mutually reinforcing
web of civic institutions—city businessmen's clubs, planning commissions, civic associations, philanthropic foundations, housing and social
reform groups—as well as through the formal structures of municipal
government. Kenneth Myer, elder son of Sidney Myer and heir apparent
to the Myer family business, had observed American approaches to city
development at close quarters, especially in Los Angeles where his father
had befriended members of its civic elite in the 1920s. Civic and philanthropic duty were an important dimension of Sidney Myer's meteoric
business success. In contributing to the social and cultural welfare of the
city, through his gifts to the University of Melbourne and his Christmas
dinners for the city's poor during the Depression, he was simultaneously
paying a debt of gratitude, reinforcing the city's prosperity and buying
future goodwill. From the early 1950s, when they returned from study

in the United States, Sidney's sons, Kenneth and Baillieu, became strong advocates for an American-style approach to the modernisation of the city's planning and development.[61] Among the lasting legacies of the family's civic duty were the Myer Music Bowl, modelled on the Hollywood Bowl, and the Myer Foundation, modelled on the great American philanthropic trusts.

Kenneth Myer was convinced that Melbourne could meet the challenge of modernisation only through the application of scientific expertise and rational planning. He joined the Town and Country Planning Association, quickly assumed its presidency, and began to shift its focus from the English garden city ideals of its founders towards a more American emphasis on efficiency and civic beautification. 'In America, planning is good business—the modern mark of civic administration', the association affirmed in its 1954 pamphlet *Meet Mr Muddle*. The villain of the story, Mr Muddle, personified the spirit of confusion and compromise that seemed to frustrate all Melbourne's modernising impulses. Nowhere was Muddle's malign influence more apparent than in the city's 'traffic tangle'. 'Everybody is angry, everybody blaming everybody else, nobody doing anything except poultice the community with more restrictions and regulations.'[62]

In November 1953 Ken Myer's uncle Norman, head of the retail firm, became president of a new body, the City Development Association (CDA), dedicated to the revitalisation of the central business district.[63] The association's concerns ranged widely. During its first two years it lobbied for slum reform, underground railways, reform of tenancy laws and shopping hours, and pressed the city to establish a civic festival, Moomba, as a magnet for shoppers and tourists. It became the power base and cheer squad for a faction of reforming Liberals on the city council, the Civic Group.[64]

In 1953 Myer sponsored a short visit from Charles Bennett, Chief Planner of Los Angeles and an enthusiastic freeway advocate. The ebullient, fast-talking and cigar-smoking visitor was every Australian's image of the can-do Yankee expert. 'The vital need for planning . . . became clear with the coming of the automobile age', Bennett declared. 'The car is here to stay . . . and there is no point whatever in legislating to restrict its activities . . . Our cities must be built around the necessity for the car.'[65]

In the following year the RACV and the City Development Association jointly sponsored a longer visit by D. Grant Mickle, a traffic engineer from the Automotive Safety Foundation in Washington and a former consultant to the City of Los Angeles. Mickle, a quietly spoken, conservatively dressed pipe smoker, was a more reassuring, and perhaps more influential, figure than Bennett.[66] The press, which covered his visit extensively, portrayed him as a kind of friendly boffin, a 'Mr Fix-it' for the city's failing traffic system.[67] He prepared a report on Melbourne's traffic problem, then at its chaotic worst, which called for the creation of a federal department of roads on the American model, the upgrading of technical training and research, and comprehensive street and traffic management plans, including the creation of a metropolitan traffic authority, possibly as a division of the Melbourne and Metropolitan Board of Works, the water and sewerage authority which had recently assumed responsibility for metropolitan planning.[68] While tactfully refusing to say that Melbourne's extensive tramway system should be scrapped, he stressed that 'all large American cities that were beating traffic tangles were getting rid of trams'.[69]

Like other traffic experts, Mickle conceived the city as a quasi-organic system and the traffic problem as a premature narrowing of its

US traffic doctor Grant Mickle arrives just in time to save a city fainting from the ministrations of feuding local authorities. (ROYALAUTO, 1954)

arteries. 'Congestion, delays and inadequate roads and streets impair free and efficient circulation and add materially to the costs of doing business and ultimately to the bill paid by the consumer', Mickle warned. Picking up this analogy, professor of architecture Brian Lewis remarked in 1957: 'We must look to America for our medicine.'[70] A cartoon in the RACV's journal portrayed Mickle as the doctor who would apply the patent Yankee cure. His primary audience was the city's business and professional elite to whom he appealed as much on a basis of enlightened self-interest, as civic idealism. 'Americans who helped promote road safety and modern highways were not "do-gooders" but cold-blooded business men,' he told an audience of Melbourne businessmen.[71] The government of the day, the Labor administration of John Cain senior, declined to endorse Mickle's plan, but under the succeeding Liberal government of Henry Bolte, most of his recommendations, including the transfer of metropolitan freeway planning and construction to the board of works, were implemented.[72]

The most constant preoccupation of the CDA was the threat of traffic congestion to the economic survival of the central business district. 'The traffic problem is hitting us like a heart attack, choking all our roads, bottling up our main arteries and congesting our central city to the point where our economy is threatened', it asserted in 1955.[73] If property values declined, then so would city revenue. Central Melbourne could be caught in a disastrous downward spiral. The note of urgency and choice of imagery were telling: the parking problem was now evidently beyond the reach of palliatives; it required the application of scientific expertise and radical surgery. The standard cures were American, most of them schemes developed by automobile advocates as early as the 1920s.[74] With the help of senior students at Melbourne High School the CDA carried out a comprehensive survey which demonstrated—to no-one's surprise—a severe deficiency in the supply of parking space, especially for shoppers and other short-term visitors to the city. To meet this emergency, the association proposed the creation of a single parking authority, with the power to compulsorily acquire property, carry out systematic studies of the parking problem, and to 'supplement and stimulate private enterprise' in the provision of parking facilities. The regulation of parking should be detached from local government and brought under a single strong authority, the police department. Planning regulations should be amended to require the provision of off-street parking in all new city buildings.[75]

The parking policies of the CDA, like the road assistance policies of the Menzies Government, and the 'Develop Victoria' policies of the newly elected Bolte Government, reflected a historic shift in the political outlook of the urban business classes. Liberals were originally attracted to the car as a freedom machine, a physical embodiment of the principles of free movement and individual choice. Mass motorisation promised to universalise those freedoms. But in the process it created an urban environment that frustrated the very freedoms they sought to promote.

It would require a comprehensive exercise of state power—in the form of traffic and planning regulations, increased charges and fines, the compulsory acquisition of private property, systematic research and rigorous surveillance—to enable every motorist to enjoy the freedom of the inner city roads. Within three years of the publication of its report, the main pillars of the CDA's traffic policy had been enacted. In 1957 the City of Melbourne amended planning regulations to require all new buildings to include off-street parking. A year later, the Traffic Commission—a three-man expert authority with power over the state's entire system of traffic control—began operations. Little by little, and with only occasional controversy, the commission has steadily assembled an immense apparatus of traffic surveillance and control: road signs, speed limits, traffic lights, roundabouts, slip-lanes, clearways, no-parking zones, radar detection devices, amphometers and red-light cameras. Between 1959 and 1968, for example, the number of traffic lights in the state more than doubled from 348 to 710. By 1969 Police Commissioner V. H. Arnold estimated that 70 per cent of police time was devoted to the enforcement of traffic laws.[76]

'He shall be forced to be free', one of the intellectual architects of the French Revolution, Jean Jacques Rousseau, had famously declared. Individual liberty was to be perfected by consulting the general will. Melbourne's motorists had learnt a similar lesson. Automobilism—the freedom to drive when and where one wished—could only be facilitated by the creation of a comprehensive system of surveillance and control. That system is now so much a part of our everyday experience of the city that we scarcely notice it, at least until the traffic infringement notice arrives in the letterbox or the traffic lights break down. From the vantage point of the rugged pioneers of automobilism, however, it represented a political revolution.

For most of the postwar years the RACV had resisted any form of regulation that appeared to fetter the free movement of the car.

On issues like owner-onus and parking meters it was usually the last to surrender. Among younger members of the organisation, however, there was a growing awareness of the need to adopt a less reactive attitude to urban issues. Modernist architect Les Perrott junior, an active member of the Town and Country Planning Association since the early 1950s, joined the council of the RACV in the late 1950s. In 1964, he used the occasion of the club's sixtieth anniversary to host a major national conference on the theme, 'Living with the Motor Car'. Premier Henry Bolte opened the proceedings and keynote addresses were given by two international experts, Burton W. Marsh, Director of Traffic Engineering and Safety for the American Automobile Association, and Colin Buchanan, Professor of Transport at Imperial College, University of London and author of the influential British report, *Traffic in Towns* (1963).[77] In personality, philosophy and style, they embodied the rival approaches to the problem of congestion then emerging on each side of the Atlantic.

Burton Marsh, a 'personal friend' of the RACV's earlier American visitor D. W. Mickle, was a breezy exponent of an expansionist, techno-logical approach to transport issues. 'Mobility has long been a desire of people', he began. The motor car was the most advanced expression of that principle. It enabled 'growing families to have homes where there is open space for play, for gardens, for more pleasant living'. Traffic congestion was an irritating, but curable, malady that accom-panied automobilisation. 'The traffic engineer is the traffic doctor', Marsh continued.

> Thinking of streets and highways as blood vessels, with traffic as blood, both the physician and the traffic engineer are concerned about congestion, about heart trouble with the central business district being thought of as the traffic heart, and about arteriosclero-sis in which the full effectiveness of the artery to carry blood is reduced by undesirable developments along the 'edges' of the artery.[78]

Since the sixteenth century, when the physiologist Robert Harvey dis-covered the circulation of the blood, the streets of the city had been likened to the arteries and veins of the body.[79] This analogy was espe-cially attractive to economic liberals, convinced of the link between the free movement of people and goods and their collective prosperity. Importantly, it also reinforced the role of technologists, planners and other experts who aspired to relieve the afflictions of the body politic.[80]

In the 1840s, Edwin Chadwick advocated pure water supplies and underground sewerage as a cure for the rampant contagion in English cities. Now the disease was traffic congestion, and the cures were parking stations and freeways.

Among an audience of late-middle-aged professionals, Marsh's jocular reference to urban 'heart trouble' may have hit a sensitive nerve. It became the conference's running joke. The CBD was 'the heart of the community', agreed Transport Minister Ray Meagher. Banning cars in the city was rather like stopping the blood flow to cure a thrombosis, suggested MMBW chief planner Alastair Hepburn. Melbourne City Council traffic engineer John Knee saw himself as a humble general practitioner, trying to keep 'this old body of ours going while [the] specialists play round with their schemes' [of comprehensive traffic planning]. By defining the urban traffic problem as one of deficient circulation, the experts had taken a long step towards the prescription of a cure.

Marsh was a personable, even ingratiating, guest. He had arrived, accompanied by Mrs Marsh, in time to tour 'your hospitable and fascinating country'. His presentation, accompanied by graphs, tables and photographs, and introduced by a short film, *Metro Mobility*, was technically polished. His opposite number, London's Professor Buchanan, arrived at the last moment and was still evidently disoriented from the long flight when he gave his opening address. 'There is something peculiarly poignant in travelling thousands of miles, and landing in a country which is really quite strange to you, and then discovering that the inhabitants speak English', he began. He introduced himself diffidently as an 'old-worlder', unsure that European experience had anything to teach Australians whose suburbanised cities so resembled those of the United States. Buchanan made no secret of his personal preferences—Los Angeles was 'the most excruciatingly unattractive place I have ever seen'. He was conscious of the contrasting 'political philosophies' that had shaped responses to the car on either side of the Atlantic. His seminal report on *Traffic in Towns* was full of practical wisdom, pithily expressed; in England it had been a best-selling Penguin special. He was tall and handsome with an attractive vein of self-deprecating humour. But as a newcomer, he seemed reluctant to contest the hegemony of the visiting American experts. While Marsh constructed the city around the apparently limitless desire of its inhabitants for mobility, Buchanan's was a characteristically European vision of a bounded city, in which demands for accessibility had to be balanced against needs to preserve the environment. Unless its use was curbed, Buchanan predicted, the car would 'kill the street'. The final goal of transport planning must be 'to produce civilised environments for city life'.[81]

Expansion or containment, accessibility or environmental conservation—these were the choices Melburnians faced as they stood on the threshold of mass automobilisation. They might decide to push their foot to the floor and follow their American cousins down the asphalt path towards 'full automobilisation'. Or they could throttle back, invest more in public transport, and reinforce a European pattern of compact, pedestrian-friendly urbanism. Among participants in the RACV's symposium opinion predictably leant towards expansion. Very few of the delegates, even including Professor Buchanan, seemed convinced that the European model could be applied to Australian conditions. More numerous than either expansionists or contractionists, however, were those who favoured a 'balanced' approach to transport development. Perhaps by steering a middle course Melbourne could avoid the pitfalls of both. 'My own view is that in our democratic way we shall end up with a compromise between the two', concluded the MMBW's Chief Planner Alistair Hepburn.[82] 'Balanced transport' looked like a solution that would satisfy everyone. Where the balance was to be struck, and whether it would deliver a transport system that would be economical and equitable for all Melburnians was the question no-one had yet even begun to answer.

6

Blood on the Bitumen

The bloodiest of Melbourne's car wars was the long campaign to stem the profligate wastage of lives on the city's roads. In 1947 the Victorian Minister for Transport estimated that 65 000 more Australians had been killed or injured on the roads between 1939 and 1946 than had been killed or injured in the war.[1] The slaughter did not end with the coming of peace. Even by later standards, the early postwar years were a violent time on the nation's roads as novice drivers in old jalopies competed for unregulated road space with cyclists, trams, horse-drawn vehicles, motorcycles, pedestrians and other motorists.

Like the carnage of war, the 'traffic toll' demanded a militant response, a campaign as disciplined and energetic as the one the nation had recently waged against the Axis. 'Australia must declare war on traffic accidents', the Australian Automobile Association trumpeted in 1946. 'They constitute an enemy which takes almost as great a toll of Australia's already sparse population as did the enemy nations in the Second World War.'[2] The imagery of battle lent a sense of urgency to the peacetime challenge of road safety. It strengthened claims for public support and government resources; it also created the comforting, but possibly misleading, impression that lives lost on the road could somehow be saved by imposing the kind of national mobilisation that had driven the war effort.

In the following half-century Victorians were among the most valiant warriors in that cause, leading the world in the introduction of such preventive measures as compulsory seatbelts and random breath testing for drunken driving. For many years they seemed to be losing that war, as the numbers of road fatalities and injuries rose year after year. New measures of law enforcement, vehicle modification, road improvement or advertising would secure a temporary improvement, but it took almost 30 years of struggle before the city's roads became safer.

Over that long campaign the war against the road toll passed through several phases, as the causes and cure of road trauma were subjected to ever-increasing levels of scientific research, legal regulation and behavioural modification. Taking a long view, the trend of policy is clear. Road accidents have been progressively redefined from a moral to a medical problem, and moral exhortation and punishment have given way to new strategies of prevention and harm minimisation. None of these developments occurred without vigorous community debate, and often spirited resistance on the part of motorists and professionals. In debating the road toll, Melburnians were grappling with issues that transcended the utilitarian logic of prevention and cure, and challenged the very values—of freedom and material progress—that inspired mass motorisation.

MORALISING MOTORISTS

In the 1940s when the numbers of road deaths first began to climb alarmingly, road safety was more a topic of morality than of science. Public discourse was governed by the assumptions of the 1920s when motor cars first made a lethal impact on the city's roads. Motorists were then a small, rich minority among a majority of pedestrians, cyclists, tram and bus passengers, and drivers of horse-drawn vehicles. When cars knocked down pedestrians or collided with other vehicles the blame was often laid at the foot of the motorist who could be charged with 'furious driving' or with a form of criminal assault. The offending motorist was often stigmatised as a 'road hog' or a 'speed merchant'.[3]

Motorists themselves, through organisations such as the RACV, had fought a vigorous counter-attack, first to gain public acceptance of the view that collisions were 'accidents' not assaults, then to limit the term 'motor accident' to incidents in which the motor car and its driver were the clear culprits. 'It is unfair and useless to issue a list of "motor" accidents without first proving that the driver of the motor vehicle was at least contributory', insisted the RACV's George Broadbent in 1925.

If motorists collided with each other, or did damage to themselves without hurting others, the damage was unfortunate but not to be considered a 'motor accident'.[4]

The best antidote to the road toll, the RACV believed, was the observance of good road manners. Since its early days the RACV had seen itself as a gallant fraternity of adventurers, the 'Knights of the Road'. Gentleman motorists pledged to uphold a brotherly code of honour. Road safety, according to this chivalric ideal, was a matter of moral obedience, of courtesy towards others. It was courtesy that smoothed out the frictions generated by the competition of free motorists for limited road space. Courtesy was a matter of both altruism and of self-interest.

> Courtesy on the road pays dividends. If we take the right view of it, we do not take payment into account, but even the self-centred driver will agree that courtesy does pay. It pays because it results in fewer accidents, fewer 'near misses', less frayed tempers, more amiability and peace of mind. Meet someone with your hackles up and his will rise correspondingly, for most of us feel that our dignity demands that we give back at least some of what we get. But if we take the other fellow in a friendly and understanding way, it is seldom that he will not as readily respond. We're a bit suspicious of people we don't know and apt to assert ourselves. What we forget is that they are likely to take the same view of us.[5]

Courtesy promoted fraternal relations among a brotherhood of gentlemen-motorists. Members of the fraternity recognised each other by common insignia, rituals and values, if not by personal acquaintance. When pioneer members of the RACV observed the club badge on the bonnet of an approaching car they were expected to salute him with a friendly toot of the horn. In making courtesy the cornerstone of its approach to road safety the RACV had sought to propagate these chivalrous ideas more widely. It was a way of maintaining the club's cardinal principle, the freedom of the road—since courtesy was a matter of individual moral choice—and of persuading the public at large—'the people we don't know'—to live up to their gentlemanly ideal.

In 1950 the editor of the RACV *Radiator* reflected on the link between the origins of motoring as a gentlemanly sport and the development, and subsequent decline, of road courtesy. When he joined the club in 1911 there was 'a spirit of camaraderie and mutual aid among

Courtesy was the keynote of road safety advertising in the 1940s and 1950s.
(ROYALAUTO, 1959)

drivers that is lacking today'. By the 1950s motoring had ceased to be a sport and had become 'almost a necessity'. As the number of drivers increased, and the sense of camaraderie declined, so had standards of behaviour on the road. Australian drivers compared poorly with their overseas, and especially their English, counterparts. 'Look out, here I come' was the average Australian motorist's motto, said Melbourne lord mayor, motor distributor and frequent overseas traveller, Sir Raymond Connolly.[6] Drivers who were perfectly courteous at the dinner table became impatient and rude when they got behind the wheel. 'It is unfortunate', the editor of the *Radiator* concluded, 'that so many drivers leave their etiquette at home'. Most motorists, he thought, were now ruled more by road rules and traffic regulations than by codes of gentlemanly conduct, but he hoped, all the same, that a vigorous educational campaign might inspire a revival of chivalry on the roads.[7]

In 1950 the National Road Safety Council launched the first of its annual Courtesy Weeks under the motto 'Courtesy is Catching'. Motorists were encouraged to sign a pledge to abstain from careless and discourteous behaviour on the roads.[8] The council circulated a booklet, *Motor Manners,* by the American motorist and authority on etiquette Emily Post, distilling the rules of courteous driving:

1. A well-mannered driver will share the road, never usurping the right-of-way from other vehicles or pedestrians.
2. A well-behaved driver uses his horn in emergencies, and never as a bad-tempered voice to threaten or scold.
3. An honourable man or woman would no more cheat traffic regulations than cheat at games or in sports.
4. Courteous pedestrians will cross busy streets at intersections, respect traffic lights and avoid darting out from behind parked vehicles.
5. An obliging driver will never fail to dim his lights when meeting other cars at night.
6. Well-bred people, whether drivers or passengers, are just as considerate of each other as are hosts and guests in a drawing room.
7. An accommodating driver parks his car so as not to interfere with the use of other parking spaces or the movement of other vehicles.
8. Orderly drivers always keep to the left, except when using the proper lane for turning or passing.
9. A courteous driver never fails to signal in time his intention to stop, turn or pull out.
10. Considerate persons always drive at speeds which are reasonable and prudent, having in mind traffic, road and weather conditions.
11. One who has consideration for the safety of others will refrain from driving when physically exhausted.
12. Kindly persons never show curiosity at the scene of an accident and always give any assistance that may be possible.[9]

Well-bred, well-mannered, considerate, kindly, courteous and orderly, the model motorist would apply the etiquette of the middle-class drawing room to the larger, more impersonal spaces of the city.

Could courtesy catch on fast enough to curb the rapidly rising road toll? At the end of the first Courtesy Week, seven people had died on the roads, well above the weekly average. 'We should not delude ourselves that campaigns of this kind, slogans or even uniform traffic codes are going to do the work of the police', the *Herald* warned. 'They can only help. There are types of drivers on the road who no advice or exhortation will curb. Some have no consideration of others; some are reckless, some are plainly incompetent and lacking in road sense.'[10] Yet both sides of the debate agreed that safety was primarily a matter of individual behaviour. A 1951 Gallup poll identified 'carelessness' as the leading cause of road deaths (37 per cent) followed by alcohol (28 per cent) and speed (22 per cent), but saw heavier penalties (48 per cent) and more traffic police (12 per cent) as more effective than licence tests (9 per cent), speed limits (8 per cent) or education campaigns (8 per cent).[11]

The code of courtesy reinforced certain features of the liberal ideal; in particular, it deflected the criticism that the motorist's freedom was an irresponsible freedom. The motor lobby was successful in its attempts to resist a tightening up of traffic laws and their stricter enforcement. In the early years of the Cold War, when bank nationalisation and the Communist Party Dissolution Bill dominated federal politics, the conflict between individualism and collectivism was also mirrored in the more mundane politics of road regulation. Labor, the party of a still largely carless working class, upheld principles of regulation against the Liberal Party, the party of a burgeoning car-owning middle class. In 1947 the Cain Labor Government had introduced a Motor Car Bill that provided for lower speed limits, blood testing for drink-driving and the creation of a special metropolitan traffic court. But when the succeeding McDonald Liberal–Country Party Government reintroduced the bill in 1948, its main provisions had been significantly watered down. The metropolitan traffic court was no more; the speed limits had been raised and the scale of penalties reduced. 'This was to have been the "Magna Carta" for the motor car user', Labor member John Cremean reminded the Assembly, 'but it appears to fall short of this political "Runnymede". Each amendment accepted by the government weakened the measure and gave greater liberties to the motorist as against the pedestrian.'[12] Attempts by the Labor government of John Cain to reintroduce a 30 mph speed limit in built-up areas and 50 mph elsewhere were greeted sceptically by the RACV. The road toll was caused 'not so much by high speeding as low breeding', responded its president T. F. McBride.[13]

In the 1920s George Broadbent had argued that it would be better to rely on the motorist's commonsense than arbitrary speed limits, 'because motor owners largely are drawn from that numerous and respectable class of successful citizens who realise the value and need for law and order, and are guarded in their actions by humane instincts'.[14] Thirty years later his son E. A. Broadbent maintained that speed limits were 'contrary to the whole concept of British justice'. Exceeding an arbitrary speed limit did not necessarily mean that a motorist was driving, in the words of previous legislation, 'to the danger of the public'.[15] At stake in these skirmishes over law and language was the attempt by the organised voice of motoring to hold on to the concept of the driver as a self-regulating individual, capable, within the broad architecture of the law, of making his own judgements of right and wrong. By the mid-1950s, however, even the 'knights of the road' were beginning to recognise that courtesy was simply not catching on fast enough. It would take stronger measures of compulsion, prevention and restraint to reduce the ever-mounting toll of lives on the road.

DETERRENCE AND SURVEILLANCE

If delinquent motorists could not be exhorted to behave, could they be terrified into compliance? In 1949 the National Road Safety Council launched a campaign under the slogan 'Death is so permanent', designed to instil among motorists a salutary fear of death and bodily mutilation. The message was meant to shock, although some of the reaction was theological as much as emotional. An Anglican clergyman 'viewed with disquiet the negation of the belief in life after death which is a fundamental of the Christian faith', although a Presbyterian, Rev. Gordon Powell, helpfully suggested that the existence of an afterlife should not 'encourage people to hasten out of this one'.[16] People still seemed to flinch from the kind of graphic realism in depictions of death and injury that would become a keynote of safety campaigns in the 1980s and 1990s. A proposal to mark the scene of fatal accidents with a red cross on the road was regarded as tasteless and insensitive.

Yet many people undoubtedly harboured a morbid fascination with the carnage on the roads. People would stop at accident scenes to stare as well as help. Throughout the 1950s, 3XY radio roundsman Tom Jones patrolled the roads with his tape recorder every Saturday night, chasing police cars and ambulances to accident scenes all over the metropolis, where he recorded the macabre soundscapes of suffering and rescue for his popular Sunday morning program, *Nightbeat*. The police, ambulance drivers and doctors who witnesssed these scenes often led the campaigns to curb the slaughter but they too were evidently sceptical or nervous about whether drivers could be frightened by horrific depictions into safer driving. Perhaps people were reluctant to imagine, even for a moment, that they could experience such trauma themselves. The connection between their own routine conduct and these terrifying scenes of slaughter was too remote to affect their behaviour.

Worse, the road toll was continuing to rise even faster than the number of cars on the ever more crowded roads. Some of these casualties were motorists, but even more were pedestrians, cyclists or passengers. In 1947–8, 126 (or 34.5 per cent) of the 362 people killed on Victorian roads were pedestrians, 50 (or 13.8 per cent) were cyclists, 35 (9.6 per cent) motorcyclists and only 45 (12.4 per cent) were drivers of motor vehicles. Not until the 1960s did the numbers of drivers dying on the roads begin to equal the number of pedestrians and not until the 1990s did drivers outnumber pedestrians among road deaths as completely as pedestrians had once outnumbered them.[17] At any time between the 1920s and the 1960s the slaughter on the roads was largely caused by collisions between motor cars, the well-protected conveyances of the middle class, and the relatively unprotected bodies of less well-to-do road users. The war on the road toll was also, in some of its aspects, a class war.

Since the 1920s motoring organisations had sought to persuade authorities that dead and injured pedestrians were largely victims of their own carelessness. While motorists were routinely blamed for the rising road toll, they complained that no similar condemnation was directed towards the 'many careless and irresponsible pedestrians, some indeed who should not be at large on the city streets'. While motorists were subject to increasing regulation and taxation, their fellow road users were seemingly exempt. They hailed the introduction of marked pedestian crossings in the early 1920s as indicating 'that every person has an equal right with every other person on a highway irrespective of whether he be on foot, on a wheel or in a vehicle'.[18]

From the vantage point of the motorist, the pedestrian seemed a random, even irrational element in the urban scene. 'The pedestrian was more unpredictable than the motorist and kept him guessing by doing unreasonable things such as ignoring traffic signals stepping unexpectedly off the footpath, deliberately crossing a road in the face of oncoming traffic and walking on the wrong side of the road', a road safety official observed.[19] Through the windscreen, the errant pedestrian often looked like a startled animal, a creature of instinct immune from the rationality of the motorist:

I'm a scientific codger
And I've quite a lot to say;
Of the Dope, or motor dodger,
Which you bump into each day.

Now this traffic dodging creature,
(Latin name PEDESTRIAN DILL);
Is an interesting feature,
Of the city landscape still.

And by that I am recalling,
That he's not extinct as yet;
Though the death rate is appalling
Of this harmless little pet.

Shy and timid, never caring,
If the lights be red or green
He will saunter, stop—eyes staring,
At a far-off distant scene.

Tooting horns will not affect him,
Swear words brush by either ear;
Would the gods-that-be inject him,
With some sense of sight or fear.

But my plea to you, dear reader,
Is to spare this simple lout;
He's a dill without a leader,
Soon the species will die out.[20]

Although pedestrians were an endangered species, no-one, it seemed, was responsible for their preservation but themselves. Either they would learn road manners or be subjected to 'rigid regulation' and severe penalties for non-compliance.[21]

Realists argued that only a greater force of police, with simpler laws, more certain methods of detection and harsher penalties for infringements would counter the rising road toll. In the 1950s, however, the growing numbers of new motorists outstripped the capacity of police patrols to survey them. 'The motor vehicle almost absorbed the policeman', the historian of the Victoria Police noted.[22] From the lone cop on his inner suburban beat the emphasis turned to the divisional van patrolling vast tracts of outer suburbia. In 1946 the police traffic branch had 22 cars and 17 motorcycles; by 1983 it had 1716 vehicles. People

often regretted the disappearance of the bobby on the beat. It symbolised, and possibly hastened, the decline of the street and the
neighbourhood as significant zones of social interaction and community
security. Confronted with the new territorial imperatives created by the
car, however, the police had little choice but to automobilise themselves.

> Although one often hears the claim that it would be better if we had
> more policemen walking the beat and consequently in closer contact
> with the public, I am afraid those who make the claim live in the past
> [replied Chief Commissioner Rupert Arnold in 1967]. Members of
> the public now generally travel by car and are not likely to be in
> contact with policemen walking beats.
>
> The expansion of the city perimeter and the vast numbers of
> shopping areas which have developed in widely separated places
> have created much larger areas to be patrolled, which can only effec-
> tively be done in mobile units. Mobility is also most essential for road
> supervision which has become one of the most important spheres of
> police work.[23]

The force grew bigger, and became more reliant on powerful new
technologies of surveillance and detection such as amphometers,
breathalysers, radar guns and red-light cameras.

The police were society's front-line troops in the war against the road
toll. Imagining the problem of road accidents as a 'war' created a
presumption that it should be waged by warlike methods. It summoned
up images of uniformed men concentrating their resources at the points
where the enemy was strongest, mounting 'blitzes' during holidays and
other seasons of high risk, for example. If the road casualties were few,
police leaders would congratulate themselves on the success of the
campaign. If not, they could blame the lack of resources or the delinquency of the motorists. The causal link between the level of police
effort and the reduction of the road toll was a tenuous one. Road accidents were a product of many factors, most of which—road congestion,
weather, vehicle or road surface faults, driver concentration, and so
on—were little affected by police vigilance. Only a fraction of those
whose 'careless' or risky driving might cause an accident would come
under the notice of the police and an even smaller proportion of such
infractions would result in accidents. The running commentaries on the
battle offered by senior police were designed more to boost morale and
enhance the image of the police than to illuminate the underlying
causes of the road toll.

DRUNKS AND DOCTORS

In the 1950s authorities took the first steps away from the moralistic and legalistic approach to car safety. Rather than waging war against the delinquent road user, they began to think of the road toll as a public health problem. Medicalising the issue of road deaths had several beneficial effects. Courtesy campaigns and other moralising approaches appealed strongly to the respectable middle class, but they probably antagonised many others, especially some young men for whom danger- ous driving was appealing precisely because it offended their elders. Shifting the language from blame to harm attempted to make the cause of road safety more popularly acceptable. If road trauma was a disease it might also be studied epidemiologically, with attention to a variety of environmental, sociological, medical, psychological, mechanical and other causes.

While external conditions could be important, most experts agreed that the prime cause of accidents was the 'human factor'. Were some persons psychologically predisposed to cause accidents? Yes, said psychologist Professor Oscar Oeser, who suggested that those who

Anti-drink-driving campaigners had to make their way against the backdrop of a society that heavily promoted drink, even on the roadside. (PHOTO MARK STRIZIC, 1967)

committed multiple road offences should be psychologically tested. As
well as the unconscious drives that made some individuals abnormally
aggressive there were also the 'accident-prone'—'unfortunate people'
who had 'a peculiar structure that makes them run unconsciously into
accidents'. Once identified, such drivers might be obliged to undergo
treatment to be 'mentally re-aligned—or barred [from driving]'.[24] In an
age of mass motoring, when a car licence was becoming almost a badge
of citizenship, proposals such as Oeser's had some unwelcome political
implications. Even if the psychologists' tests could pick the 'accident-
prone' with certainty, was it fair to deny them a driver's licence? It is not
surprising that, after a brief flurry of discussion in the mid-1950s, the
idea was quietly shelved. It was one thing to disqualify a repeat offender
for what he or she *did*, but quite another to debar them on the basis of
what a psychologist said they inherently *were*.

It was much easier, morally and politically, to deal with 'the human
factor' when it appeared in the form of such antisocial behaviour as the
excessive consumption of alcohol. While everyone decried the evil of
drink-driving and wanted to punish offenders, there was wide disagree-
ment about the extent of the problem. In public opinion polls of the
1950s 'drunkenness' (28 per cent) ranked next to 'carelessness' (37 per
cent) and above all other factors, including speed (22 per cent), as a
cause of accidents.[25] Yet in official police returns on the causes of accidents it hardly ranked at all: 'inattentive driving' (often about 30 per
cent), 'excessive speed', 'not giving way', 'disregarding traffic signals'
and other breaches of the road code all exceeded 'intoxication' (about
2 per cent) as causes of accidents. But this was a primitive and cautious
form of analysis: accidents could have multiple and complex causes
('inattention' could be caused or aggravated by 'intoxication', for
example) and police at the scene of an accident were reluctant to attri-
bute a collision to intoxication unless there was irrefutable evidence.[26]
Other circumstantial evidence, such as the peaking of road deaths in
the hours immediately after the closure of hotels, suggested that the
effects of drink-driving were much greater than official figures showed.[27]

In the 1940s and 1950s trying to secure a conviction for drink-
driving was among the most unrewarding forms of police activity. How
was the constable arriving at an accident scene to obtain evidence of
intoxication? The driver might be incapacitated by injury or unwilling to
cooperate in the officer's attempts to administer one of the rudimentary
tests for intoxication: walking a chalk line, standing on one leg, picking

up car keys, telling the time or repeating the phrase 'six thick candle-sticks' without slurring. Even when drivers failed the test, their legal representatives often succeeded in casting enough doubt on the tests themselves to secure an acquittal. In 1951 Judge Leonard Stretton threw a drink-driving case out of court, arguing that 'the sort of day a man had on the job could affect his ability to pass a physical drunkenness test'. Police attempts to secure a conviction of one allegedy drunken motorist fell to the ground when he beat them in a game of noughts and crosses. A woman who had been intercepted on her way back to Melbourne from Cockatoo, and had failed all the usual tests, got her doctor to testify that her condition had been influenced by medication for blood pressure and nerves. (The two empty bottles of gin on the driver's seat suggested otherwise, however, and the court convicted her.)[28] Even when a conviction was secured the penalties were relatively light. A trav-eller who allegedly downed 40 beers in an hour before getting behind the wheel received a £20 fine but avoided gaol and kept his licence.[29]

In 1955 the new Liberal premier Henry Bolte and his chief secretary Arthur Rylah made the first of a series of determined legislative assaults on the problem of drink-driving. The most vigorous opposition to drink-driving had come, predictably, from the temperance lobby. Neither Bolte nor Rylah was a wowser. They liked a drink, a smoke and a bet but they were also political pragmatists who recognised that Victoria's stringent drinking laws could only be liberalised if longer drinking hours did not bring more road deaths. They proposed to increase penalties for driving under the influence of alcohol to a maximum £700 fine or two years' gaol or both and to institute voluntary blood alcohol tests. The public response to this modest proposal was cautious. Were the blood tests reliable indicators of driving competence? Where, in the suggested range from 0.05 to 0.15 blood alcohol, did a motorist become incompetent to drive?

Shortly after Bolte's accession to power a former military officer, Major-General Selwyn Porter, was appointed as Chief Commissioner of Police. A self-conscious moderniser, Porter introduced a stronger emphasis on police training, traffic issues and public relations.[30] In 1957 Rylah appointed 33-year-old John Birrell, a former pathology lecturer and assistant government pathologist, as Victorian Police Surgeon. He was appointed by Governor-in Council and retained a right to private practice, giving him a degree of independence that his employers later sometimes may have regretted.[31] His duties included a

wide range of forensic inquiries, but from the first he gave priority to
the gruesome and exhausting task of on-the-spot investigations of
serious road accidents. A month after his appointment the *Herald*
reported that 'this doctor with a footballer's frame [he was a former
public school goal-kicking record-holder] has amazed police headquarters with his tireless enthusiasm for his new job'. Birrell worked
a sixteen-hour day, spending mornings in the magistrate's courts,
afternoons on paperwork at Russell Street police headquarters, and
evenings, especially the two hours from six to eight after the city's notorious 'six o'clock swill', taking blood alcohol tests from suspect drivers
at police stations, hospitals and accident scenes. At first he relied on
police patrol cars to drive him to the accident scene, but he soon
persuaded Porter to supply him with a radio-equipped car for his own
use. Even before he came to the job, during his time at the coroner's
court, Birrell had become convinced of the strong link between road
accidents and drink-driving. He now patrolled hospital casualty wards
and carried out 'sneak' blood tests on dead or injured motorists. More
than half of the victims admitted to casualty wards, he discovered, were
under the influence of liquor.[32]

The young police surgeon quickly became a media hero. He invited
journalists to spend an evening accompanying him on the road. He
appeared on the national weekly television interview program *Meet the
Press*.[33] In 1959 the *Age*'s feature writer and later editor, Graham Perkin,
wrote a hard-hitting series of articles, 'Blood on the Bitumen', exposing
the impact of alcohol on the road.[34] Television reporter Michael Schild-
berger made a documentary *Seven-Tenths of a Second* featuring Birrell's
work. Birrell invited politicians to join his nocturnal tours of the
suburban killing fields. The Bolte Government's Assistant Chief Secretary Lindsay Thompson accompanied him one Saturday night to
the Oaklands Hotel just beyond the city's northern limits to witness the
horrifying mass exodus of tipsy motorists from its carpark.[35] On one
occasion, Birrell recalled, he was driving a party of observers back along
the road towards Melbourne when they passed three pedestrians
walking beside the road. 'They'd better look out', someone casually
remarked. Only minutes later the message came over Birrell's radio that
all three had been knocked down and killed.[36] The offending motorist
was found to have a blood alcohol reading of 0.16. Such experiences
reinforced the crusading instincts of younger members of the Liberal
Party, such as Thompson, Walter Jona and Brian Dixon, who began

to exert pressure on a party hierarchy reluctant to offend powerful interests in the liquor industry or to align itself too closely with wowserism.

Birrell was zealous in his pursuit of the drunken driver, but insisted that he approached the issue of road trauma from a strictly medical, rather than moral, point of view. 'Drinking drivers were as bad as any deadly disease and must be treated like one', he maintained.[37] In the many talks and lectures he gave to school and community groups he usually began by explaining that he enjoyed a drink, had been inebriated in the past, and 'in the right circumstances might be so again'. Humour, sometimes of a rather black variety, spiced his slide presentations. To illustrate the efficacy of seatbelts he compared the effects of rolling an egg (and by analogy, a human skull) down a sliding surface, with and without, a restraining belt. He showed a photograph of a light pole covered with the bloody residue of a fatal accident. But he shrewdly recognised the inoculating effects of excessive 'shock-horror'. 'What you do is you arouse anxiety with the shock-horror. But then you show how you get away with it, and how you avoid it. That way you don't turn people off completely.'[38]

A young man in a hurry, with the pathologist's characteristic bluntness, Birrell was impatient with the legal niceties and political sensitivities that had made the government's 1955 proposal for voluntary blood testing all but a dead letter. Blood tests administered without the consent of the patient were technically an assault; yet, lawyers argued, most road accident victims were unfit to give informed consent. Many doctors were also reluctant to administer blood tests, either because they doubted their validity or were reluctant to testify against their patients. Lawyers objected that a suspected person should not be obliged to incriminate himself. Yet, as Birrell perceived, only compulsory tests would provide definitive evidence of intoxication. 'I am convinced that if a compulsory blood test were given to everyone associated with a serious accident this State would be rocked by the results', he predicted.[39]

Birrell had taken a courageous stand in advocating compulsory blood testing. While Gallup opinion polls showed a growing public readiness to 'get tough' with drunken drivers, support grew more slowly among the press and the professional and political elite. Doctors were still divided on the reliability of blood tests and lawyers and politicians nervous about the legality of a compulsory test. Professor R. Douglas

Victorian police surgeon Dr John Birrell (centre with beer can) is pictured among a group of leading international road safety experts who met in Bethesda, Maryland, USA in 1968. They include his 'hero', Dr Bill Haddon Jnr (second from left), first administrator of the US Highway Safety Bureau and an early advocate of airbags, and Professor Robert Borkenstein (second from right), inventor of the breathalyser.
(PHOTO COURTESY JOHN BIRRELL)

('Pansy') Wright, physiologist and outspoken civil libertarian, contended that the tests were not a reliable test of intoxication. Opinion among his colleagues in the British Medical Association was divided.[40] In 1959 Birrell's former boss, the government pathologist Keith Bowden, travelled to the United States to investigate the latest methods of combatting drink-driving, including the new breathalyser machine that gave an instant reading of blood alcohol from an analysis of the subject's breath. Bowden canvassed a range of alternative preventive and punitive methods including voluntary and compulsory blood testing, but declined to make definite recommendations.[41] Birrell was 'disappointed' with the report but continued his public campaign, sometimes in the face of public rebuke by a government still waiting to be convinced.[42] In 1960 he published an article in the *Medical Journal of Australia* presenting strong statistical evidence for the link between alcohol consumption and road trauma that his roadside experience had long since made plain.[43] His case gained new authority when a Senate Select Committee on Road Safety, to which he gave evidence, came down firmly on the side of compulsion. 'While the growing trend towards submerging personal rights might be regarded with disfavour in many quarters it appears completely justifiable in such an important instance as this.'[44]

In July 1961, in the midst of an election campaign, the Bolte Government promised, if it was returned, to legislate for compulsory blood tests for motorists suspected of drink-driving. Police would be specially trained to administer breathalyser tests which the government believed were gaining acceptance as evidence by the courts. (Within days a magistrate had called that assumption into question by treating as hearsay the evidence of an officer who had administered a test.) The government decided to proceed with the bill but to delay proclamation until doubts about the reliability of the breathalyser had been resolved. The idea of compulsory blood tests created complex divisions among politicians. Liberals, the traditional guardians of liberty, were also the party of the respectable urban middle class. Labor, the party of state intervention and control, was also the party of the trade unions, jealous of the working-man's right to a drink. The Country Party, the voice of the man on the land, knew how inhibiting the new law might be for rural-dwellers heavily dependent upon car travel. When the bill came to parliament in October, the main parties reversed traditional roles. Opposition leader Clive Stoneham opposed it on libertarian grounds ('There has to be a hard line of demarcation between what constitutes the free way of life . . . and the police state and totalitarianism') while Premier Henry Bolte mocked civil libertarian concerns about self-incrimination ('Is it incriminating for a person to be asked to walk a straight line or say "Woolloomoloo"?').[45]

The new act came into force just before Christmas 1961. A Gallup poll showed 53 per cent of Victorians in favour of compulsory blood tests and the number of deaths over the ensuing holiday period showed an encouraging decline.[46] But while the people and their representatives had apparently accepted the new law, its validity would be tested severely in the courts in the ensuing months.

Meanwhile the government was eager to tackle the reform of the state's drinking laws, especially its increasingly antiquated six o'clock curfew on hotels. After a referendum to abolish six o'clock closing in 1955 was defeated by a NO campaign led by the Protestant churches, Bolte gave an informal undertaking that no change would be made without a second referendum.[47] Knowing the difficulty of securing a referendum majority, Bolte and Rylah now set out to convince the

Liberal Country Party and the churches to drop their opposition. Trading hours, they argued, were only one factor in a broader picture of alcohol abuse. Liberalising hotel hours might be achieved with safety if coupled with more stringent policing of alcohol abuse.

In 1963 P. D. Phillips QC conducted a royal commission on the sale and distribution of liquor. His report recommended both a liberalisation of hours and the introduction of a 0.05 blood alcohol limit for drivers. Fixing a blood alcohol limit was no different from fixing a speed limit, Phillips argued, and no more difficult to justify. 'A driver of a motor car who drives his vehicle when he has a blood alcohol concentration of more than 0.05 per cent is acting in a selfish, reckless and anti-social manner.'[48] Other authorities regarded such limits as too arbitrary, too hard to police and too likely to provoke disobedience. 'We Australians have a strong streak of independence, some would say rebellion', Justice John Starke observed. 'I feel that the ordinary, easy-going Australian may view with jocularity, even contempt, the suggestion that if he drinks four beers in twenty minutes, or six beers in 50 minutes, he is unfit to drive. He is, you know, something of an expert on the art of drinking.' Phillips reacted sharply to the learned judge's unsolicited opinion. 'Community support for the 0.05 blood alcohol law would not be increased by judicial encouragement to disregard it.'[49]

In 1965 the Victorian Parliament enacted the recommendations of the Phillips Royal Commission by passing laws to extend hotel trading hours to 10 pm and to introduce a 0.05 blood alcohol limit, the two laws coming into effect simultaneously. Victoria was the first Australian state, and one of the first in the world, to introduce 0.05 testing, a record now often cited with pride as evidence of its progressive approach to road safety. Yet these reforms reflected a need to accommodate a still-powerful strain of moral conservatism as much as to promote a new liberalism. A journalist aptly summarised the social contract underlying the new regime: 'If Victoria was to have 10 o'clock closing then it also had to accept 0.05.'[50] Since the goldrushes, Victorian politics had been strongly shaped by two currents of thought—a radical liberalism that embraced state power in the service of social betterment, and a moral conservatism, sometimes known as 'wowserism', that sought to curb human appetites in the service of family and community morality.[51] Since the 1960s the force of both these creeds has steadily diminished. But in 1965 they had each contributed to the creation of laws widely seen as novel.

The introduction of the breathalyser and the 0.05 alcohol limit enabled police to prosecute drunken motorists with greater prospects of success but the new laws had little apparent effect on the steadily rising road toll. The risks of detection and the penalties for offenders were low by later standards. Drivers convicted under the law faced fines of up to £50 for a first offence, but could keep their licences and third-party insurance. Refusing the test carried a fine of only £20.[52] The extension of hotel hours cut the number of deaths in the hour or two following the notorious 'six o'clock swill' but created another 'swill' and another peak in drink-related accidents later in the evening. A careful statistical study showed that in the year following the legislation 34 of the 40 lives 'saved' in the hour between 6 and 7 pm were 'lost' later in the evening between 7 and 11 pm.[53]

Data collected by the breathalyser tests provided a disturbing confirmation of the link between alcohol consumption and road deaths. Many of those apprehended for drink-driving were males with blood alcohol concentrations of 0.15 or more, and multiple convictions for a range of criminal offences as well as drink-driving. Some were professional drivers.[54] Identifying these problem drinkers posed a problem for law-makers and revived the issue posed by Professor Oscar Oeser and since sidestepped by legislators. Could these delinquents somehow be detected before they caused maximum harm and either treated, re-educated or barred from driving?[55] If so, would the adoption of 'scientific' methods to identify this minority also threaten the civil liberties of the innocent majority? In 1968 criminologist Duncan Chappell urged the adoption of random breath tests on the whole motoring population, accompanied with more severe penalties including suspension or even cancellation of the offender's driver's licence. 'If we really do want drinking and driving laws which are effective, laws which do save lives and prevent injuries there is no alternative but to introduce random tests of motorists.'[56]

The utilitarian logic of prevention was steadily winning ground against traditional common law objections to arbitrary or random interference with the liberties of the individual.

PREVENTING TRAUMA

Through bodies such as the Road Trauma Committee of the Royal Australasian College of Surgeons, the medical profession exerted growing influence on the road safety debate. Their experience on the front-line in attempting to save the lives and repair the mangled bodies of road crash victims gave them the moral and scientific standing to lead a debate that was increasingly framed by medical paradigms of prevention and harm mitigation. 'In the past', one surgeon observed, 'road safety has been almost exclusively in the hands of road engineers who were given the impossible job of attempting to make roads idiot-proof. This is obviously beyond the "bitumen boys".'[57] Only a resolute assault on the 'human factor' would bring the epidemic of road deaths and injuries under control. Working through the Joint Committee on Road Safety, the surgeons had won a certain amount of bipartisan support for measures of more rigorous surveillance and compulsion. In 1970 medical evidence given before the committee persuaded all political parties to support legislation, the first in the world, compelling Victorians to install and wear car seatbelts.[58]

The RACV and other motoring organisations had long publicised the use of seatbelts and public opinion polls had supported their fitting as standard equipment to new cars since 1959.[59] Surveys of road accidents by the Traffic Commission in the early 1960s had shown that seatbelts could reduce the chances of death or serious injury by as much as one-third.[60] In 1964 the government legislated to make seatbelt anchorages a compulsory fitting to new cars, and in 1969 required lap-sash belts to be fitted as well. Requiring motorists to *wear* the belt was seen as just another step along a path already well travelled, and although an RACV survey showed a bare majority of the public in favour of the measure, it passed through parliament without opposition. The infringement of personal liberty involved in wearing the belt was regarded as insignificant compared with the potential harm to the community, through hospital care, insurance payouts and so on, of not doing so.[61]

Seatbelts might reduce death and injury among drivers and passengers involved in serious accidents but they did nothing to curb the number of accidents. Restraining people's bodies was one thing; regulating their behaviour, the troublesome 'human factor', was much more difficult. As with the seatbelt legislation, the safety advocates proceeded step by step. In 1971 the government enacted recommendations of the Joint Select Committee on Road Safety to link spot checks of drivers' blood alcohol with mandatory periods of licence disqualification for offenders: three months for exceeding 0.05, six months for exceeding 0.10 and twelve months for exceeding 0.15. Those with a concentration of 0.1 or more, or with a repeat offence of exceeding 0.05, could not be issued with a new licence except by order of a magistrate.[62]

The new law aimed to secure three objectives. By introducing spot checks of blood alcohol it increased the chances of detection. By linking blood alcohol levels with automatic penalties it increased the chances of conviction. And by automatically disqualifying offenders from driving it greatly increased the level of deterrence. Only drivers already selected by police as exhibiting some sign of being affected by alcohol were supposed to be subjected to spot checks, but the onus of proof lay with the police and during the early 1970s the numbers of tests and convictions steadily increased. In 1976 the drink-driver's chances of escaping detection were further narrowed when Victoria became the first state in the world to legislate random blood alcohol tests. The loss of personal liberty involved in these measures did not go without remark. A person should not be obliged to incriminate himself, Labor's Frank Wilkes had objected in 1971.[63] 'It is a severe intrusion into the rights of people [when] . . . the ordinary citizen can be pulled up for no other reason than to ascertain whether he has been drinking', said the National Party's Bruce Evans.[64]

But these objections quickly dissolved as the success of the new measures became apparent. The numbers of road deaths and accidents had risen steadily through the 1960s, more or less in line with the growing number of vehicles. The peak occurred in 1969–70 when, for the first time, more than 1000 people were killed on Victorian roads. From 1971 accidents, injuries and fatalities all began to fall. From 17 030 accidents (or 498 per 100 000 population) in 1969–70 the number fell to 12 591 (or 337 per 100 000 population) in 1975–76—an overall fall in the accident rate of about one-third. Police attributed most of the fall to the seatbelt law and their own vigorous policing; yet, oddly, the fall in the accident rate (32 per cent), which should have been relatively unaffected by the seatbelt law, was much greater than the fall in the death rate (22 per cent) or the injury rate (10 per cent).[65] The lives of some of those who figured in the injury statistics may have been saved by the seatbelt law, but the major feature of the statistics—the big fall in the accident rate—may have been caused by exogenous factors, such as the economic downturn of the early 1970s.

Not all of this improvement was attributable to random blood alcohol tests. After the mid-1970s, the toll slowly began to rise again, but random breath testing was almost certainly the major factor in the short-term decline, and more than enough to confirm the effectiveness of the new measure. Many drivers who had previously backed their ability to drink and drive, yet elude police detection, now knew that the odds were increasingly stacked against them. By 1983 a national survey of road trauma by the Royal Australasian College of Surgeons noted that that 'there can be no argument that Victoria has out-performed all other States in the field of road safety'.[66]

SHOCK TACTICS

Since the 1950s, when the cost of road trauma first began to attract scientific interest, road safety campaigners had concentrated their attention on the 'human factor', the multiple sources of human failure that caused collisions. If they no longer believed that it was possible to moralise motorists through courtesy campaigns, the conviction that motor accidents were caused by individual human failure remained strong. The war on the road toll was a war on all those factors, such as bad driving skills, alcohol and fatigue, that contributed to human failure. The delinquent motorist also remained the foundation of legal approaches to compensation for road injuries; the 'victim' had to prove a 'fault' against the perpetrator of the so-called 'accident'.

Already by the 1970s students of road crash statistics had recognised that the 'human factor' was only one among a complex of factors contributing to the chances of a crash.[67] Weather and road conditions, traffic signalling, the mechanical efficiency of the vehicle, its ability to withstand a crash, and the simple density of traffic on the road were as important in accounting for longer-term trends in road accidents and fatalities as those factors within the voluntary control of the driver. Road trauma was coming to be seen as a characteristic of the urban system, as much as a sin of the individual motorist. Lowering the road toll meant re-engineering the system, as well as re-educating the driver. In a city where the car had become a necessity it was no longer sufficient to treat the individual motorist in isolation.

One of the most striking illustrations of this shift is found in the way Victorians have handled the issue of road accident compensation. Since the 1970s all car owners have contributed a proportion of their regis-tration fees to compulsory 'third-party insurance'. These funds were originally administered by an independent board, the Motor Accident Board, and paid, as cash or medical and rehabilitation services, to compensate the injuries of road accident victims on a 'no-fault' basis. During the 1970s and early 1980s the number of successful applications to the board grew spectacularly, from 8959 in 1973 to 54 200 in 1984–85 while the funds distributed increased from $734 000 to $87.1 million.[68] While the motorist was insured on a 'no-fault' basis, victims could still sue them through the courts, and by the 1980s a significant proportion of funds were being consumed in legal costs. In 1984 the Labor government of John Cain introduced reforms designed to radically reshape the scheme. A new Transport Accident Commission (TAC) would have the power to determine compensation for long-term injuries without resort to the courts and in accordance with standardised estimates of loss. It would also have the power to apply its funds to the prevention of road injuries. After some resistance from lawyers, who objected to the loss of the victims' 'common law rights', the TAC got under way in 1986.

In 1989 the TAC inaugurated the most expensive, vigorous and controversial road safety campaign in Australia, perhaps anywhere.

'Bush Telegraph' (1996) was one of the most graphic of the series of shocking television road safety advertisements produced by the Traffic Accident Commission in Victoria in the 1990s. (PHOTO COURTESY TRAFFIC ACCIDENT COMMISSION)

During the summer of 1988–89 the commission screened a series of hard-hitting television commercials under the slogan 'If you drink and drive you're a bloody idiot'. The first commercial begins with graphic footage of a crash, cuts to an overturned burning vehicle, and concludes in a hospital emergency ward where the young drink-driver is glimpsed, shocked and remorseful, as he learns of his passenger's (girlfriend's?) death.[69] Forty years after the Road Safety Council's 'Death is so Permanent' campaign, the TAC had returned to mass advertising as a weapon in the battle against the road toll. But the stark realism, colloquial style and emotional appeal of the new campaign were a striking contrast with the stiff moralism of the old. Drink-driving, the campaign suggested, was not just antisocial; it was stupid. It didn't just threaten your own life (something, after all, you might never live to regret) but the lives of those you loved. Later advertisements in the campaign graphically depicted the distress of physical disablement ('Belt Up or Suffer the Pain') and the lethal effects of speed ('Speed Kills'). Viewers surveyed by the TAC found the advertisements shocking, but agreed that the shock was salutary. Ninety-eight per cent of respondents agreed with the statement: 'I admire them for getting right down to the problems rather than beating around the bush.'[70] More importantly, the commercials seemed to work: in the following months road fatalities, and especially the numbers of alcohol-related deaths, declined sharply. Between mid-1989 and mid-1992 the Victorian road toll fell from almost 800 deaths per annum to approximately 450 per annum. There even appeared to be a rough correlation between the intensity of the advertising campaign and the fluctuations in the number of road deaths.[71]

The television commercials were only one facet of a more comprehensive attack on the road toll. The TAC also sponsored the 'Black Spot' program, designed to remove road hazards already known to have been the scene of fatal accidents. While powerful new weapons, such as random breath testing and shocking safety advertisements, could produce spectacular short-term results, their effects could quickly become blunted.[72] Only by massive publicity (the TAC's promotional advertising expenditure grew from $3.2 million to $16.5 million between 1989 and 1991) and vigorous application of the full armoury of weapons could the toll of fatalities be lowered and kept low. The introduction of compulsory breath testing signalled a fundamental change in the legal regulation of road behaviour. In the 1920s otherwise law-abiding citizens were affronted to be pulled up by a constable for speeding. Even in the 1940s and 1950s the Chief Commissioner of Police regularly received letters from irate members of the middle class, who had been apprehended for a road offence, asking for the stain on their character to be removed. By the 1980s the language of the law had become more neutral but its operation had become more rigorous. Rather than simply punishing offences it aimed, though a graduated system of penalties (the points demerit system), to modify driver behaviour. A more rigorous law was combined with a more efficient and impersonal system of surveillance and detection, including red-light cameras and radar guns.

Probably nowhere else in the world was the conduct of the individual motorist more closely monitored or more rigorously controlled. Yet, with only occasional grumblings, motorists overwhelmingly accepted these measures. Their acceptance attests to the enduring strength of the progressive utilitarianism that had once made Victoria a famous social laboratory. It also shows just how much privacy, money and personal independence we are prepared to surrender in order to preserve that most cherished and illusory of our liberties, the freedom of the road.

7
Dream Highways

If autopia had a symbol it was surely the dream highway or freeway. Its sweeping ribbons of carriageway, with their flyovers, clover leafs, underpasses and exchanges, crowded with motor cars, each self-directed yet moving in swift tidal flows, gave monumental form to the new order brought into being by the car. The freeway seemed to have resolved the competing principles of freedom and order. It permitted individuals to go where and when they wished, without the imposition of timetables, speed restrictions or delays. Yet it also enabled a complex technological society to anticipate, plan and channel those desires into orderly patterns of traffic movement.

The freeway did for the city what Henry Ford's production line had already done for industry. Industrial management called for a rigorous analysis of the component phases of production and their reprogramming into a smooth logical sequence. The freeway was the outcome of a similar process in which engineers first measured and analysed the flows of traffic, plotted and predicted their volume, then designed complex systems of roads, traffic signals, parking lots and policing to accommodate them.[1]

While motels and drive-in shopping centres were products of individual enterprise, the remaking of the urban highway required bigger changes in social and political organisation. America not only invented the technologies of the motor age, such as freeways and parking meters, but the research paradigms, methods of analysis and forms of political organisation required to implement them. It was the knowledge systems

'A continuous, free-flowing, three-dimensional whole': the F19 (Eastern) Freeway cuts a wide swathe through Melbourne's eastern suburbs, from North Balwyn (lower left) to the central business district (top left). (PHOTO VICROADS)

as well as the technologies, the politics as well as the practicalities, of road design that America exported to Australia in the 1950s and 1960s.

In the 1960s Melbourne embarked on the most extensive and expensive freeway experiment in Australian history. The 1969 Melbourne Transportation Plan (MTP) has often been characterised as one of Australia's great planning disasters, a product, Leonie Sandercock argues, of 'laissez-faire policies that cater for the rich and strong and ignore the poor and weak'. The lobbying of car and oil companies, she suggests, combined with the ideology of the technical experts, to skew public investment towards the car and away from public transport.[2] A leading international study, J. M. Thomson's *Great Cities and their Traffic* (1977), damned the MTP as an 'unconvincing work . . . a highway plan [rather than] a transport plan', a verdict echoed by later writers.[3] In this chapter I seek to excavate the origins of that plan, listening to the voices of its creators as well as its critics, and describing the ideas that inspired it as well as the political interests that finally shaped it.

THE LURE OF THE FREEWAY

Australian planners and road engineers had long looked to the United States as a model of highway design and administration. In 1924 the Chairman of the Victorian Country Roads Board (CRB), William Calder, returned from an overseas visit convinced that the American road system was 'one of the outstanding wonders of modern transportation'.[4] In 1937 Calder's successor as chairman of the CRB, William McCormack, inspected American highways on both the west and east coasts, visited the US Bureau of Roads in Washington and returned with the hot gospel of American road construction. 'Design', McCormack wrote on his return, quoting his American advisers, 'must keep as the main objective directional, free-flowing lines that give velocity and rhythm, and no obstruction to traffic'.[5]

The idea of the freeway, already implicit in the theory of prewar highway design, took a powerful hold on the imagination of the postwar Australian motoring public. From the late 1940s Australian motoring magazines offered tantalising glimpses of the joys of freeway driving. In 1947 a photograph of the Arroyo-Seco highway in Los Angeles appeared in the *Radiator* with the caption: 'American highway speedways: 60 mph "minimum": 70 mph "desirable"'.[6] Two years later it argued that 'the development of the great highways of the United States should give our road authorities food for thought. Highway development there is in the direction of greater widths, more under and over passes, easier curves and less steep grades to increase sighting distance.'[7] In the accompanying illustrations sweeping multi-laned highways weave across the page, merging and dividing, leaping over and diving under each other, like strands of white ribbon strewn casually across the countryside. In its 1959 call for a 'Detailed City Plan for Melbourne' the City Development Association (CDA) juxtaposed a picture of Melbourne's peak-hour 'traffic chaos' with a panoramic shot of Boston's city expressway. 'Sky-rocketing car-ownership makes such roads an absolute necessity for city survival', read the caption.[8]

The lure of the freeway was not just technological but aesthetic.[9] In 1974 the Chairman of the Country Roads Board, Robert Donaldson, was asked by a journalist about his artistic interests. He replied with the single word: 'freeways'. 'I really believe the freeway is a work of art', he continued. 'They are beautiful things. They are not evil things. They are things which enhance the beauty of the countryside not desecrate it.'[10] From the Olympian height assumed by the traffic engineer, these concrete cordons had a pleasing fluidity of line, a delicacy of form that belied their massive bulk.[11]

> The aesthetic value of the freeway [according to *Country Roads Board News*] lies in the designer's ability to organise the component parts of the alignment in a continuous, free-flowing, three dimensional whole, properly proportioned and consistent in scale. The well-designed freeway merges with and forms an integral part of the environment and does not spoil or detract from it. In many places the freeway opens up vistas on a scale not provided by conventional roads.[12]

The new highways looked best at a distance and the standard publicity shots taken by the highway authorities emphasise the engineer's sense of pride and mastery. Groups of youngish engineers in ties and shirt-sleeves stand on the top of a hill; two hold a plan while a third points proudly into the distance, where the newly constructed freeway sweeps towards the horizon. The text invites the reader to admire the skill with which the engineers have blended natural and man-made forms. Roads should 'follow the lines of nature', McCormack had advised his fellow engineers, and his successors—though often portrayed by their critics as soulless technicians—were ardent devotees of modernism, as exhilarated by the free-flowing forms they sculpted in reinforced concrete as any Brancusi or Picasso.

The primary appeal of the freeway, however, was economic. Australian businessmen returned from the United States full of praise for the Californian highway system. In 1951 the electrical goods manufacturer Keith Healing reported that 'California's highway and road maintenance are splendid . . . America as a whole realises that her automobiles are an asset and does all that is humanly possible to keep the traffic flowing so that car production need not be restricted.'[13] Frank Beaurepaire and Charles Butt of the Olympic Tyre Company observed the 'excellence of the highways' in the United States and called for a master plan of national highways similar to that constructed under the Eisenhower administration.[14] The real estate and housing developer J. R. Buxton, returning from a trade mission to promote Victoria in the USA, told of a conversation with a Californian businessman. 'How far out of Los Angeles do you live?' he had enquired. 'His answer was in minutes and he explained that you did not speak of miles any more because a person living 20 miles out could be quicker to his place of work than someone only 10 miles out not having access to a fast through highway.' Australia, Buxton concluded, should study what was happening in the United States and 'plan ahead for the inevitable similar happenings in this country, and perhaps save ourselves millions of pounds'.[15] Another traveller, Victorian premier Henry Bolte, confessed that he was 'impressed with the USA where people thought big and tackled big jobs in a big way. There is a lesson for everybody to be learned by visiting the USA, particularly in problems associated with traffic.'[16]

Not all the lessons from America were positive. In the mid-1950s motoring writers were divided on the question of whether the American toll road was an acceptable solution for Australian road congestion. 'There is a very strong case for extending the turn-pike toll system to this country in order to relieve our more pressing road problems', suggested *Modern Motor* in 1954. 'It is doubtful if Australia can afford the expensive toll-type roads being made in the USA', replied *Wheels*. 'Dream highways have their headaches', it commented two years later.[17] The toll road, it appeared, was not necessarily a cure for the road toll. The pay-as-you-go highway was also a rude assault on a long Australian tradition of publicly funded, publicly accessible roads and railways. If freeways were to come then they would necessarily be on a smaller scale, most Australians thought. Yet the conviction remained strong that America's today was Australia's tomorrow and, although there was a formal readiness to recognise that America might have made mistakes in coping with the car, there was little readiness before the mid-1960s to identify clearly what they were.

'ALL-AMERICAN BOYS'

The American highway system was not just a distant dream. By the early 1960s Victorian road authorities employed a growing number of young traffic engineers who had themselves been trained in the United States. In 1954 Melbourne City Council's Deputy City Engineer Len Frazer returned from a tour of the United States, convinced of the need to increase the flow of American expertise. He supported his protegé John Bayley's application for an International Road Federation fellowship to study at the annual Traffic Engineering course at Yale University.[18] After his return, retailers Kenneth and Baillieu Myer, already active in city traffic issues, sponsored a scholarship to send an Australian engineer to Yale University each year. Over the following decade more than a dozen Australian engineers would attend the Yale course, which became the main conduit of American highway expertise into Australian road construction and planning organisations.[19] Most of the Myer scholarship-holders were young men, often from the country, or educated in provincial technical schools, and later at Melbourne University, who sometimes found their way into traffic engineering, then a lowly branch of the profession, almost by default.[20] Short-back-and-sides, practical, hardworking country boys, they gravitated to Melbourne's middle-distance eastern suburbs, becoming stalwarts of the golf and football clubs, the service organisations and churches.

Going to Yale in the 1950s was a big break, a chance not only to see the world, but to glimpse the future. Joe Delaney, who took the Yale course in 1956–67, recalls: 'I think the American experience of traffic, and volumes of traffic, [was] far advanced in one sense . . . the whole thinking well ahead ten years. I remember thinking: we'd better learn quickly from the American experience and not make the same mistakes.' 'My introduction to traffic engineering has been, really, the "all-American boys" approach', agreed Neil Guerin, who followed a year later.[21]

In New Haven the Australians were introduced to the infant science of traffic engineering. They studied the characteristics of traffic behaviour, methods of recording and interpreting traffic phenomena, such as flow, speed and road capacities, methods of regulation and control, traffic law, administration and planning and the economics of highway operation.[22] Basic to all their training was the conviction that traffic was a phenomenon, akin to the flow of rivers, that could be studied with the precision of a science. It was something, said Joe Delaney, 'that you could measure and analyse, and come up with theories that could be replicated'. One of his later bosses, Jack Thorpe of the Traffic Commission, was fond of quoting Lord Kelvin's dictum: 'If it can't be measured, it's not real.' 'Study everything', John Bayley was taught. 'Nearly everything in traffic will form a statistical curve. So everything was studied—studied to death statistically.'

Traffic engineering, like market research, scientific management, project building, and the other new American forms of expertise that were transforming the Australian urban environment in the postwar era, was shaped by the ubiquitous principles of Henry Ford. Ford had shown how human activity could be broken down into its constituent units, measured and analysed then reconstituted, temporarily and spatially, into step-wise sequences of activity in the form of production lines, sales floors, marketing campaigns, housing assembly plans, fast-food outlets and highway interchanges. The main objective of all these activities was to reduce uncertainty, effort, dead time and wasted space; to streamline decision-making and to increase the volume and accelerate the flow of transactions, trips and decisions.[23]

But not all the young engineers' education was purely technical. It was impossible to separate the science of traffic from the broader experience of American life. The Australians were encouraged to get out of the classroom and travel the country observing traffic and highway developments. 'The roads are made of concrete and are generally in excellent condition so high average speeds are effortless', an elated John Bayley wrote home in 1955. 'A trip of 118 miles on the New Jersey Turnpike from Scranton, Delaware took me 118 minutes.'[24] They came under the personal influence of charismatic teachers, like Wilbur Smith, chief consultant to the American road lobby and an influential writer on urban transportation.[25] 'He was a very personable character', Delaney recalled. 'I couldn't help liking the guy . . . He was a farm boy originally, and he had this basic, hard, down-the-line, no bull-shit [way], and sufficient of the theory to be able to apply it, and to come up with solutions which were politically balanced.' The young engineers, often farm boys themselves, admired Smith's informal style: 'He [would] walk into the room with his hands in his pocket, sit up, put his feet on the table . . . and then give us an hour lecture', Robin Underwood recalled.[26]

In Australia, the engineers had often made their way up under the guidance of senior members of the profession who they often portray as hard but fair taskmasters. John Bayley had worked under Len Frazer at the Melbourne City Council. 'He was called "Little Hitler"', Bayley remembered. 'He was a person with very strong views. When he made up his mind that was it. He would support his staff to the hilt.' The hallmark of the good engineer was the ability to 'get things done'. The emotional hardness they came to admire in their mentors was perhaps another face of the respect for 'hard data' they identified as the scientific foundation of their expertise.[27]

Through example if not through precept, the Yale graduates also learnt that traffic engineering took political craft as well as technical skill. Politics was not necessarily a dirty word to the engineers, although over the following twenty years they often had occasion to curse the ignorance or weakness of their political masters. 'Keep the press and the business community on side', was one of the lessons John Bayley learnt from his Yale instructors. He put it to good use back at the Melbourne City Council in the 1950s when the town hall press office was next door to his own and the press and engineers became regular drinking companions. Bayley made it his business to know the needs and demands of influential central city stakeholders like Sir John Williams, editor-in-chief of the *Herald,* and big retailers like Coles and Myer. As a 27-year-old, just back from Yale, he was already helping to spread the gospel of automobilism. In 1955 a gathering of 200 city decision-makers organised by the new Traffic and Parking Committee 'watched wonderingly and sighed at times as colour films unrolled magic carpets of American super-highways, flyovers, underpasses, double-decked bridges and geometrically-patterned parking lots'.[28]

Joe Delaney was born in Victoria's Western District 'of Irish background' and, as he recalls, 'automatically interested in politics, and therefore in things other than simple nuts and bolts'. After completing his engineering degree he studied town planning and was prompted to think more deeply about the relationship between transport, land-use and politics. His Catholic faith had also reinforced his aspirations to a concept of 'community' with a 'Christian shape'. At Yale, and on later visits to the United States, he had 'gained a bit of a line on the development of American politics', and struck up enduring friendships with several American traffic engineers. He observed the success of Wilbur Smith as a consultant and Washington lobbyist, a path from the technical to the political he was to follow himself.[29]

In the early 1960s, Delaney read a book by Catholic apologist Hillaire Belloc, *The Road*, which helped him articulate an ethical rationale for his profession. 'Movement', he wrote, 'is essential to the living of a full life. In fact the United Nations quotes "freedom of movement" as one of the four freedoms of mankind.' In widening the opportunity for human movement, the engineer was promoting the flow of commerce and ideas, and enhancing the potential for human betterment. Delaney observed the steady rise in car ownership and predicted that if Melbourne's car ownership levels had risen to American levels by 1985, the city would require a trebling of its road system. There was only one efficient and safe means of achieving such a dramatic increase in road capacity: the urban freeway.[30]

THE FREEWAY APPROACHES

For almost two decades, Melbourne's modernisers had dreamed of freeways, but it was not until the mid-1950s, and the election of the Bolte Liberal Government, that the dream began to be realised. In 1955 Melburnians experienced a foretaste of the freeway era when 'Australia's first major overpass' was commenced at Clifton Hill.[31] A year later the Bolte Government heeded then advice of visiting American expert D. Grant Mickle and placed responsibility for metropolitan highways and bridges with the city's main planning authority, the Melbourne and Metropolitan Board of Works (MMBW), which in turn began work on a comprehensive survey of the city's traffic needs. 'The solution of the city-suburban traffic problem lies in the progressive development of a system of "freeways" designed to permit rapid and uninterrupted movement between the city and the main suburban areas', the board's chairman, Richard Trickey, declared in 1957.[32] He foreshadowed a program of road widenings and bridge improvements, especially on the access roads to the CBD, to be followed by more costly freeway projects. Beginning with the south-eastern freeway, it would later include a city ring-road, a freeway to the city's new airport at Tullamarine, a Sydney road bypass and an eastern suburbs bypass along the route of the disused Outer Circle railway.[33]

Melbourne's freeway ambitions may have been spurred in part by its old rivalry with Sydney. Sydney was already a city more burdened by congestion and inaccessibility than the southern capital. With its narrow winding streets it had more incentive to build freeways, but the cost of building them in a rocky, undulating terrain, broken up by rivers and harbour, was also higher. In 1932 the opening of the Sydney Harbour Bridge had given Sydneysiders a glimpse of the power of engineering to transcend urban distance. The Cahill Expressway (opened in 1958) was Australia's first elevated urban freeway, designed to relieve congestion at the city end of the Harbour Bridge. By the late 1950s the New South Wales Department of Main Roads (DMR) had a number of other expressway projects on its drawing boards. Several, like the Warringah Expressway and the Western Distributor, were designed to handle the growing volume of traffic across Sydney's waterways. In 1959 the DMR increased the length of its projected expressways from 87 miles to 147, a target further increased to 185 miles in 1965.[34]

The South-Eastern Freeway at Richmond, 1963. (PHOTO MARK STRIZIC)

Melbourne's ability to follow in Sydney's ambitious path was curbed by a shortage of funds and a wasteful rivalry between the state's main road construction authorities, the Country Roads Board and the Melbourne and Metropolitan Board of Works. The MMBW had only the $250 000 per annum provided through the Metropolitan Improvement Rate to pay for its $19.5 million projected roads program. By contrast, the Country Roads Board, which had the responsibility for main roads beyond the metropolitan area (defined by the limits of the Melbourne tramway system) was the recipient of the state and Commonwealth road funds.[35] By the mid-1960s each authority could claim successes in freeway construction: the CRB in the completion of the rural Maltby Bypass (1961) and the MMBW with the completion of the first stage of the South-Eastern [Monash] Freeway (1962). By American standards, the development of the freeway system was slow and beset by political opposition and fiscal uncertainty.[36] Within the government and the rival bureaucracies pressure mounted for a more coordinated approach to transport planning.

In 1963 the government legislated to establish the Metropolitan Transportation Committee (MTC), an unwieldy amalgam of the many competing state and local governments and special-purpose statutory authorities that had dominated the state's political landscape since the late nineteenth century. Representatives of the Railways, Tramways, Melbourne City Council, MMBW and CRB, each dedicated to the defence of its own turf, confronted their rivals across the table. The commercial and consumer interests represented by such bodies as the City Development Association and the RACV, which had often participated directly in American planning commissions, were excluded, at least officially, from Melbourne's transport planning process. The MTC had no sooner convened than the CDA offered its expertise to the committee, but the offer was politely declined.[37]

An early decision of the committee was to conduct a million-dollar study of Melbourne's transport as a basis for a comprehensive plan of the city's needs into the mid-1980s. The public transport authorities, already under pressure through declining patronage, approached the committee's deliberations as a rearguard defence. For the road authorities, on the other hand, there were larger spoils at stake. 'The CRB and the MMBW were . . . each *secretly*—at each other's throats, because they were both competing to be the metropolitan road builder', Joe Delaney, first technical director of the Melbourne Transportation Study (MTS) recalled.[38] Rather than concede an advantage to one or the other, the committee assigned staff from the main constituent organisations. Delaney, an employee of the MMBW, who had previously worked for both the CRB and the Traffic Commission, was considered acceptable to both sides as director of the project. When he left in 1966 to join the new Commonwealth Bureau of Roads, he was replaced by another compromise candidate, the Melbourne City Council's John Bayley.

To sidestep these entrenched rivalries, the committee devised a convenient fiction. It would separate the science from the politics of planning by delegating the initial stage of the inquiry to a group of experts who would scientifically analyse and project the transport habits of the people, while leaving the plan itself to the senior bureaucrats on the committee. In the heyday of modernist planning this was a more credible and attractive approach than it might seem today. Even so, from the very beginning, some members of the committee feared that too much politics would infect the science. One of the committee's first decisions was the selection of a consultant to carry out a comprehensive study of the city's transport patterns and needs. Four firms were considered but it was clear from the outset that Wilbur Smith and Associates, the firm headed by the charismatic Yale instructor Wilbur Smith, was the leading contender. (The firm later won similar contracts in Brisbane, Sydney and Hobart.) In 1961 Smith had published an influential textbook, *Future Highways and Urban Growth*. Beginning with an analysis of urban population and land-use patterns, he forecast an urban environment of increasing affluence, mobility and suburbanisation. 'The multiple-centred community appears . . . increasingly to be meeting the needs of the 20th century city . . . It appears to be a natural consequence of urban expansion.' A 'modern, well-planned system of express-highways' was the best form of transport for such a dispersed city.[39]

Wilbur Smith was a name that already aroused misgivings among some members of the committee. 'Wilbur Smith and Associates have been more particularly concerned with highways and freeways and I must be frank in saying we prefer someone with more experience towards public transport', warned Robert Risson, the redoubtable chief of the Tramways Board. 'They are very freeway minded', agreed Railways commissioner Robert Brown. But the other consultants' bids were weak and the best the critics could achieve was an undertaking that the consultant should be hired only to conduct the survey, not to devise the plan.[40]

All-American boys. Australian members of the MTS study team Len Frazer (centre) and Joe Delaney (centre left) confer with representatives of the American consulting organisation, Wilbur Smith and Associates. (PHOTO VICROADS)

The foundation of the MTS was a comprehensive survey of the travel habits of households throughout the metropolis. The Traffic Commission had previously estimated the volumes of traffic along specific transport corridors but no previous survey had collected data on travel modes, origins and destinations, frequencies and travel times, or analysed it sociologically by sex, age and income level. In 1964 Melburnians began to observe men in white coats standing by the roadside and flagging down motorists to ask them where they had come from and where they were going. Female interviewers visited people's homes to enquire about their travel habits.[41] From this data the consultants generated maps and tables showing the aggregate patterns of daily movement across the city. The data was then used in combination with forecasts of population, geographical dispersion and travel habits to project patterns of demand, by the various transport modes, over the following two decades. The committee had debated the interval over which it should attempt to plan. In selecting the year 1985, rather than 1975 or 2000, it sought an interval long enough for meaningful decision-making, yet short enough for realistic projections.[42]

The statistical method used for predicting future travel patterns, the

Motorists were surprised, and—as Herald *cartoonist WEG (Bill Green) suggests— sometimes embarrassed, when MTS staff flagged them down to ask where they had come from and where they were going.* (HERALD AND WEEKLY TIMES)

'gravity model', assumed a high degree of stability in travel patterns. It assumed that new growth would simply increase the flow of traffic along existing travel corridors. Yet, as critics pointed out, travellers might adapt to growing congestion in a variety of ways. They might change mode or route, move house or reduce their travel habit, for example. It would require a more interactive model, and much more computer power than was available in 1964, to model these more sophisticated assumptions. In 1967, when the MTS was well under way, the Harvard transport planner John F. Kain visited Melbourne and offered a pene-trating critique of the standard methodology adopted by the committee. Such studies, he argued, were captive to premature constraints and predetermined conclusions. By adopting long time horizons and low-level criteria for congestion they tended to create a planning framework favourable to grandiose technological solutions, such as freeways. With-out directly criticising his colleagues at Yale, he counselled his Australian audience to remember that:

> Current usage represents consumer demand for the facilities only under a particular set of circumstances and does not indicate what consumers, if given the choice, would be willing to pay for a higher level of service or the construction of additional capacity.

There was usually much more capacity in the existing road network than the freeway advocates assumed.[43]

From the beginning, and long before the Metropolitan Transport Committee reported, almost everyone assumed that the centrepiece of its plan would be an extensive urban freeway system. In 1965 Premier Henry Bolte had forecast massive new expenditure on metropolitan highways.[44] The engineers' models projected an ever-declining share of travel on public transport, and the public transport authorities seemed fixated on projects designed to solve the transport problems of the 1930s rather than those of the sprawling metropolis of the 1960s and 1970s. (For example, they gave almost no attention to the possibility of extended suburban bus services.) Within the committee a tacit consensus emerged: the Railways would get their long-awaited loop, but most of the projected $2 billion funds would be expended on an extensive metropolitan freeway system.

The traffic survey gave the engineers a wealth of data on the origins and destinations and volumes of movement across the city, but designing an appropriate road system to carry it was, as Joe Delaney observed, 'a matter of judgement'. The committee had not begun with a clear slate. History and geography had already limited the range of potential transport corridors. In the late nineteenth century railways engineers had identified the fingers of ridges and creek valleys radiating from the Yarra as the lines of least resistance and the 1929 Metropolitan Planning Commission had further reinforced this pattern by selecting the creek valleys as potential routes for a system of New York-style parkways.[45] The 1954 MMBW Planning Scheme had introduced a new element: a proposal for a ring-road encircling the inner city and distributing traffic to a grid of wide arterial roads.[46]

In designing the new road system, the MTC planners sought as far as possible to utilise the road corridors already reserved under the 1954 scheme.[47] This, they believed, would minimise both the financial and social costs of compulsory land acquisition. The assumption that creek valleys and parklands were unoccupied, and therefore 'free' to be used for roads, struck only a few observers as questionable. 'They don't cost much because they go through parkland, costing nothing, only a bit of a moan from the people living near', observed Railways commissioner E. H. Brownbill sarcastically. 'If parklands are available for freeways, why are they not available for housing? I'd like to get a block myself in some of the parks.'[48]

About half the new freeway system was to be built along existing road reservations. Since the reservations were generally located along creek

Planned Melbourne freeway system, 1969.

and river valleys, they tended to reinforce the radial pattern of the existing rail and tram networks. The most radical and important components of the new system were a series of outer ring-roads (the F5, F6 and F7 freeways), designed to carry traffic around the city, and two major north–south arteries (the F2 and F6 freeways) designed to enable traffic to move north and south through the inner city. From a functional point of view, these north–south links were crucial to the transport plan, since they facilitated cross-city movement rather than duplicating the radial patterns of movement already serviced by train and tram routes. 'Wouldn't it be better to concentrate the available resources on improving both inner and outer ring [freeway] routes

where the car shows up to greatest advantage rather than waste our
resources on radial freeways that cause more problems than they solve
and merely duplicate a task that public transport can do much better?',
asked Brownbill.[49]

However, the inner city ring-roads, which ran mainly through residential and industrial property, were also the most costly and socially
disruptive to build. Since much of this property was perceived as run-
down and substandard, the engineers anticipated that the process of
building the inner city freeways might proceed in tandem with the
equally desirable processes of 'slum clearance' and 'urban renewal'.
'The inner urban areas were still largely considered to be "slums" and
therefore we were improving the area by putting a road through', Joe
Delaney recalled. By the mid-1970s, however, perceptions of the inner
city and of the cost-benefit ratio of building inner city freeways had
changed dramatically. 'Let's face it', John Bayley admits, 'putting an F2
through that area of the world would have been pretty traumatic'.[50]

In the bureaucratic battle between the CRB and the MMBW to
become the city's main road constructor, the CRB was also, implicitly,
a force on the side of radial rather than cross-city freeways. As the
authority with responsibility for country roads they looked at the city
from the outside in. Their freeway ambitions naturally took the form of
city-bound extensions of state highways, such as the Geelong, Calder,
Tullamarine, Hume and Maroondah highways. 'We couldn't just
increase the capacity [of] the Maroondah Highway through Ringwood,
and just land it up at . . . the tram terminus, without some interest in
what was going in on the city side', observed the CRB's Neil Guerin.[51]

In order to test its efficiency, the model of the city's future transport
system produced by the technical staff of the MTS was 'matched to the
expected demand throughout the design area'.[52] The MMBW's planning branch had estimated that the metropolitan population would
grow by almost 90 per cent to 3 654 100 over the following two
decades. Jobs in the inner area would grow by about 40 per cent. In
order to accommodate these pressures, the Housing Commission had
embarked on a massive program of urban renewal. (As it turned out,
the 1985 population was over a million short of the MMBW estimate,
but the projected car population was close to the study's projection.)

Using the data furnished by the survey conducted by the MTS in
1964, the engineers computer-tested various combinations of alternative highway designs to determine which gave the most satisfactory

performance. In estimating the carrying capacity of the road system
the engineers had relied very largely upon standards derived from
American cities where vehicles were generally larger and travel habits
were different from Australia. Like many American cars, the planned
freeway system was probably over-designed. 'There was about thirty
per cent more travel projected than there should have been', Joe
Delaney now concedes. 'We were heads-down tails up, naive guys,
doing what we thought was right, and applying standards we were
given', recalled Bill Saggers, a member of the design team.[53]

Not all the experts were enchanted with the methodology or conclusions of the MTS. In 1966 Ted Barton returned to the Country Roads
Board from Canada, where he had worked with a Toronto consulting
firm, and became involved in the final stage of the project. Working in
Toronto, he had seen how an integrated system of radial subways and
circumferential freeways could transport people more efficiently and
with less environmental damage than the American pattern of cross-city
freeways. He had also visited England, and read Colin Buchanan's
Traffic in Towns (1963) and other textbooks on European traffic design.
The emerging recommendations of the MTS team struck him as
'grandiose' and politically impractical. 'I was absolutely horrified at the
freeway network that they were proposing!' he recalled.[54]

Little account was taken, at least until the final stages, of the economics of construction, or indeed of the consequences of not building
the system, the so-called 'no-build' option. Only two brief pages of the
final report were devoted to the cost of the proposals.[55] At the eleventh
hour, the committee had briefly considered a scaled-down version of
the plan, but it was quickly rejected. 'One member of the Committee
proclaimed that it was the engineers' job to advise on the best engineering solution [but] the Government's job to find the money', Delaney
recalled.

By 1969 the politicians were beginning to push for the project to be
completed. 'It was virtually extracted out of us by instructions that this
study was going to be wound up', Guerin recalled. Part of the reason
for the haste was the Commonwealth Government's recent decision to
change the formula for the distribution of road funds, which had previously favoured rural roads, to include urban highways. The proportion
of Commonwealth grants going to urban arterial roads suddenly
increased from zero to over 50 per cent.[56] All at once, it seemed, there
was a stream of money for roads, sufficient to meet the ambitions of

everyone. Instead of having to choose between highways and rail loops, or between radial freeways and ring-roads, the committee could include them all. 'It was just too much of a temptation', Guerin ruefully admitted. The government accepted the plan, subject to planning, consultation, heritage and environmental considerations.

'Balanced transport is the only hope', wrote Minister of Transport Vernon Wilcox in his introduction to *The Transportation Plan*. In striking that balance the plan's creators had been able to draw upon the most extensive and expensive program of transport research in Melbourne's—perhaps in Australia's—history. It had employed the most modern techniques of quantitative analysis and modelling. When the plan appeared, however, it was clear that the 'balance' was as much a product of politics as science, economic optimism as sane analysis, rival bureaucratic ambitions as public interest. Its centrepiece, absorbing $1675 million or 75 per cent of the total estimated $2.6 billion funds, was a 307-mile urban freeway system. Of the $355 million devoted to public transport, $80 million was devoted to a single project of dubious value, the Underground Loop. Not since the land boom of the 1880s, when politicians indulged in a reckless spree of railway construction, had Melburnians indulged their dreams so extravagantly. It would not be long before they emerged into the clear light of day.

8

The Walls of Jericho

Melbourne's Metropolitan Transportation Plan of 1969 marks the high noon of the modernist dream in Australia. A new generation of planners and engineers, imbued with scientific zeal and equipped with American know-how, envisaged nothing less than the wholesale transformation of the Australian city. In 1944 Liberal leader Robert Menzies had exalted the suburban ideal of living on 'a little piece of earth with a house and garden which is ours, to which we can withdraw, in which we can be among our friends, into which no stranger can come against our will'.[1] The planners expected that their 307 miles of freeways would speed thousands of commuters to happy homes in burgeoning new suburbs. But in their path were thousands of other households who surveyed the approach of the new road with growing alarm.

In Britain and the United States urban freeways were simply the latest chapter in a history of continuous, and often radical, urban redevelopment. Great disasters—earthquakes, fires, wars, floods, revolutions—had occasionally required the reconstruction of entire neighbourhoods, sometimes even of the city as a whole. Lisbon was half-destroyed by earthquake in 1755; Chicago and San Francisco were devastated by great fires; war and revolution preceded Baron Haussman's comprehensive reconstruction of modern Paris. British cities, whose history has been among the least troubled of European cities, nevertheless underwent massive dislocation and rebuilding during the industrial revolution when thousands of hectares were cleared to make way for new canals, factories and railways. In the course of the

nineteenth century more than 76 000 Londoners had been expelled
from their homes to make way for railway development, and possibly
another 100 000 for street reconstruction.[2] Hundreds of thousands
more were terrified and dispossessed by Hitler's Blitz.

Australia's cities escaped these convulsions almost completely. No
great urban catastrophes scarred our urban fabric—until Darwin's
cyclone in 1974 and Newcastle's earthquake in 1989. No wars or revolutions disturbed our sleepy suburbs. Australia's railways were built
before the cities had grown large enough for any demolition to be
required. In 1900 an outbreak of plague in the crowded waterfront
areas of inner Sydney prompted Australia's first scheme of slum clearance, imposed on a largely compliant populace of wharf labourers by
the powerful Maritime Services Board.[3] In 1937 a parliamentary
inquiry led by the Methodist reformer Oswald Barnett recommended
the compulsory clearance of tracts of slum housing in Melbourne's
inner suburbs, but not until the 1950s were these draconian powers
invoked. By 1958 Victorian housing authorities had cleared some 47
acres (19 hectares) of land and demolished 568 houses in block clearance schemes, and a further 275 acres (111 hectares) and 3788 houses
were to be cleared by 1970.[4] To most Australian city-dwellers, used to
the security of their own freehold homes, it came as a shock to discover
that the state could actually take their homes away and force them to go
and live somewhere else.

Conscious of the scale of their proposals, the creators of the 1969
plan had first attempted to disguise its social impact. By announcing its
grand plan for the future highway system without detailed maps or
timetables the Metropolitan Transport Committee had unwittingly
strengthened opposition among local communities. 'Was it necessary or
wise to leave the routes of the proposed new freeways as vaguely
defined as they are in the plan's fold-out maps?' the *Age* asked.

Defining them in detail would certainly have brought immediate
howls of protest from those whose businesses and homes lay in their
path. But, sooner or later, the objections will have to be heard. In
the meantime, the planners appear to have placed whole blocks under
a cloud. Many people would have been angered if they had been
told the worst at the outset. Many more will be needlessly alarmed,
and reluctant to spend money on their properties, until the present
uncertainty is removed.[5]

FREEWAY WAR MAP
October 1977

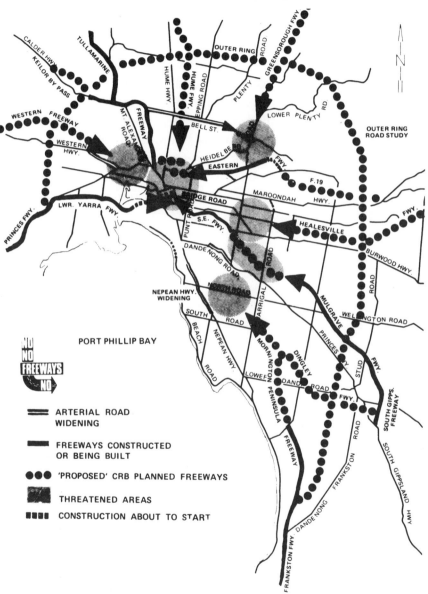

To residents of Melbourne's 'threatened' inner suburbs, the prongs of the planned freeway system seemed like arrows aimed at the heart of their communities.
(RILEY AND EPHEMERA COLLECTION, STATE LIBRARY OF VICTORIA)

By creating a generalised sense of threat within highly localised communities, the MTC had increased the likelihood that its plans would strike vigorous opposition.[6]

The Metropolitan Transport Plan presented only vague estimates of the economic and social costs of property acquisition and redevelopment. It acknowledged that some 12 300 acres (4977 hectares) of property would have to be resumed to build the system, more than half of it outside previously reserved land, but it gave no indication of the numbers of houses involved, where they were located or how their residents were to be compensated or relocated. In 1973 the Commonwealth Bureau of Roads made the issue a little more concrete when it estimated that Melbourne's inner city freeways would require demolition of approximately 560 houses per year or about 5600 over the following decade.[7] In 1954 when the MMBW had first proposed the construction of a network of inner city arterial roads it had taken a philosophical view of the consequences. 'Many of the properties in this area are old, and near the end of their useful life . . . and the location of the new road route can best be carried out in conjunction with a comprehensive scheme of redevelopment.'[8] As late as the mid-1970s the MMBW continued to regard the inner city as a zone characterised by physical decay and 'social dysfunction'.[9]

This, needless to say, was not how the inner city communities thought of themselves. Many of the neighbourhoods considered ripe for wholesale redevelopment were already being renewed piecemeal by new immigrants and young professionals. In 1963 poet Chris Wallace-Crabbe noted the striking influence of Italian and Greek immigrants on the inner zone of the city:

> The terraces and brick cottages have been repainted in bright extroverted colours that make no concession to the formal demands of taste; ironwork blossoms forth in pink or yellow or pale blue; tiny front and back yards are made to cultivate tomatoes, beans and espaliered grape-vines; old streets appear populous, rejuvenated.

With the migrants, too, came a new appreciation of the delights of urban living—of the square, the corner shop and the verandah. 'The city's cold heart is thus surrounded by the ebb and flow of Mediterranean life.'[10] In the wake of the migrants came a younger generation of Australians, students and academics, like Wallace-Crabbe himself. By the early 1970s the Italians and Greeks had begun to move out, and the young professionals to move in. Between 1966 and 1976 the professional and managerial proportion of the workforce of the inner ring of Melbourne doubled from 10.7 to 21.9 per cent. In the academic enclave of North Carlton it rose even more dramatically, from 9.4 per cent in 1961 to 40.2 per cent in 1976.[11]

THE ROAD AND THE COMMUNITY

When inner city residents contemplated the approach of the urban freeway, they regarded it, first and foremost, as a threat to their own neighbourhoods. They predicted that freeways would 'divide', 'disrupt' or 'destroy' local 'communities'. While road engineers saw them as an aid to the economy of nature, relieving the city's 'blocked arteries' and 'ailing heart', their opponents demonised the new roads as 'monsters' that inflicted bloody injury upon the organic communities of the inner

'An amazing mix of people': Carlton Street scene, c. 1973.
(FROM LES GRAY, *CARLTON*, SUN BOOKS, 1973)

city. Their favourite images were of bodily mutilation: their 'closely-knit communities' were being 'raped', 'vandalised', 'put on the chopping block', 'gouged', 'severed', 'carved up', 'cut into pieces', 'disrupted' or 'torn apart' by the 'concrete tentacles' of the freeway. Freeways were 'like a dagger pointed at the hearts of these people', said Labor leader Clyde Holding.[12] The freeway was an inanimate or unnatural intruder into communities that were portrayed as 'close-grained', intimate and organic.[13]

Often the speaker was a 'community leader' defending the members of a community apparently unable to speak for themselves. 'We may not rate very highly on the social scale—but we feel very strongly about what they [the Country Roads Board] are doing to our community', said Fr Phillip Smith whose parish lay athwart the Lower Yarra Freeway in Spotswood. 'We do not object to the freeway being built . . . but [it] is cutting a swathe through our community.' Twelve local streets had been blocked off with forbidding high wire fences; now only one circuitous road and a footbridge linked the two halves of what had been a single working-class suburb.[14] To the north of the city local MP David Bornstein complained that the F19 freeway 'would split the closely-knit North Carlton community'. 'Freeways destroy the delicate fabric of an area', agreed John Goatley, leader of the protest against the F2 freeway in Coburg.[15]

Highway officials were sceptical of these claims. The districts bisected by the new roads, they claimed, were not longstanding organic communities, but 'areas' of mixed industrial and residential, freehold and leasehold property already in flux. Many local residents were tenants accustomed to moving on: the resumption of properties for the freeway and the flight of residents from blighted areas were just another phase of the volatility characteristic of the inner city property market. Freeway construction might even hasten the pressures for beneficial redevelopment begun by the Housing Commission's Urban Renewal program.

Social scientists have often turned a sceptical eye on the claims of professionals to 'nurture' or defend local communities. 'Community', they suggest, was a construct of the local teachers, clergymen or politicians who gained their own identity in caring for 'the community', rather than something intrinsic to the experience of those they cared for.[16] In Melbourne's inner suburbs the language of community resonated strongly with the aspirations and interests of a newly arrived professional middle class, the 'gentry' or the 'trendies' as they were sometimes called.

Many of them were refugees from the suburbs, free spirits consciously seeking closer social bonds than they had found in the 'soulless' streets of Box Hill and Beaumaris. Some had come from the bush, seeking to reproduce the intimacy of the small town in the streets of the big city. Some had lived in Europe as students, backpackers or campervanners where they caught a glimpse of cities whose vibrancy derived from the crowded life of the square and the street. A few may have dipped into the writings of American critics, such as Lewis Mumford and Jane Jacobs, who celebrated the virtues of diversity, density and adaptation and decried the false hopes of modernist planning. One or two activists had caught the spirit of American advocates of 'community power', like Chicago's Saul Alinski.[17]

But 'community' was not just a figment of their hopes; it was also something the activists had experienced for themselves as students and young professionals living alongside European immigrants in the share-houses of Carlton and Fitzroy. Here, often for the first time, children of the sprawling suburbs and open spaces of the bush began to recognise the delights of density. From immigrant neighbours they learned the pleasures of the street, the corner shop and the public square.

In the early 1960s Trevor Huggard arrived at the University of Melbourne to study engineering. He had grown up in the bush, the only European boy on the Aboriginal station at Cumeroogunga on the Murray. Coming to Melbourne was a moment of discovery. He was fascinated, as an 'inlander', 'to find that the world had an edge, and lots of water', a discovery that primed his lifelong enthusiasm for yachting. This was also his first experience of city life. He lived in a series of student houses in South Carlton, then a vibrant mixed neighbourhood of older working-class Australians, university students and recent Southern European immigrants. 'There was an amazing mix of people', he recalled.

[The immigrants] had their little clothes lines with pulleys going to the elm trees to the middle [of the street] to hang their washing, which dripped on your car. They sat on the front doorstep and played the accordian on a summer's night because the backyard was full of junk . . . And everybody talked to everybody, even if it was the most basic acknowledgement.

You walked to the corner shop. The little Greek guy who was there was the most amazing man. He was building a boat which grew bigger and bigger, leaning over the fence . . . You could get anything there. Credit. When you were a student very important if you were broke

and needed to see the week out. And he'd fix you up. You could go
in at ten o'clock at night—in those days [of] six o'clock closing [of
hotels]—and get a flagon of red. Everyone that was in the square
knew . . . they could get their flagon of red . . .

I was told when I left the country that the city is a cold, soulless
place. Nobody spoke to anyone. You all shuffled around and you
didn't ever get to know your neighbour. And I stumbled into a place
that was more of a village than where I had come from. Everybody
helped everybody. Everybody would make sure that the elderly were
okay, knock on their door. There'd be street parties. There'd be people
helping one another. Everybody talked and everybody seemed to be
incredibly happy, very satisfied with their lot.

And then it became apparent that this heart was being ripped out.[18]

Huggard's nostalgia for the vitality of Carlton's community life in the
late 1960s is heightened by awareness of the threats even then looming
over it. In 1966 Trevor and his wife Lorraine returned from their
honeymoon to find that a Housing Commission 'Not Fit for Human
Habitation' order had been placed on the front door of the little terrace
house they had just purchased in Macarthur Place. The Ministry of
Housing had marked a large tract of 'run-down' housing, including the
Huggards' terrace, for 'urban renewal'. Even Jimmy Watson's famous
Lygon Street Wine Bar was slated for demolition.

During 1968 and 1969 the Huggards joined other local residents in
a strenuous campaign to save South Carlton from urban renewal. In
1969 the residents had formed themselves into the Carlton Association.
Like its Sydney counterpart, the Glebe Society, formed in reaction
against the New South Wales Department of Main Roads' inner city
freeway proposals, the Carlton Association represented a new kind of
grassroots politics. Each sprang from an intense engagement with the
aesthetic and social qualities of a newly gentrified historic suburb; each
exhibited the same formidable combination of political and professional
know-how.[19] While the academics wrote a constant stream of reports,
letters and petitions they also drew upon the more volatile support of
their immigrant neighbours.

At the height of the campaign against the Housing Commission over
3000 people attended a public meeting. The organisers, concerned not
to antagonise the authorities, were all 'saying the nice, right things'
when an immigrant man, 'a Rumanian of Italian extraction', jumped to
his feet, quivering with rage:

I can't understand you Australians. I come . . . to Australia, the Lucky Country, supposed to be where we have a democracy. If they took our house from us in Rumania I would be out in the street with a gun. What is fucking wrong with you Australians?

Some old ladies, 'hearing a word of that strength in those days', nearly fell off their seats, Huggard recalled. 'But they realised he was right. Here we were pussy-footing around . . . but this man said "I am ready to fight".'

It was in such moments that Carlton's sense of 'community' was crystallised. Community, Huggard suggested, was something woven through the everyday experience of inner city residents meeting in streets and corner shops ('everybody talked to everybody', 'everybody helped everybody'). It became powerfully manifest during a common struggle against the men in suits—the planners, engineers, politicians, bureaucrats and policemen—whose modernist projects threatened to destroy it. And it took ideological shape around European ideals of civility, urbanity and cosmopolitanism. 'We need an André Malraux in Australia', suggested Dudley Phillips, invoking the name of de Gaulle's Minister for Culture and saviour of modern Paris. Lygon Street should model itself on European cities like Paris and Berlin by planting street trees and allowing café tables to project onto wide pavements, a Melbourne University architect suggested. Carlton deserved to be cherished for its 'charming terrace houses and cosmopolitan atmosphere'.[20]

In 1970 the Committee for Urban Action, an investigative body formed from representatives of the Melbourne City Council and inner suburban councils, produced a brief report, *Transport Melbourne—The Inner Area Crisis*. It noted the distinctive character of the inner area, such as its 'close-grained mixture of factories, shops or other workplaces and residences', its narrow streets and narrow-fronted houses, and the devastating impact of rising volumes of motor traffic on its social and physical fabric. Echoing the writings of Jane Jacobs and Hugh Stretton, whose *Ideas for Australian Cities* (1970) had just appeared, it stressed the value of rehabilitating existing housing stock and preserving a 'mixture' of nationalities, age groups, occupations and income levels. While not ruling out the construction of inner city freeways, the report emphasised their tendency to divide communities, spread noise and pollution, force the pace of demolition and generate increased congestion in the inner city. Any inner city road system, it argued, must be constructed so as to minimise these threats. Roads designed to bypass the inner city should provide only very limited access anywhere in the CBD. The F19 freeway should not terminate near Alexandra Parade but connect with the F12 along the northern edge of Royal Park. The F9 freeway, designed to join the Westgate and South-Eastern freeways should be diverted to the north bank of the river rather than cutting through the Domain. If inner freeways were inevitable they might be run, as far as possible, through railway reservations or on stilts above existing arterial roads.[21]

The Town and Country Planning Association presented similar proposals in its 1971 transportation policy document, *Melbourne Transportation*.[22] The policy had been drafted by a subcommittee including Communist and North Melbourne resident Maurie Crow, architect, clergyman and Australian Labor Party Collingwood councillor Andrew McCutcheon, engineer and ALP Fitzroy councillor Barry Pullen, and Carlton Association member and architect Peter Sanders. The policy made no objection to the MTC's recommendations for the outer suburbs. But transportation should be designed to preserve the character and 'community fabric' of the inner city. The committee sought to establish an alliance between municipalities whose interests were potentially opposed. Keeping an unwelcome freeway out of one's municipal backyard might be another way of pushing it into someone else's.

Even so, some local areas clearly had more to lose than others. Collingwood, long Melbourne's Cinderella suburb, was the biggest loser. Since the 1850s it had copped more than its share of the city's industrial pollution, jerry-built housing and middle-class contempt. Now, lying directly in the paths of both the north–south F2 and the east–west F19 freeways, it was about to be ravaged again. Residents, accustomed to being put upon, surveyed the approach of the new roads almost fatalistically. 'The council has little hope of keeping freeways out of its area', the *Age*'s Neil Jillett reported in 1971.[23] Some councillors seemed more interested in the $300 000 of rate revenue they would lose through property resumptions than the noise, air pollution and social dislocation suffered by their constituents.

Collingwood lacked the professional clout of Carlton. Its representative on the Committee for Urban Action, Andrew McCutcheon, had come to Collingwood more as a kind of missionary than a cosmopolite. McCutcheon had grown up on the other side of town, the son of prominent architect and staunch Methodist, Sir Osborn McCutcheon. He followed his father to Wesley College and Melbourne University Architecture School and then into theological studies at Queen's College where he was a contemporary of another future urban activist and anti-freeway campaigner, Brian Howe. In the late 1950s Andrew and his new wife Vivienne had joined the Iona Community, a radical experiment in Christian discipleship, founded by the Scottish visionary George MacLeod. With other young ministers, McCutcheon alternated summers spent labouring on the restoration of the ancient abbey of Iona, with experience as an assistant parish minister in Bridgeton, a working-class district of Glasgow. It was impossible, MacLeod insisted, to disguise the political imperative of the Christian gospel, the pursuit of a 'Kingdom . . . whose shape is a city and whose pattern is community'. Within any Christian community itself, he suggested, there would be both shepherds—'practical men who will become politically concerned by their service in the rehabilitation of houses'—and wise men 'who will find their place in the cut and thrust of political action'.[24] McCutcheon carried his vision with him back to Melbourne where, for the next decade, as shepherd and wise man, he sought to build a community in the inner suburbs.

In 1960, McCutcheon was posted, at his own request, to the Collingwood Methodist Church, a traditional inner city mission, 'a bit of a hand-out joint', dispensing firewood, blankets, food parcels and spiritual consolation to residents of a suburb long regarded as the toughest in the city. Coming to Collingwood, so far as the McCutcheons were concerned, was a long-term commitment. They declined to live in the parsonage provided for the minister across the river in Kew and moved with their young family to a Housing Commission walk-up flat in Dight Street in the middle of the Collingwood Flat. With other local activists—clergymen, teachers, youth workers, migrants—he began 'to try and understand the community and its needs'. He collected social data and made contact with local community leaders, including those from the rapidly growing immigrant groups. MLA Clyde Holding, with whom he had had regular breakfast meetings to discuss local issues, persuaded him to stand for the Collingwood Council. The council was a tough school of politics. Although an official member of the ALP caucus, McCutcheon was at first sidelined from a political process dominated by the deal-making of local bosses still operating in the style of the old John Wren machine.

Gradually, he began to win some ground. The issue that united Collingwood and its councillors was their resistance to the great modernising state bureaucracies, such as the Housing Commission and the

Country Roads Board. As a Methodist and an architect, McCutcheon was steeped in the reforming legacy of Oswald Barnett's anti-slum campaigns of the 1930s. Vivienne's aunt, Frances Penington, had been a member of the first Housing Commission imbued with its vision of public housing as a form of guaranteed income. But as a Collingwood resident, the young minister saw the results of the commission's newest ventures in slum reclamation from a fresh angle:

> There seemed to be a huge gap between what was happening on the ground and the way it affected you and what the bureaucracy seemed to be firing at us. And a huge lack of understanding. You know, I'd go and talk to the Housing Commission people and they didn't really have a clue what they were doing. And the longer I was there the more I saw my parishioners locked into a slum reclamation area, and being told that they had to get out and their houses bulldozed . . . I'd known an awful lot of the people in those little cottages, and it drove home to me that this slum reclamation thing was missing the significance of what was going on—the community networks and the privacy that they had, even in the tumble-down cottage and the fact that they all knew their neighbours and they supported each other, [that] uncle was round the corner and gran was there to mind the kids. All that was swept aside, and it wasn't replaced by the housing that was put in its place. In the interim between knocking down the old and building the new stuff those people got scattered all over the place. And goodness knows what happened to them and how they survived.[25]

'Community', for McCutcheon, was both something that he had found among an old Australian working class and the new migrants, and an ideal that he had consciously sought to articulate and represent.

Carlton, which had led the protests against the Housing Commission's slum reclamation schemes, reacted more slowly to the apparently less imminent threat of urban freeways. The Metropolitan Transportation Plan showed the F19 freeway emerging from Yarra Bend National Park across the river into Alexandra Parade in Clifton Hill then dipping south through the 'urban renewal' area of South Carlton to join the F14 in North Melbourne. In 1970 a meeting convened by the Carlton Association was addressed by academic Nicholas Clark and veteran Communist and planning advocate Maurie Crow who called for greater expenditure on public transport and the construction of parking stations on the edge of the inner city to facilitate modal transfers from road to rail. This proposal also found its way into the Town and Country Planning Association's 1971 report on Melbourne transport which Crow, McCutcheon and Peter Sanders helped to write.[26]

In October 1971 the government cancelled plans for the F1 freeway through East Melbourne and ordered the MTC to substantially modify its plan 'with a view to minimising its sociological impact'. A joint committee of the MMBW and CRB was appointed to develop detailed suggestions. The inner suburbs breathed a collective sigh of relief. 'With the F1 scrapped and the F19 [designed to carry its traffic south around the city] unlikely to be built Carlton retains its unity', the *Carlton News* exulted.[27]

Their congratulations were premature. In cancelling the F1 freeway the government had inevitably increased the pressure of cross-city traffic on the other proposed north–south linkages, especially the parallel F2 freeway, which was expected to run from St Kilda to Clifton Hill on an alignment just east of Punt Road and Hoddle Street. In 1971 Local Government Minister Rupert Hamer had emphasised the significance of the F2 to Carlton Association representatives. 'The F2 must be built. Provision must be made to move the increased volume of traffic.'[28] To take the increased traffic the F2 might have to be widened to twelve lanes, some experts suggested. The CRB was determined to press ahead with the F19 freeway but rather than pushing it through the urban renewal area of South Carlton, the highway planners now proposed a diagonal route through the wide, tree-lined streets of North Fitzroy and Princes Hill.[29] The old route had targeted the students and migrants of South Carlton; now it was the young professionals themselves who were in the engineers' sights. Four hundred indignant residents attended a 'rowdy' meeting at Princes Hill High School. Jeers greeted the attempts of CRB engineers to explain their scheme. An action committee was formed to ensure that 'every possible means was used to prevent any freeway coming near Carlton'.[30]

Municipalities along the proposed route joined in opposition. 'If it's good enough to throw out in East Melbourne [the F1] it should be chucked out in Richmond, Collingwood and Fitzroy', protested Richmond councillor Jimmy Loughnan.[31] To the technical experts such arguments were nonsensical; restricting the flow of traffic through one artery would only increase the pressure on another. Politically, however, they were hard to gainsay. For if noise and air pollution were unacceptable to the burghers of East Melbourne, twice the volume of pollution was surely even more unacceptable to the working people of Richmond and Collingwood.

The young professionals from the inner suburbs often talked the same language as the engineers, but sought to persuade them to different conclusions. 'The Carlton Association is not necessarily opposed to the construction of freeways', a report of its Freeway Action Group declared in March 1972. The problem was that current transport plans were 'uncoordinated', unbalanced and oblivious to the effects on local residents.[32] But finding common ground with the transport engineers was politically hazardous. In agreeing to consider an alternative route, for example, residents in suburb A were likely to antagonise those in suburb B who copped the increased traffic. Rather than alienate neighbouring municipalities, the residents' associations were drawn, ineluctably, towards a policy of blanket opposition to all freeways. When the Freeway Action Group's report was presented to a general meeting of the Carlton Association in March 1972, the members rejected it outright, expressing their 'total and absolute opposition to the freeway concept of mass transport'.[33]

Inner suburban residents were often stung into action by the apparent complacency of their elected representatives. 'It is inevitable that freeways will go through South Melbourne', local mayor Arthur Leggo predicted in July 1972, as he announced a planning study to determine the least disruptive routes for the F9 and F14 freeways.[34] Within days, groups of residents—'young professional people who [had] moved into South Melbourne's Victorian and Edwardian houses in the past five years'—had formed the Emerald Hill Freeway Action Group. They were concerned with the human as much as the physical effects of the projected new roads. 'In my belief this is a real community', said banker Peter Mitchell. 'I think coming here I've met more people than in any place I've ever lived in.' 'Freeways carve through suburbs dividing them in two; people suddenly find their lifestyle of 50 years destroyed', observed newly arrived housewife Merilyn White.[35] By leaping, unbidden, to the defence of the area's older residents the newcomers endowed their own recently discovered sense of community with the aura of local tradition.

Many of the inner suburban activists were young mothers, whose ties to the local community were strengthened through their children's links to kindergartens and schools and their friendships with other mothers. Fashion designer Sally Browne was worried that if the proposed freeway went through, she would no longer be able to push the pram round to her old schoolfriend's house on the other side of Montague Street or join her on shopping expeditions to South Melbourne market. With her elegant terrace house on the north side of St Vincent Place, the most prestigious precinct in South Melbourne and less than a block from the proposed freeway route, Sally was worried, too, about noise, motor fumes and the prospect of plummeting real estate values. Like their counterparts in Carlton the residents knew the value of expertise, and planned a survey to assess the sociological effects of the freeway. 'We've got plenty of emotional reasons why freeways are wrong', Sally Browne acknowledged. 'What we're doing now is researching the matter so we've got good logical arguments.'[36]

In the months since the MTP was unveiled there had been a rapid shift in the public mood. The highway engineers, who seemed to be surfing the crest of a wave in 1969, were suddenly swimming for their lives in an undertow of public scepticism and resentment. The protests of inner city residents defending their patch against urban renewal and freeways had merged with wider currents of counter-cultural protest. The Club of Rome report *Limits to Growth* sounded a first warning bell against the prodigal consumption of finite natural resources such as oil. Ecologist Paul Ehrlich and consumer advocate Ralph Nader made successful tours of Australia preaching this new ecological conscious-ness. In the United States itself residents in New York and New Orleans were rising to oppose the extension of inner city expressways.[37] In Sydney, the campaign against the Department of Main Roads' plan for freeways through Sydney's inner west had followed a similar curve, forming in 1969 and rising to vociferous strength during 1971.[38]

The slogans of the era—'Small is Beautiful', 'Make Love not War', 'Burn the Bra'—expressed a reaction against the artificiality and complexity of a mechanised modern society. Overshadowing and imparting a deadly urgency to all these movements was the growing public disenchantment with the American and Australian military involvement in Vietnam. The anti-freeway movement was radicalised, not just by the assault on its home turf, the inner suburbs, but by a mounting unease with the kind of mechanised, mobile, wasteful, violent society that the war and the freeway each, in their way, seemed to epitomise.[39]

In August 1972 chief secretary Rupert Hamer succeeded Henry Bolte as premier of Victoria. The transfer of power from the ebullient

farmer to the more conciliatory and urbane lawyer marked an ideological as well as a political divide. From the outset of his premiership
Hamer set out to meet the environmentalist challenge.

> Economists gave us the concept of Gross National Product and
> interest has centred on the rate at which that grows. Is it time to think
> more about Gross National Well-being? Is it time that our proper
> concern with growth should be tempered with a greater emphasis
> on the very essence of the quality and purpose of life itself—of the
> relationship of man to his environment?[40]

A more significant change in the political landscape came a few months
later with the election of the federal Labor government of Gough
Whitlam on 2 December 1972. Sensing the shift of political opinion
the United Melbourne Freeway Action Group—a coalition of some
26 progress associations and residents groups—organised a mass rally
in the Melbourne Town Hall, to coincide with a similar rally in Sydney.
A barrage of freeway critics—academics, architects, planners, sociologists, even a dissident traffic engineer—called into question the
cherished assumptions of the freeway planners. How did the freeway
plans square with the government's revised planning goals? asked
veteran planning advocate Robert Gardner. Was social mobility an
unequivocal good? asked Fitzroy clergyman, sociologist and budding
politician, Brian Howe. Was road congestion an evil if it forced more
people to use public transport? asked the visiting traffic expert Professor Ross Blunden of Sydney. Carlton Association activist and planning
lecturer Trevor Tyson produced a map plotting the residences of MTC
members and staff. 'Funnily enough the homes of many freeway officials are near freeways but not one stands in their path', he observed.
John Bayley, technical director of the Melbourne Transportation Study,
attended the meeting incognito, listening with mounting irritation to the
cheers of an audience which 'was not of a type to listen to objective
reasoning . . . predisposed against freeways and indeed all authorities,
public bodies and public servants'.[41]

  The most telling contribution to proceedings came from two absen-
tees. The first Whitlam ministry had yet to be sworn in, but its shadow
spokesmen on urban affairs and transport (Tom Uren and Charlie
Jones) sent a telegram to the meeting pledging the new government to
withhold Commonwealth funding for inner city freeways. Without
federal funding the plan was simply unattainable. Within days Hamer
had promised to stop further freeway construction in the inner suburbs

'where their construction would involve substantial loss of housing and community disruption', to upgrade the arterial road system, and to foster increased public transport usage, especially in the inner city 'by deliberate policies of inducement'.[42]

This decision, which looked to have been forced on the state government by pressure from the community and the Commonwealth, was actually little more than a ratification of plans already being prepared in response to the government's instructions to the MTC in October 1971. Four days after the election of the Whitlam Government and a week before the town hall meeting, the Executive Director of the Metropolitan Transportation Committee, Robert Risson, had written to the Victorian Minister for Transport Vernon Wilcox outlining the committee's thinking. Financial constraints, he explained, would oblige the government to cut the cost of the proposed freeway network by approximately two-thirds. Whether the 'quadrangle' of inner freeways comprising the

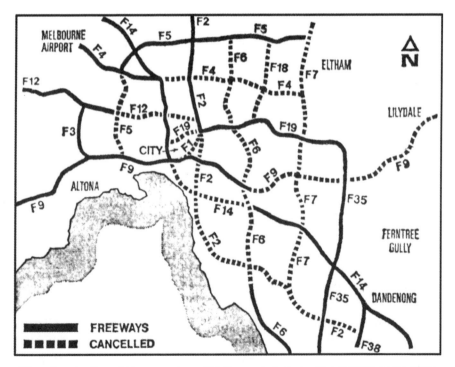

When Premier Rupert Hamer reviewed Melbourne's freeway plan in 1973, some of the most contentious inner city freeways were deleted, but radial freeways serving the outer suburbs, and sometimes disgorging traffic into the inner city, were retained.

F2, F19, F14 and F9 would be retained was still uncertain, but there would be no freeways inside the quadrangle.[43]

When the government's revised plans were announced in March 1973 more than 150 miles of freeway had been cut from the original 1969 plan. These included the eastern leg of the F1 (cancelled in 1971); the F2 south of the Eastern Freeway to Moorabbin; the F5 from the Calder Freeway to the Lower Yarra Freeway (the present western section of CityLink); the F6 north of South Road, Moorabbin; the F7 from Dandenong to Hurstbridge; the F9 South-Eastern Freeway link from Glen Iris to East Burwood; the F12, the system that runs east from Sunshine (similar to the current Western Bypass); the F14 from the Lower Yarra Freeway to Warrigal Road, Chadstone; the F18 from Watsonia South to Bourke Road; and the F19 from North Melbourne to Collingwood.

Press and public applauded the government's decision to 'put people before cars'. Among the car lobby, however, it was received more coolly. 'The new freeway plan will not solve congestion problems in the inner suburbs of Melbourne', predicted the RACV.[44] The engineers who had created the 1969 plan viewed its miscarriage as a disillusioning example of bad logic and political expediency. Pilloried by their opponents in the anti-freeway movement, they had been obliged, as public servants, to suffer in silence. They saw themselves as defenders of the public interest against the noisy minority of inner city activists. Theirs, they believed, was the larger, longer-term view, one informed by fuller information and more scientific expertise than that of the protesters. 'It is obvious that the anti-freeway section of our community has a disproportionate amount of material circulating around Melbourne', one of John Bayley's junior officers observed.

> I am convinced that the public as a whole acknowledges the need for freeways. Since it is unlikely that they will ever be as vocal as the anti-freeway group, it is up to us to maintain as much public support for our proposals as we possibly can.

To reassure the silent majority of freeway supporters he proposed the publication of an up-to-date summary of the latest proposals, with a map ('The scale shall be such that people will not be able actually locate the freeway routes') and an approximate timetable of projected construction ('Many people cease to be worried about a particular route location when told that it is unlikely that work will commence inside say 10 years').[45]

When engineers asked CRB chief Robert Donaldson in February 1973 whether local councils should be shown the projected route for the F2 freeway, he replied in terms that left no doubt about the authority's ultimate goals.

> I greatly dislike postponing decisions and adopting a course of no action, but believe that we should go quietly on freeway matters at the moment, particularly inner area freeways . . . It is imperative that we do not give away the concept of building inner area freeways, and I would agree with the deputy chief engineer and the chief engineer in their recommendation for an extension of the project engineer's responsibilities to include all sections of the F2 on which planning is proceeding.

Planning would also continue on outer circle freeways. 'I hope they will create a public appetite for high-capacity roads to take traffic through inner areas . . . These are frustrating times for us all', he concluded, 'but the pendulum will swing our way again'.[46]

The freeway planners and the protesters spoke two different languages. While the engineers appealed to the 'public', the protesters appealed to 'the people' or 'the community'. It was said of Robert Moses, the master-builder of modern New York, that: 'He loves the public but not as people.'[47] The public, to him, was impersonal, amorphous, a complex of the *needs* he could meet *for them*, rather than of the *wants* they expressed *for themselves*. None of Melbourne's highway planners achieved the power, or succumbed to anything like the megalomania of Robert Moses, but by the early 1970s they were themselves beginning to recognise that even the best of plans could not be imposed upon a resistant people.

'Community consultation' became the new buzz word. It was the price to be paid for political consent to plans which, so far as the engineers were concerned, were largely beyond discussion or negotiation. During 1974–75 rumours continued to circulate that the Country Roads Board, now the sole metropolitan authority for freeway construction, was stealthily pursuing its freeway plans. While the government had announced the cancellation of several freeways, the road reservations proclaimed under the 1955 metropolitan plan to build them were still intact.[48] The CRB continued to acquire property along other projected freeway routes, including the F12, F3/5 and, most contentiously, the F2, through Northcote and Brunswick, and the F14 through the built-up middle-class suburbs of Malvern and Chadstone.[49] In October 1974 it commissioned a new study of the F2 freeway, ostensibly to show whether traffic from the northern section of the Hume Freeway could be handled by the local roads system; in reality, to reopen the case for building the southern section through Northcote and Fitzroy.[50] Trevor Huggard, now almost a full-time anti-freeway activist, had compiled an extensive file of internal memos and plans revealing 'the CRB's secret masterplan for the inner suburbs'. The engineers, he claimed, were now a law unto themselves. 'Calling no man its master, the CRB is a permanent unelected bureaucracy dedicated to the one aim—maintaining and constructing roads and freeways.'[51]

The engineers had accepted the government's decision—what else could they do?—but their frustration showed through their weary responses to the government's new demands. The politicians expected that only a few nips and tucks were required to revise the estimates of traffic demand and highway provision in the original plan. But as John Bayley reminded Risson, the 1969 plan had been based on the assumption that people could choose their mode of travel without constraint. Now it was 'expressly stated . . . that there will be some restraint on the use of the private motor vehicle. This means that the whole 1969 plan is in need of revision.'[52]

To the Barricades

Rupert Hamer's decision in 1972 to prune the 1969 road plan had postponed, but not avoided, the looming confrontation between the road authorities and the inner suburban activists. In 1973 the government resolved to proceed with the principal eastern route, known as the F19 freeway, linking Doncaster and Templestowe with the inner city. Emerging from a deep cutting in the Yarra Bend National Park the freeway swooped across the Yarra, under Hoddle Street and onto Collingwood's finest (indeed only) boulevard, Alexandra Parade.

A hundred years ago Alexandra Parade was known as Reilly Street and a wide stone-lined drain ran down the centre of the carriageway. Storm water, sewage, industrial wastes, even 'stones, dead cats, pots and pans' were deposited in the drain. In winter, it often overflowed into the surrounding streets. 'Occasionally', historian Bernard Barrett laconically notes, 'someone fell in and was drowned'.[53] Early in the twentieth century the drain was covered over and the council adorned the central plantation with elms and peppercorns. Now in the 1970s the boulevard was about to become a drain again, an overtaxed conduit for the thousands of cars and trucks streaming from the eastern suburbs towards the city. As the concrete pillars went up on the Hoddle Street overpass, and the tarmac edged closer to Alexandra Parade, Collingwood surveyed its approach with mingled anger, resentment and dismay. Soon the stream of traffic would overflow, like water through irrigation ditches, into the narrow side streets of Collingwood and Fitzroy, seeking egress towards the city. 'Just as a large tap will transport more water, so an eight-lane freeway will deluge the city with cars', predicted Collingwood Residents' Association president Bob Hogg in April 1974.[54]

Nothing, it appeared, could stop the advance of the freeway; yet local residents refused to lie down and accept their fate. They held protest meetings on the median plantation. A delegation of placard-waving protesters 'disrupted' a meeting of the Board of Works.[55] Collingwood Council instructed its officers to draw up contingency plans for street closures, cul-de-sacs and one-way streets to repel the unwelcome 'invasion'.[56] Some residents declared their readiness to stand in front of the bulldozers rather than see their precious street trees uprooted.

Collingwood's defence, like Carlton's, was being led by newly arrived young professionals—the 'Academics' as some locals ironically called them. A *Herald* reporter who visited the area late in 1974 found that the old working-class Collingwood was often less indignant (or more fatalistic) than the new.

> With sardonic resignation, many of the old-timers wonder why the residents' association is going to such trouble. They regard association members with reserve because most of them are middle class and newly arrived in Clifton Hill where they are doing up old houses.[57]

Not all the newcomers were youngsters. Marion Miller was already in her sixties when the anti-freeway campaign began. Daughter of an English architect and town planner, she had worked for the Leftist publisher Victor Gollancz before migrating to Melbourne in the 1930s and marrying journalist Forbes Miller. In retirement the Millers had come to live in Clifton Hill where Marion's organisational flair and passion for the local community soon brought her to the fore in campaigns against the Housing Commission and against the relocation of the Collingwood High School. She helped found the Collingwood

Residents' Association and in 1976 was elected to the Collingwood City Council.[58] Marion Miller and her fellow campaigners were conscious of the need to mobilise a wider constituency of locals. They felt the suburb's long history of wrongs as though it were their own. They were 'fed up with Collingwood being used as a doormat', protested Mayor Ray Coverdale.[59] They translated their pamphlets into migrant languages and knocked on the doors of neighbours throughout the municipality. Among other newcomers, the city's large Greek and Italian communities, they scored some success. Milk bar proprietor and local councillor Theo Sidiropoulos estimated that his fellow Greeks made up more than half of those attending street protests over the freeway.[60]

In Australia, as throughout the Western world, the early 1970s were a political watershed. The Vietnam War and the campaigns of students and intellectuals against 'American imperialism' had crystallised oppositional movements around a wider range of environmental, social and economic issues. The Left began to recognise a new set of class issues based in the urban environment. From their traditional concern with workplace issues Marxists began to theorise what one of them defined as 'the relations of collective consumption'—including such issues as transport, housing and public health.[61] In 1971 the Australian Communist Jack Mundey persuaded his Builders' Labourers Federation to support the campaign of middle-class housewives in Sydney's Hunter's Hill to save a small patch of bushland. By banning construction on the site—the first of the famous 'green bans'—Mundey forged a powerful new alliance between the environmentalists and militant trade unionists.[62] In October 1975 a meeting of over 1000 inner suburban residents called on the Victorian Trades Hall Council to ban work on any extension of the F19 freeway into Collingwood and Fitzroy, blocking the highway at Hoddle Street. Building and Construction Workers' boss Norm Gallagher promised: 'We are not going to have people thrown out of their homes for motor cars.'[63]

By 1974, the language and militancy of the Marxist Left began to influence the anti-freeway movement more strongly.[64] 'The fight against freeways is only part of the overall struggle against overseas domination of our country', declared the Worker–Student Alliance in its bulletin *Stop Freeways*.[65] Freeways, it argued, were a creation of the American oil and motor companies who had conspired to destroy public transport systems and to make everyman and woman, willingly or unwillingly, into a motorist. The energy crisis, precipitated by the OPEC oil price rise in 1974, was a further manifestation of their monopolistic influence and a startling proof that the days of the automobile were numbered. A petrol strike in April 1977 gave Melburnians a brief foretaste of the carless world they might soon inhabit. By the mid-1980s, experts believed, Australia's own supplies of crude oil would be exhausted. Then, one freeway activist suggested, the concrete dinosaurs would be good for nothing but to be converted into bicycle tracks.[66] As the construction of the freeway proceeded, the rhetoric of its opponents became increasingly apocalyptic: the struggle now was not just to stop the F19 but to challenge the system that sustained it.

'Garden State or Asphalt State?' asked *Freeway Fighter* in response to Premier Hamer's launching of a campaign to promote Victoria as 'The Garden State'. Was the slogan an attempt to divert public attention from the fact that freeways were destroying parks? it wondered.[67]

As the date for the completion of the freeway approached, MMBW chairman Alan Croxford sought to 'clean up the loose ends' by offering Collingwood and Fitzroy councils $400 000 each, as compensation for lost rates, and a package of abatement measures such as overhead pedestrian walks and 'aesthetic schemes'. 'The board tried to buy us off alright', Bob Hogg responded.[68] An expert inquiry was appointed into the problem of the western approaches of the freeway, but local residents boycotted meetings with the consultant when it became clear that the 'no-open' option—scrapping the freeway or confining its use to buses—was not under consideration. 'All they're asking us is which way do you want to die: you can choke, suffocate or shoot yourself', remonstrated Trevor Huggard. 'Our answer is that we don't want to die.'[69] Even the residents' less preferred alternative, a T-junction at Hoddle Street, was eventually ruled out as likely to cause more congestion, accidents, noise and pollution than other alternatives. The only route that could take the traffic was the one that brought maximum disruption to the inner suburbs: the seemingly inevitable eight-lane freeway down Alexandra Parade.

'HAMER MAKES IT HAPPEN'—the Liberals' slogan for the 1976 state election—sought to create an image of activity for a premier who had sometimes seemed too conciliatory for his own good. The freeway issue seemed to bring out all the contradictions—between economic development and environmental responsibility, wealth-creation and quality of life—that had beset the efforts of the Liberals to remake themselves in the post-Bolte era. Conscious of the complexities of the issue, Hamer seemed unable either to transcend or bypass them. By 1977, with unemployment rising and economic realists once more in the ascendant in Canberra, the mood of the Victorian Government began to harden. Ministers Bill Baxter (Roads) and Ray Meagher (Transport) were pressing for a resolution of the impasse.

'Stop the F19!' screamed the headline of *Freeway Fighter*, the news-letter of Citizens against Freeways (CAF) in September 1977. The government's long procrastination had convinced some activists that they had only to maintain the pressure and the government would buckle. Each side prepared to do battle. Collingwood, Fitzroy and Brunswick councils appointed special 'anti-freeway organisers'. Citizens against Freeways organiser Andrew Herington announced the forma-tion of a Civic Defence Committee to prepare 'aggressive' protective measures against freeway traffic.[70]

The time for compromise had passed. On 14 September Minister Bill Baxter announced the government's determination to push ahead with the opening of the Eastern Freeway by the end of the year. 'The decision is certain to bring a storm of protest', predicted the *Age*.[71] Fitzroy and Collingwood councils authorised roadworks to restrict traffic on Alexandra Parade to one lane each way. The government responded by proclaiming it a state highway, thus removing it from local government jurisdiction. The car wars were headed for a dramatic climax.

On 9 October 1977, 3000 local residents occupied the median strip along Alexandra Parade for a 'Community Day' with dances, music and 'barricade building'. They reaffirmed their stand against the opening of the freeway and resolved to keep a vigil, day and night, on the threat-ened thoroughfare. Fitzroy Council stationed a caravan as a bivouac to supply cups of tea and sympathy for the weary protesters. The pro-tective sense of community that had drawn local residents into the anti-freeway struggle was made tangible through the struggle itself. Leaders of the protest had organised a 'telephone tree', a network of communication that enabled supporters to be mobilised almost instantly for battle. The vicar of St Mark's Anglican Church volunteered to sound his church bell at the enemy's approach.[72]

On 25 October CRB workmen began work on the installation of traffic lights at the Gold Street intersection. Protesters stood in the path of their bulldozer and filled in the workmen's trenches as fast as they were excavated. The CRB men retired. A fortnight later they returned in strength to resume their labours. The residents had been

anti-freeway community day

SUNDAY NOV. 6

ALEXANDRA PARADE

3pm BARRICADE BUILDING

New Theatre   Puppets and Clowns
Greg Hildebrand   Christos and Tassos
Ben Witham   Turkey Rhubarb
                     Hopeless Romantics

5pm B.Y.O. BARBEQUE

7pm EVENING ROCK CONCERT

NO NO FREEWAYS NO
Yasmine and the Tealeaves
Flying Tackle
Red Hot Peppers

Tree-lined Alexandra Parade, the frontline in inner Melbourne's resistance to the freeway, became the setting for a desperate, joyous celebration of community solidarity. (RILEY AND EPHEMERA COLLECTION, STATE LIBRARY OF VICTORIA)

forewarned (by a mole within the CRB) of their arrival, and more than 300 protesters, including the mayors of Fitzroy and Collingwood dressed in their mayoral robes, gathered in the darkness on the morning of Monday 7 November to await the expected confrontation. At 9.40 am when most of the protesters had left for work, the CRB contractors arrived, escorted by hundreds of police in cars, vans and paddy wagons. A Cyclone Wire fence was hastily erected around the work site. In the ensuing melée some dozens of protesters, including the two mayors, Bill Peterson and Theo Sidiropoulos, were forcibly removed by police.[73]

As news of the confrontation spread, local residents assembled outside the wire compound. They were divided about what to do next. Some, including most of the CAF leadership, proposed a meeting of the inner group that evening at the Fitzroy Town Hall to discuss future strategy. A more radical group called for the crowd to begin the construction of a barricade across the street. In the angry aftermath of the police action, theirs was the voice that prevailed. Some observers would later suggest that this was the moment when 'outsiders'—Trotskyist and Maoist exponents of 'direct action'—wrested control of the movement from the middle-class professionals. Certainly, events now took on a more 'spontaneous' course. Under the cloak of darkness, young protesters emerged from the surrounding streets and suburbs, pushing derelict cars, carrying old doors and lengths of corrugated iron. A truck driver contributed a lump of concrete. The protesters piled them, head-high, across the Wellington street intersection, decorating the crumpled duco with their slogans:

STOP THE FREEWAY NOW
THE F19 STINKS
WELCOME TO THE GARDEN STATE

A policeman upbraided one young man who carried a sign incorporating a four-letter word. Fellow protesters, including a clergyman and several lawyers, came to his aid, chanting the offending word and daring the police to arrest them. Next day the young man was back, with his sign reversed: FREE THE FUCKWAY.[74]

The barricade was the last stand of the inner suburbs against the freeway menace. A wall of wrecked cars, lying helplessly on their backs like capsized beetles, it was a potent symbol of the inner suburbs' rejection of autopia. A gesture of defiance, the barricade was also a

THE CRB AND POLICE FORCED THROUGH THE F 19 . . . . . THEY GO NO FURTHER!

MARCH TO PROTECT YOUR STREETS
SATURDAY 15 APRIL 10:30

Memories of the F19 barricade continued to inspire gestures of community resistance to inner city freeways. (RILEY AND EPHEMERA COLLECTION, STATE LIBRARY OF VICTORIA)

reckless and joyous celebration of the community solidarity that the anti-freeway struggle had brought into being. At night, the campaigners gathered around a great campfire singing protest songs, sharing sandwiches and homemade lemonade.

Slash go the freeways, slash, slash slash
Down come the trees and the houses go crash[75]

A few people pitched their own tents in the protective lee of the barricade itself. 'There were a few romances down there too', recalled one participant who was still 'going steady' with the 'lady' he met on the barricades.[76]

Trying to defuse the conflict, Premier Hamer proposed the formation of a working group of CRB officials and local representatives to examine the effects of the freeway opening. Mass meetings of protesters debated the proposal. Moderates, conscious of the dangers to life and limb and intent on moderating the effects of the freeway, even if they could not stop it, favoured its acceptance. Militants, who preferred glorious defeat to compromise, vowed to fight to the bitter end. In a confused and heated debate the moderates narrowly prevailed.

When the working group assembled, it soon became obvious that there was little room for compromise. The residents had come with a range of suggestions—restricting freeway exits to two lanes, confining use initially to buses and taxis, limiting the overall number of vehicles per day. The CRB was prepared to consider noise abatement and traffic management schemes but on the central issue—the widening of Alexandra Parade to take most of the freeway traffic—there was no budging. Hamer had undertaken not to cease work on the Alexandra Parade approaches to the freeway, but on 24 November, after four days of discussions, the working party's report had still to be finalised.[77] Early that morning residents' representatives received a tip that police and CRB employees were about to arrive on Alexandra Parade to dismantle the barricade. Andrew McCutcheon called on the CRB, the Minister for Roads and eventually the Premier to seek an assurance that no such move was planned. After much toing and froing Hamer agreed.[78]

Meanwhile, alerted by the rumours, local residents flocked back to the defence of their barricade. Young men were piling old fridges and chairs on the cars, sitting on top and defying the police to get them down. A young woman chained and padlocked herself to a car. Shortly after one o'clock the police arrived and began to drag protesters from the barricade. A bulldozer advanced on the Fitzroy Council caravan, the protesters' unofficial headquarters, tipped it over and smashed it apart. By the end of the afternoon most of the cars had been cleared from the roadway. During the evening some of the more ardent protesters tried to rebuild the barricade, but by one o'clock in the morning, when private tow trucks arrived to clear the remaining wreckage, only a handful of diehards remained. 'The walls of Jericho are down', Victorian Commissioner of Police Mick Miller declared next morning, 'and as far as we are concerned they will stay down'.[79]

Sporadic protests—sit-downs, vigils, marches, benefit concerts, even a Carols by Traffic Lights service—continued over the following weeks, but by the end of November the residents' power, if not their will, had effectively been broken. Four days before Christmas 1977 the first cars roared down the new freeway, under the Hoddle Street overpass and

On 24 November 1977 police dragged protesters from the barricades. Next morning, a battle-scarred veteran of the struggle displayed his wounds and medals. (*AGE* PHOTOS)

along the crowded carriageways of Alexandra Parade. Next day 42 000 more followed. The freeway planners were pleased. Traffic on other arterial roads was down, but the overall number of cars descending on the inner city was up.[80]

Long before the freeway had opened, some residents had been forced to move out. Joyce Tsakalofas and her three children had occupied a small weatherboard cottage in Maugie Street close to the western terminal of the F19 until the Board of Works decided in 1973 to demolish it to make way for an off-ramp. 'I've lived here for 18 years, and my children have lived here all their lives—why should I move?' she remonstrated. The board had offered her £8000 and two years' free rent in a nearby house, but she was holding out for £12 000. By the time it moved to evict her, all her neighbours had gone and the cottage was perched precariously on a little mesa 6 metres above the newly excavated exit ramp.[81]

Those who went, however unwillingly, and received compensation were probably better off than those who had to stay. Graham Retallick had been arrested during the last days of the barricade. Eight months after the freeway opened his worst fears about the effects on local residents were fulfilled. 'We can't get to sleep for the noise of the traffic shooting off the freeway . . . sometimes it gets you so mad you feel like rushing out with a big board with nails in it and putting it across the road.' Almost two-thirds of residents on Alexandra Parade complained of loss of sleep, asthma, heart strain and other ailments, a finding confirmed by a local pharmacist who observed a sharp increase in prescriptions for insomnia, bad nerves and eye and ear complaints. Attendances at a nearby Greek Orthodox Chapel had fallen from 60 to five or ten because the congregation could no longer hear the priest. The Isobel Henderson Kindergarten had closed down. Two-thirds of the households on Alexandra Parade wanted to move but could not sell their houses at anything like their original value.[82] Almost five years after the project began some families were still waiting to be offered realistic compensation.

WINNERS AND LOSERS

Who won the car wars of the 1960s and 1970s? In 1973 when the Hamer Government lopped the Bolte Government's grand plan in half, the inner suburbs seemed to have won a famous victory. Most of the projected inner city freeways have remained unbuilt, although some widened arterial roads (such as Hoddle Street/Punt Road) carry almost as much traffic as some freeways. Several of the anti-freeway movements' leaders—Brian Howe, Trevor Huggard, Andrew McCutcheon, Barry Pullen, Bob Hogg[83]—were launched on successful political careers. The inner suburbs, once threatened with urban blight, have become some of the most coveted real estate in the city. Range Rovers and BMWs now line the streets where battered Holdens and Volkswagens once parked. No-one lives more than five minutes from a strong cappuccino.

When veterans of the barricade look back they take pride in their achievements and in the robust health of the neighbourhoods they fought to save.[84] But they are puzzled and troubled too. They miss the old sense of political urgency, the vibrant sense of community that once united them with their youthful comrades on the barricade. Their own children, priced out of Fitzroy and Carlton, are moving further out to Northcote and Preston.

With hindsight, and perhaps too much cynicism, the anti-freeway campaigns may look like a successful campaign to secure the amenity and property values of the new middle class. The young professionals had astutely anticipated a new trend ('trendies' was their nickname, after all) and, as the old industries closed down and the working class moved out, they bought up their houses and used their political muscle to erect protective barriers against unwelcome traffic and redevelopment. 'Community', according to this cynical reading, was the watchword of collective self-interest.

But hindsight can distort as well as illuminate. Looking through the lens of the selfish 1980s and 1990s can blind us to the power of ideals that inspired a more generous and confident era. Only the most prescient of the 1960s generation banked on the revolution in property values that would transform the inner suburbs by the 1980s and 1990s. The discourse of the anti-freeway campaigns reveals a rich web of meanings that transcends individual or collective self-interest. It is about identity as much as property, reciprocity as much as collective self-interest. Sometimes it looks back to the rural or suburban places from which the campaigners had come ('more of a village than the place I had come from') or across the street to migrant families whose ways of inhabiting the spaces of the inner city seemed somehow more natural than their own. 'Community' was an ideal that expressed the aspirations of student radicals rebelling against the corporate, bureaucratic or technological forces that curbed their aspirations for more spontaneous and unselfish forms of living. It was a pivotal idea in the outlook of those, like the influential group of clergymen, who came as caretakers to the lost and powerless of the inner city, and of the women who constructed networks of mutual support through their common task of child-rearing. 'Community' was also something drawn vicariously from the history of the localities in which they had come to inhabit. But, above all, it was a product of the activists' shared struggle against the powerful and impersonal forces that threatened to 'divide' or 'erase' it.

'Community', the American historian Thomas Bender wisely observes, 'can be defined better as an experience than as a place. As simply as possible, community is where community happens.'[85] As the rueful veterans of Melbourne's car wars now realise, community was not something inherent in the territory they defended. It was something that 'happened' in the process of resisting its extinction, and that began to die at the very moment success came in sight.

9

The Serpent in the Garden

The urban freeway was a heroic attempt to resolve a dilemma at the heart of industrial civilisation. Since the 1830s, when the piercing whistle of the locomotive first shattered the calm of the English countryside, human progress seemed to have been set at odds with the moral and aesthetic principles of nature. Roads, railways, cotton mills and smokestacks were seen as unwelcome invaders of a pastoral Eden. 'The contrast between the machine and the pastoral ideal dramatizes the great issue of our culture', says Leo Marx in his perceptive study, *The Machine in the Garden*.[1]

Planners and engineers have long aspired to enable the Machine to dwell more harmoniously in the Garden. In the 1920s Robert Moses, the godfather of modern New York, endowed the metropolis with a magnificent network of landscaped highways, or 'parkways'.[2] Moses' ingenious amalgam of high-speed roads and picturesque countryside created (in Marshall Berman's apt phrase) a 'techno-pastoral garden' only minutes from the soaring skyscrapers of Manhattan.[3] By following the serpentine course of streams and rivers, easing its massive pavements, ramps and bridges into the contours of the land, planting its grassy verges with water-smoothed rocks and native vegetation the parkway seemed to have effected a new marriage between nature and technology. In its subtle blend of organic and inorganic forms the freeway seemed to promise the speeding motorist that he could enjoy the best of both worlds—the excitement of mechanised automobility and the pleasures of communion with nature. It was a seductive idea,

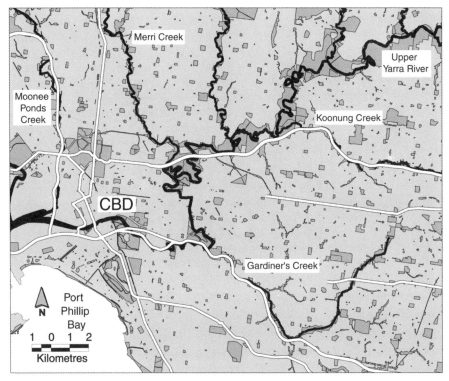

*The green ribbons of park and farmland along the River Yarra and its tributaries
became the main corridors for Melbourne's urban freeways. The Tullamarine Freeway
follows Moonee Ponds Creek; the Eastern Freeway weaves along the Yarra River and
Koonung Creek; while the Monash (Eastern) Freeway borders Gardiner's Creek.*

although more plausible, perhaps, to the man behind the wheel than to
the sedentary souls who heard the distant roar of traffic from the green
fringes and interstices of the metropolis.

In faraway Melbourne planners and engineers sought their own
accommodation between the Machine and the Garden. As in Moses'
New York, the city's waterways were to play a crucial role in that experiment. Melbourne stands on the banks of the Yarra River, about
3 kilometres from the sea and at the centre of a wide alluvial basin
drained by creeks and rivers that rise a hundred kilometres or so away
in the foothills of the Great Dividing Range. From colonial times the
city expanded first along the hills where the highest and best-drained
land was found. Stock routes first extended like the fingers of a great
hand, linking the new suburbs. In the valleys between these fingers were
several creeks. Those to the west, like the Kororoit and Moonee Ponds

creeks, drained to the Yarra's main tributary the Maribyrnong, while those to the north and east, like the Merri, Darebin, Plenty, Koonung and Gardiner's creeks emptied directly into the Yarra itself. Meandering through shallow valleys of tussocky grass and eucalpyt, the creeks carried only a trickle of water for most of the year. In winter they sometimes flooded, in summer they often ran dry. Sometimes enjoyed, often abused, usually ignored, these humble waterways have nevertheless shaped the city's development.

By the end of the nineteenth century, when real estate developers had annexed most of the high and dry land, the river and creek valleys were almost the last continuous ribbons of undeveloped land in the metropolis. In the late 1880s Chief Commissioner of Railways Richard Speight, a man with ambitions almost as grand as those of Robert Moses, spotted their potential, planning new railways from Flemington to Pascoe Vale along the valley of the Moonee Ponds Creek, along the Yarra and Koonung creeks to Doncaster, and along Gardiner's Creek from Kooyong to Holmesglen.[4] The 1890s depression blocked his plans and it was not until the late 1920s that the waterways again came under notice when the Metropolitan Planning Commission, alert to Moses' example, selected them as routes for a future system of 'parkways'.[5] Depression and war deferred these plans too until 1954 when the MMBW's Melbourne Metropolitan Planning Scheme proposed a network of radial highways designed to carry workers from the suburbs towards the main centre of employment in the city centre. The planners sought to avoid disruption to existing centres of population by locating the proposed 'controlled access roads' in the old creek valleys 'where there is often substantial space not built upon'.[6]

So when the planners of the 1960s drew their maps of the future highway system they built upon more than half a century of unfulfilled dreams. Their scheme largely followed the recommendations of the 1954 plan, utilising the river and creek valleys to carry several of the main freeways.[7] The Tullamarine Freeway (F14) followed the Moonee Ponds Creek. The Hume Freeway (F2) ran from the Yarra at Clifton Hill northward along the Merri Creek through Northcote and Coburg to Craigieburn. The South-Eastern (F14) ran along the northern bank of the Yarra until it diverged along Gardiner's and Scotsman's creeks. The Eastern Freeway (F19) bisected the Yarra Bend National Park then followed the Yarra along the border between Camberwell and Doncaster to North Balwyn where it swung up the Koonung and

Mullum Mullum creeks towards Ringwood. Flowing towards the lower
Yarra from the surrounding hills, these 'creekways' naturally tended to
reinforce the radial pattern of the city's public transport system.

The planners anticipated that these radial freeways would be
complemented by an overlapping system of circumferential or 'box'
freeways (F2, F4 and F6) designed to facilitate cross-city journeys from
north to south or from east to west. From the vantage point of the transport planner, these cross-city roads were possibly more important
than the radial freeways, because they enabled journeys that could not
easily be made by rail or tram. But because they had to forge new paths
through densely populated inner suburbs they were costly and disruptive to build and, as we have already seen, provoked vigorous opposition
from well-organised residents. Radial freeways running down unpopu-
lated creek valleys, on the other hand, involved low costs of property
resumption and provoked fewer protests. Their opponents were
dispersed along a ragged suburban frontier, unlike the more easily
mobilised radicals of the inner city. In the political equation that would
govern Melbourne's transport future, the yabbies of the creek valleys
had less clout than the yuppies of the inner suburbs.

THE GEOPOLITICS OF HIGHWAY PLANNING

In December 1972 when Prime Minister Gough Whitlam forced
Premier Hamer to scrap plans for inner city freeways, he dealt a heavy
blow, not only to the professional ambitions of the highway engineers,
but to the integrity of their transport plan. While the cuts minimised the
financial and political costs of the road-building program, they left
the city with a curiously truncated transport system. The proposed
roads that survived the cuts duplicated the existing radial public transport system and potentially undermined their economic viability. Faced
with a choice between rail and road, an increasing number of suburban
commuters preferred to drive rather than ride. They converged towards
an inner city that would no longer have the ring-roads and bypasses to
draw traffic away from its congested local road system.

Not all the engineers were displeased with this compromise, however.
Throughout the postwar period two strong bureaucracies—the
Melbourne and Metropolitan Board of Works and the Country Roads
Board—had engaged in a strenuous and sometimes bitter contest to build

the city's new road system. Since the 1920s, the CRB had been the state's premier road construction authority, but its legal responsibilities stopped on the fringes of the metropolis, a boundary formally defined by the reach of the electric tramway system. Already in the 1960s the board's metropolitan ambitions had been encouraged by some large highway projects joining Melbourne and its hinterland, such as the Maltby Bypass on the Geelong Road (1961) and the northern section of the Tullamarine Freeway (1968).[8] Looking inwards from the urban periphery to the centre, the CRB was a natural advocate for a radial approach to freeway planning. Meanwhile the MMBW, the city's main planning authority, had built its first freeway, the South-Eastern (1962) and was far advanced on designs for the main inner city components of the freeway plan, the F2 and F4. The rivalry of the two authorities had not escaped notice and in 1974 the government ratified the advice of two official inquiries by handing responsibility for metropolitan freeways to the CRB.[9] The MMBW felt, with some justification, that it had been punished for having to bear the disgrace of an unpopular inner city freeway plan. By excising the cross-city freeways and delivering planning responsibility to the CRB, however, the government had effectively reinforced the already strongly radial pattern of the city's transport system.

Freeways, the politicians now decided, were good for sprawling outer suburbs even if they were bad for crowded inner ones. Many of the 'creekways' were originally conceived as bypasses designed, the engineers claimed, to carry traffic around the CBD to the airport or the western industrial zone. There was something disingenuous about these claims: planning documents emphasised their bypass function but a 1969 promotional film for the Melbourne Transportation Study showed a typical commuter driving his car from Doncaster down the F19 to his city office. Once the cross-city freeways were scrapped the outer suburban freeways were left, as one observer noted, like lengths of garden hose waiting for someone to connect them. Beginning on the outskirts and heading towards the centre of Melbourne they had no obvious destination but the CBD. Sooner or later, the residents of the inner suburbs feared, the floods of commuters would pour into their already crowded streets. A meeting of the United Melbourne Freeway Action Group in March 1973 condemned the government's compromise, rejecting the distinction between outer and inner suburbs. 'The disruption of outer communities was just as disruptive as pouring traffic into inner suburbs.'[10]

By 1973 several of the radial freeways—the F9 and F19—had been completed or were under construction. Already they were attracting traffic and creating a demand among frustrated motorists for their extension. Inner city residents who already lived close to their jobs had little to gain and much to lose from a freeway in their backyards. But outer suburban residents were divided between the minority who suffered the noise and pollution of the freeway, or deplored the loss of native vegetation and wildlife in the creek valleys, and the majority, who cared less for the bellbirds and stringybarks than for shaving a few minutes off their journey to work. The inner suburbs, led by young professionals, had already been mobilised in defence of their environment by the slum clearance programs of the 1960s. The outer suburbs, often Liberal electorates, were less militant and harder to mobilise in protest.

Even so, the passage of the roads along the creek and river valleys was not as smooth as the highway planners may have anticipated. Attracted by their delightful views of river and bushland, suburban home owners had often already built on the slopes overlooking the waterways. At some points suburban backyards almost backed on to the river or creek, leaving little room for the highway to pass. It was here especially that the plans of the freeway engineers clashed most sharply with the aspirations of local residents. The Battle for the Creeks was fought on different terms from the Battle of the Streets. In Carlton and Collingwood young professionals and migrants mobilised the people of Labor-voting electorates in defence of communities that were more social than natural. The anti-freeway campaigners of Ivanhoe, Doncaster and Malvern were more likely to be middle-class Liberal voters, roused in defence of a picturesque natural environment, or sometimes just to resist an attack on their own property rights. Every battle was different, being fought for different stakes and on different battlegrounds. But some features recur. One was the prominent role played by women as defenders of home and hearth.

DEFENDING THE LANDSCAPE: THE YARRA VALLEY

The battle had begun even before Hamer's decision to scrap the inner city freeways. Ten miles north-east of the city, where the Yarra joins Koonung Creek, the course of the river flows south through a wide flood

An Important Choice For All Victorians

this

or this

GARDINERS CREEK VALLEY ASSOCIATION

Environmentalists joined with middle-class property owners to resist the despoliation of the Gardiner's Creek Valley by the projected South-Eastern Freeway extension.
(RILEY AND EPHEMERA COLLECTION, STATE LIBRARY OF VICTORIA)

plain overlooked from the west by steeply rising hills. From the first days
of European settlement it was a noted beauty spot. Gentleman settlers
including the writer Rolf Boldrewood planted the village of Heidelberg
as a rustic retreat on the slopes overlooking the river in the 1840s. Forty
years later when the railway reached the town, landscape painters
including the young Tom Roberts, Arthur Streeton and Fred McCubbin
visited the valley on weekend painting expeditions.[11] They became
known collectively as the 'Heidelberg School'. Early in the twentieth
century suburban development spread across the valley, merging the
village into the familiar tapestry of houses and gardens. The famous
American architect Walter Burley Griffin designed two new estates,
'Mount Eagle' on the heights overlooking the river and 'Glenard' on the
flats beside the newly constructed Boulevard, a scenic road that followed
the meandering course of the river from Burke Road to Heidelberg
village. In the 1920s and 1930s the valley remained a semi-rural retreat
but suburban development boomed in the early postwar years. By 1969
it was one of the city's most delightful suburbs, a haven for the city's
business and professional elite.[12]

When the Metropolitan Transportation Plan was unveiled, much of
the lower Yarra had already been appropriated for new roads. The F9,
or South-Eastern Freeway, occupied the north bank of the river from
Punt Road to Burnley where it diverged along Gardiner's Creek. The
F19 cut through the Yarra Bend National Park before following the river
itself from Kew to North Balwyn where it turned east along Koonung
Creek. Here, near the junction with Burke Road, Melbourne's longest
north–south arterial, another high-speed road, the F18 or Greensbor-
ough Freeway, was projected to strike north along the Yarra Valley
through Heidelberg towards Watsonia and the Diamond Valley. The
strip of land reserved for the road under the 1954 MMBW Plan was
uncomfortably narrow, less than 120 metres between the Boulevard
and the river at some points. Nowhere in the city was the conflict
between the Garden and the Machine as stark.

Local residents were alarmed by the prospect of a freeway dividing
their valley, cutting off views of the river and hills, and polluting the air
with petrol fumes. Ivanhoe, the state electorate, was traditionally Liberal
but in 1970 the local member Vernon Christie, Speaker of the Legislative Assembly, relied on Democratic Labor Party preferences to win
the seat. A middle class increasingly sensitive to environmental issues
might easily swing against the government. In July 1971 Ann Bunbury,

Citizens Against Freeways bumper sticker.
(RILEY AND EPHEMERA COLLECTION, STATE LIBRARY OF VICTORIA)

who lived with her management consultant husband Alan at 607 The Boulevard, wrote to the *Age* expressing concern that the valley was to be 'used up' for a freeway. Concern mounted when it was revealed that the MMBW had recently acquired $250 000 of property along the proposed route. Meetings were held among local residents and in March 1972 the Valley Freeway Action Group (VFAG) was formed at the home of surgeon Sir Benjamin Rank in Vine Street, beside the river in the old Heidelberg township.

The activists saw themselves as defenders of the scenic and recreational values of the valley on behalf of posterity. 'This open space will be of increasing value as Melbourne grows. Future generations of Melbournians should be able to enjoy the advantages of the Yarra Valley and be protected against piecemeal useage [sic] by public authorities.' Since the foundation of the Commons Preservation Society in England in 1865, defence of public land for recreational and aesthetic purposes has been an impeccable conservationist cause. But among the defenders of the Yarra Valley private interest and public responsibility were closely intertwined. Most of them were local property-holders financially threatened by the freeway, and much of the land they sought to preserve was inaccessible to anyone except those, like the Ranks and Bunburys, who were lucky enough to own allotments backing on to the river flats.

Support for the group among local residents grew quickly. By October 1972 more than 250 members had subscribed, most of them residents of the narrow strip of prime real estate in the endangered zone between Lower Heidelberg Road and the river.[13] They joined, often as husbands and wives together, following the lead of the group's president Alan Bunbury and his energetic wife-secretary Ann. Of the members listed in the group's newsletters the vast majority were professionals and business people: doctors, lawyers, engineers, university professors, architects, company directors and managers and an occasional secretary, teacher or car dealer.[14] A feature article under the title 'Asphalt Threat to Melbourne Pastures' was accompanied by a pleasantly nostalgic portrait of Ian Fleming, a dairy farmer whose cows had been grazing the Yarra Valley since 1924; he was the sole rustic among the bourgeoisie. In addressing their concerns to the government, the group spoke in the manner of injured friends—firmly, sometimes vigorously, but always politely and within a common framework of conservative values. The highlight of the first phase of their campaign was an art exhibition, showing the work of artists from the Heidelberg School onwards who had cherished the scenic qualities of the valley. Transport Minister Vernon Wilcox accepted an invitation to attend. 'With your interest in both transport and the Yarra Valley, we would very much appreciate an opportunity to meet you', Alan Bunbury gracefully proposed.[15] Photography exhibits, nature tours, letters and deputations rather than noisy public meetings and blockades, were their standard methods of persuasion.

From the beginning it was clear that the government was anxious to placate the concerns of a group they regarded as friends. In June 1972 Rupert Hamer, Minister for Local Government, wrote to assure VFAG that 'I agree fundamentally with the Group's beliefs about the unique value of the Yarra Valley' and that he had directed the MMBW to examine other routes for the freeway. An invitation to the group to suggest alternative routes was firmly rebuffed: 'THE VFAG IS NOT IN THE BUSINESS OF PUSHING A FREEWAY FROM ONE SIDE OF THE RIVER TO THE OTHER.'[16]

Conscious of the votes to be won from disaffected Liberals, as well as their own supporters in the inner suburbs, the Labor Party called for a stop to the construction of all freeways within 400 metres of the Yarra upstream from Princes Bridge.[17] In August 1972 Hamer succeeded the long-serving Henry Bolte as premier. Bolte had been a vigorous advocate of economic development but his appreciation of environmental issues was more limited. Asked to define what he understood by 'quality of life'—the environmental catchcry of the early 1970s—Bolte replied: 'Quality of life is peace of mind based on a home and garden.'[18] As the electors of Ivanhoe apprehended, however, the peace of one's home and garden could easily be destroyed by the noise and stench of a nearby freeway. Bolte's successor, Rupert Hamer, was sympathetic to the environmentalists but he led a government in which pro- and anti-development forces were still delicately balanced. With an election rapidly approaching the government was anxious to keep its options open. While Hamer had reassured the electors of Ivanhoe that he would not allow a freeway to despoil their valley, his successor as minister for local government, Alan Hunt, was hopeful that the road could still be built without damaging the environment. 'There is no reason why a properly planned and landscaped road may not enhance the Valley as does Alexandra Avenue and the Boulevard.'[19]

Local protesters were unconvinced. Any route through their valley—whether it was a 'freeway' or just a 'road'—was unacceptable. Both Liberal and Labor candidates for the Ivanhoe seat pledged themselves to oppose the freeway. In December 1972 the Minister for Transport (Jones) and the Minister for Urban and Regional Development (Tom Uren) in the newly elected Whitlam federal government announced the suspension of Commonwealth funding for inner city freeways and in March the Victorian Government fell into line by cancelling more than half its slated projects, including both the F4 and F18 freeways. In the May election the Liberal candidate, Bruce Skeggs, just squeaked home: his predecessor's majority shrank from a comfortable 9 per cent to just 0. 2 per cent.[20] Without the government's timely concession the seat would almost certainly have changed hands, though the government itself might have survived. Residents of the Yarra Valley breathed a sigh of relief, but the VFAG remained vigilant, believing that until the 1954 road reservation was also removed the valley was in jeopardy. Membership of the group fell away, and meetings became less frequent. In 1976 the government at last announced the cancellation of the road reservation and the group disbanded.

The VFAG was among the smallest and least militant of the anti-freeway protest groups. Its ranks were full of lawyers, engineers and other professionals, but it shrewdly avoided the kind of technical debates on freeway design and traffic flows that engaged the inner city activists. It took the high aesthetic ground, challenging its political friends not to mutilate a landscape hallowed by the canvases of Streeton, Roberts and McCubbin. It kept well clear of the street protests of the Fitzroy and Collingwood anti-freeway action groups, joining the coalition of freeway action groups only after declaring its reservations about the tactics of the militants. Its strength lay in its

strong informal connections with the Melbourne business and professional elite, its astute personal lobbying of politicians, and its potential
influence upon the result of a closely fought local election.

DEFENDING NATURE: THE MERRI AND KOONUNG CREEKS

The Yarra Valley had been protected by its good looks and its friends in
high places. Its northern tributary, the Merri Creek, had no such advantages. Wending its sluggish way across the northern suburbs, past
factories and beneath power lines, through a stony valley littered with
the carcases of abandoned cars and dead animals, the Merri was the
ugly sister of the Yarra. Awakened to its environmental plight by plans
for the Hume Highway, a group of radical students and young academics, the Victorian Public Interest Research Group, took pity on it. Their
report, the *Merri Creek Study* (1975) contains an astute review of the
environmental and social condition of the valley and the implications of
the proposed new road. A survey of local residents showed that support
for the freeway increased with distance from the inner city. While 48 per
cent of the residents polled in Fawkner and Reservoir thought that the
freeway was necessary, and a further 24 per cent were uncertain, only
20 per cent of the residents of Fitzroy and Northcote considered it
necessary. The researchers looked back nostalgically to the 1929 Metropolitan Town Planning Commission's grand vision of a continuous belt
of parkland with a scenic four-lane road along the Merri. Now, it
seemed, the scenic potential of the valley might be destroyed by a road
more than twice as wide. Even in its degraded condition, the researchers
argued, the valley was an under-appreciated recreational resource:

> Children gather in small groups to play, European women select
> weeds and vegetables, men and families walk their dogs, yabbies are
> sought, birds are watched, car bodies explored, and picnics held.
> Creek-side activities are often at variance with suburban norms and
> these non-conformists are fragmented with no common bonds, beside
> the creek, and no leadership.[21]

There was a hint of romantic identification between the student radicals
and these 'non-conformist' denizens of the Merri valley. Whether
together they could have saved the Merri is unlikely. The fate of the
Hume Freeway, and of the Merri Creek, hinged more crucially on

Koonung Creek flows beside translucent sound barriers on the Eastern Freeway.
(AUTHOR'S PHOTO)

'No Freeways Here': fading relics of resident protests still adorn the back fences of homes along the Koonung Valley. (AUTHOR'S PHOTO)

that of the F2 freeway, the inner city ring-road to which it was joined. When Hamer cancelled the inner city freeways the threat to the Merri receded, even if it did not entirely disappear. As traffic on Sydney Road becomes more congested, the Merri Creek corridor could again become a battleground.

Further to the south-east, where the F18 turned north along the wide flood plains of Yarra Valley, the F19 was expected to continue eastward along the narrower valley of Koonung Creek. On the flatter southern side nearer the rail and tramways lay the suburbs of Balwyn and Box Hill; on the slopes to the north was the new suburb of Doncaster. With its sprawling ranch-style houses, swimming pools and three-car garages Doncaster was the favourite suburb of Melbourne's new rich. Nowhere else in the metropolis were there as many cars per household.

The Koonung was a pretty valley, its grassy bottom dotted with stands of eucalypt and grazed by cows and horses. It was more picturesque than the Merri and it probably had more friends, but they were more than outnumbered by the silent majority of local car users. Much more was at stake, moreover, in the extension of the F19 than in the construction of the F18. The second was the southern end of a freeway that might never be built; the first was the vital link between a freeway already under construction and a projected outer eastern ring-road. The freeway extension would require the demolition of very few homes but it threatened to disturb the domestic tranquillity of many others built along the valley in order to enjoy its bushy environs.

'My husband and I spent several years looking for an area within reasonable proximity of Melbourne which contained natural Australian bushland with its inhabitants', one resident of the valley, Maureen Ostrowski of Donvale, recalled.

> We found it and worked very hard to plan a house so as to not disturb the natural environment . . . Our children are delighted with their first experiences with nature. They see rabbits every day; the trees are alive with bellbirds, magpies, whipbirds, and they are always coming into the house with stories of how those birds and animals react to one another.

She was one of several residents along the valley who wrote to the Victorian Minister for Planning (Ray Meagher) deploring the approach of the freeway. They were pleading, not just for themselves, but for their fellow inhabitants, the native birds and animals of the valley. 'It seems to us it's the birds as well as us who will be losing their homes', said one resident. Identifying with the world of unspoiled nature, the locals were natural enemies of 'the monstrous freeway'.[22]

Local residents appealed to the municipalities to turn the creek valley into a linear park, preserved for native species and passive human recreation. The consultants appointed by the CRB to investigate planning options for the valley predictably pooh-poohed the residents' ideas. 'Within the Koonung Creek area there are few areas that could designated as of good landscape quality', the consultants found. The valley was in 'an environmentally depressed state' and 'stable native plant communities' could be re-established only with 'great difficulty'.[23] From a strict ecological point of view they were probably right. The creek had long been polluted by seepage from septic tanks, much native vegetation had been destroyed by mowing and grazing, and most of the original trees had been cut down. But the locals were not comparing the valley as it was with the one that the first European settlers found; they were holding on to a precious remnant bushland and resisting, as best they could, the 'concrete monolith of man's progress' that would soon overrun it.

Even so, their fight was in vain. More than two decades would pass before the freeway was actually open along the full length of Koonung Creek, but local resistance had collapsed years before. Today the Eastern Freeway wends its way along the valley between miles of high earth barriers and artfully contoured glass and concrete sound walls. Boulders have been rolled into creeks to create ponds and waterfalls, a new home for yabbies and waterbirds. Cyclists pedal along a winding path between newly planted eucalypts and across the rustic wooden footbridges that now span the highway. But the bellbirds and whipbirds have departed, and, despite the tonnes of insulating earth and concrete, there is nowhere in the valley that the dull hum of traffic cannot be heard.

DEFENDING HEARTH AND HOME: GARDINER'S CREEK

The longest and hardest battle for the city's creek valleys was fought further to the south in the no-man's-land along Gardiner's Creek between the South-Eastern (F9) and Mulgrave (F14) freeways. The MTP had envisaged four major east–west freeways carrying the traffic to Melbourne's expanding eastern suburbs: the F19 to the north-east, the F9 through Hawthorn, Camberwell and Box Hill, the F14 extending the South-Eastern Freeway along Gardiner's Creek into South Box Hill and the F2 through the south-eastern suburbs to Dandenong. When Premier Hamer cut the freeway program in March 1973 the integrity of this plan was fatally compromised. The South-Eastern Freeway now stopped at Toorak Road. The most controversial section of the F14 freeway, through the densely settled suburbs of South Melbourne and Caulfield, was cancelled, but work continued on the outer section from Warrigal Road to Dandenong, the so-called Mulgrave Freeway. Between the end of the F9 and the beginning of the F14, from Toorak Road to Warrigal Road, was a 10-kilometre gap linked only by an overcrowded arterial road. It was as though the two gushing hosepipes were connected only by a thin drinking straw.

Motorists were frustrated by the slow drive along an overcrowded arterial road. A growing number of local residents began to think that the visual blight of a freeway along the creek might be better than putting up with angry motorists rampaging through local streets. Perhaps, some critics suggested, the highway planners had even arranged this debacle, trusting that public frustration would achieve what their own advocacy could not.[24]

Beyond Toorak Road, Gardiner's Creek ran through a tattered landscape of brickyards, playing fields, powerlines and industrial sites. On its southern bank was the main Mount Waverley railway line. Towards Warrigal Road, however, the factories and powerlines disappeared and the creek valley became, one of its defenders claimed, 'a stream of great beauty'.

> It is the habitat of waterbirds. It is a bustling little creek, flowing between trees presently attired in marvellous spring growth. There is a path winding amongst a close wood of oak trees, spreading everywhere a dappled light, effusing a damp scent of leafy mould. It is so still, so quiet, so sacred.[25]

Besides the waterbirds and oak trees, Gardiner's Creek had also attracted middle-class residents, many of whose homes lay either athwart, or uncomfortably near, any prospective freeway. They included the local Liberal member and deputy premier Lindsay Thompson, whose home in Allenby Avenue was just a stone's throw from the creek.

For almost a decade local residents agonised about whether, and how, to link the two freeways.[26] Mindful of the pitched confrontations of the early 1970s, and the potential political damage for the government, the Country Roads Board initiated a detailed environmental and social impact study of the projected road. Premier Rupert Hamer was some-times nicknamed 'The Mirror' because, it was said, his standard response to questions was 'I'll look into it'. For almost three years a perplexed government looked into the problem of the Gardiner's Valley freeway. Every aspect of the project was studied—noise, air, traffic, safety, open space, the financial and human costs of property acqui-sition, 'community severance'. Residents were encouraged to contribute to the study through letters and public meetings. 'We want to hear from you', the study's *Bulletin* reassured local householders.[27]

As the study got under way the road authorities attempted, in not-so-subtle ways, to reassure local residents. Although humans might fear the approach of the new road, the birds and animals in its path were said to be untroubled by its impact. The *CRB News* reported a project conducted by pupils at Pinewood Primary School on the effects of the already completed Mulgrave Freeway. They had interviewed local resi-dents, taken photographs, made models and written an information book containing a comic strip entitled 'Bellbird and Foxy':

> Bellbird and Foxy were two little characters the children found in a reserve named Bellbird Gully, off Forster Road, adjoining the Freeway.
> Bellbird and Foxy left their homes while the freeway was being built, but returned when work was finished.
> Bellbird: 'The road is beautiful with all the trees.'
> Foxy: 'I didn't think it would be like this.'
> 'We will stay here now, won't we Foxy?'
> 'Yes, Bellbird.'

If Bellbird and Foxy could live happily with the freeway then surely the human inhabitants of the valley would adapt as well.[28]

The planners knew that in an expanding city with finite space, restricting access in one place increased pressure somewhere else. In seeking the 'road ideas' of citizens in the Gardiner's Creek corridor, they hoped to persuade nervous householders to rise above self-interest and accommodate the interests of others. 'Individual attitudes to each of the ideas is affected by where the individual lives and what use he or she makes of the road system', the *Bulletin* reminded its readers. As though to demonstrate the point it published a selection of readers' letters canvassing a bewildering range of viewpoints. 'The problem which besets every proposal is that of sharing space. Space for homes, schools, parklands, sport, bike-riding, parking, shopping, driving cars and everything else which at present is competing for space.'[29] Residents were invited to contemplate a range of alternative routes, each with their corresponding balance sheet of advantages and disadvantages. They were encouraged to ponder the trade-offs between conserving houses and conserving green space, between abating local traffic and minimising the visual impact of new structures. The language of the study team's bulletins was studiously neutral, non-technical, reassuring. But by offering a range of road plans, some even more devastating than the planners' own preferred option, the study paved the way towards a seemingly sensible compromise. Only one alternative—the 'no-build' option—was not seriously studied.

The planners themselves favoured the scheme known as C3, a six-laned freeway along the southern side of the valley between the original 1955 road reservation (C1) and the railway.[30] Moving the road away from the creek was designed to placate conservationists' fears that the natural beauty of the waterway would be lost, but it only increased the exposure of local householders to the engine noise and petrol fumes of the freeway. Somewhere between 40 and 180 buildings, three-quarters of them houses, would have to be demolished and perhaps 230 others would suffer within the house traffic noise above 65 decibels—generally regarded as the threshold at which conversation becomes impossible.[31]

The hardest hit were those who lived directly in the path of the freeway or within a narrow strip of blighted land sandwiched between the railway and the highway in Glen Iris. In January 1978 Mr J. S. B. Rosair wrote to the Victorian Minister of Planning, Alan Hunt, to protest 'the wilful destruction of my home'. Like many of his middle-class neighbours, Rosair was a staunch conservative, a fervent believer in the rights of private property and the sanctity of Home. (He even cited the opinions of those bastions of English conservatism, Sir Edward Coke and Sir William Pitt.) As a former army officer and public servant, Rosair had served his Queen and Country in war and peace.

> Surely, Sir, I am now entitled to expect that I shall be allowed to reside quietly, without let or hindrance, in the peaceful enjoyment of my home, and in the company of my esteemed wife 'for as long as we

both shall live'. And I am sure there are hundreds of other people, with homes under threat, whose entitlement to these blessings and benefits far exceeds my own. Are all of our lives to be disrupted, our homes destroyed, and our future in jeopardy, just to build a road? Would that not represent a frivolous, unbecoming, and unjust use of an awesome power of the State? And how, Sir, would you like to find our positions, yours and mine, reversed?

Rosair had touched a sensitive nerve. In an age of growing environmental consciousness Liberal politicians had learnt to listen to conservationists worried about the despoliation of the natural environment. They even paid polite attention to the protests of inner city radicals defending vibrant immigrant or working-class communities. But nothing stung them quite so sharply as the accusation of fellow Liberals that they were using the 'awesome power of the State' to attack private property and desecrate the 'Homes Spiritual' that their leader, Sir Robert Menzies, had once exalted as the foundation of society.[32]

The plight of home owners subject to compulsory purchase was bad enough; even worse was the lot of those whose homes lay in the so-called 'buffer zone' close to the new road. When the C3 alignment was chosen as the route of the freeway, Frank and Margaret Gottstein of York Street, Glen Iris woke up to discover that the road they had been expecting to be built at the bottom of their street would now be just a few metres from their side fence. In an instant the value and amenity of their home had been all but destroyed; yet all the government could offer was a landscaped earthern mound to minimise visual and noise pollution. 'What a sorry situation this is when a long-term resident of Malvern, who has lavished care and love on his family home, should be pleading to have it destroyed', Gottstein exclaimed in one of his many appeals to officials and politicians. For four and half anxious years the Gottsteins waged paper warfare until in 1984 Labor minister Steve Crabb at last agreed to purchase their home.[33]

By the time the Gottsteins' cheque arrived, the resistance of the last objectors had been bought off or defeated and the long-anticipated highway along Gardiner's Creek was under construction. But the long years of conflict had dented the resolve of the politicians too. While the Liberals were prepared to brave the opposition of Labor-voting residents of the inner suburbs, they were more circumspect with their own supporters in Malvern. Only after the defeat of the Thompson

Government in 1982, and the election of the Labor government of John Cain junior, was the impasse at least partially resolved.

Labor had come to power on promises to revitalise public transport, and to oppose further freeway construction. Meanwhile the ever-swelling traffic from the Mulgrave Freeway continued to discharge into the side streets and back streets of Malvern, generating almost as much frustration among local residents as it did among motorists seeking passage towards Toorak Road where the South-Eastern Freeway began. The new Minister for Transport, Steve Crabb, pledged not to build a freeway but he did the next best thing. The 'South-Eastern Arterial' was a four-lane, dual carriage highway. It followed the same route as the projected F14, but, without the grade separations of a fully engineered freeway, the traffic regularly stopped at traffic lights. A freeway with traffic lights was like a striptease show: it simultaneously stimulated the desire for mobility while frustrating its satisfaction. Sooner or later the pressure of traffic and discontent would become irresistible and the South-Eastern Arterial would grow up into a full-scale freeway. In the meantime, nothing could have better symbolised the difficulties of Melburnians in the 1970s and 1980s in attempting to reconcile the realities of the machine age with the ideals of the Garden State. By the early 1990s a new and turbulent political force appeared, ready to deliver them from their dilemma.

10
On the Move?

The urban freeway was a road paved with good intentions. It symbolised the modernist dream of a city endowed with the power and
efficiency of a finely tuned machine. To its friends it signified speed,
opportunity, material prosperity. Its enemies feared that, for all those
good intentions, the freeway led to an urban hell of environmental
waste, pollution, noise, social fragmentation and isolation. As fast as
the car accelerated personal movement, it divided neighbourhoods,
deepened social divisions and wasted scarce resources. In the 1970s and
1980s Melbourne was transfixed by this dilemma, caught, as a visiting
transport planner observed, between 'strong-centred' and 'weak-
centred' policies of development.[1] Its truncated freeways and run-down
public transport were a monument to that unresolved dilemma.

By the early 1980s the postwar Keynesian model of development that
had sustained Melbourne's growth through the 1950s, 1960s and 1970s
was running down. For almost 30 years, the city had enjoyed a long
postwar boom based on high levels of immigration, foreign investment,
tariff protection, full employment and state provision of roads, public
housing, schooling and other public services. No industry was more
fundamental to this process than the car industry. No technology
was more critical to the process of metropolitan expansion than the
car itself.

In the 1970s public opinion underwent a seismic shift. Disenchantment with the Vietnam War, deepening gloom about the depletion of
natural resources, and the slowing of the world economy reinforced a

growing conviction that the old engine of development was becoming obsolete. In 1981 John Cain, son of a former Labor premier, became the first non-Liberal to head a Victorian government for almost 30 years. Like its Liberal predecessors, the Cain Government sought to reconcile the demand for renewed economic growth with care for the environment. Public investment and state planning remained pillars of government policy. Melbourne enjoyed a new surge of growth in the late 1980s, fuelled largely by a speculative boom in property and shares. The stock market crash of 1987 sounded a first warning. Then, in the early 1990s, the boom collapsed. In scenes reminiscent of the great land boom and bust of the 1890s, several major financial institutions, including the Pyramid Building Society and the State Bank, were forced into liquidation or sale.

Cain resigned and was replaced by Victoria's first female premier, former community activist Joan Kirner, in August 1990. Kirner's grass-roots skills and maternal style made her a leader better able to absorb the shock of change than to redirect it. With rapidly escalating state debt and a stagnant economy, the Kirner Government was desperate to staunch the outward flow of capital and population, to kick-start the main engine of growth, metropolitan Melbourne, and to stem the loss of revenue from the state's depleted coffers. In an era of free trade and global competition, Melbourne could no longer hide behind tariff walls or run up further debt. Yet without public investment in infrastructure, cultural institutions and tourist facilities its capital might fall off the international map of tourism and investment.

Desperation forced the Kirner Government to abandon some cherished local traditions. Braving the wrath of the wowsers, it invited bids for the state's first casino licence. Abandoning a long tradition of state enterprise, it investigated the feasibility of inviting private companies to build and operate a new system of urban roads, to be financed by a 3 per cent petrol levy. In May 1992 it announced its intention of constructing the Western and Southern bypasses and in September, just before the state elections, it released the short list of preferred developers. How the $1 billion road system was to be paid for was still vague, although one of the consortia indicated its interest in an electronic toll.[2] The Kirner Government was also eager to reposition Melbourne in the competition for global commerce. It appointed businessman and former lord mayor Ron Walker to coordinate a program of major events designed to lure tourists and investors to the city. The foundations of a coming revolution in public management were dug by a Labor government prepared to shred its traditional principles in a desperate effort to hang on to power.[3]

In October 1992 Liberal leader Jeffrey Kennett won government in a landslide victory over an exhausted and discredited Labor Party, the 'Guilty Party' as the Liberals dubbed them. Like Labor's John Cain, Kennett was an old Scotch Collegian, but his road to the premiership, via army service in Malaya, his own suburban advertising agency and ten frustrating years in and out of the Opposition leadership, had reinforced his impatience with the inertia and compromise of his predecessors. His brash populist style invited comparisons with the state's longest-serving Liberal leader, Henry Bolte, who had presided over the city's last heroic era of expansion in the 1950s and 1960s. In homage to his mentor, Kennett even reinstalled Bolte's old desk in his office at Parliament House. Both premiers had a passion for promotion, for 'selling Victoria' and an ability to reach beyond the Liberals' traditional middle-class constituency.

From the first, Kennett displayed a determination to break with the past. Victoria had resisted the neo-liberal reforms associated with Thatcher and Reagan longer than most Australian states, but in the early 1990s it quickly outpaced all others in its zeal to downsize, privatise, outsource and deregulate state activity. Many of the old state bureaucracies, including the Country Roads Board (Roads Corporation) and Metropolitan Board of Works (Melbourne Water), were pruned and corporatised. Trams, trains, electricity and gas were turned over to private companies. Melbourne's 55 local government areas were reduced to 31, the membership and powers of their elected councils curtailed and their services compulsorily let out to tender.[4]

Jeff Kennett's was a cultural as much as a political revolution. As an old advertising man, he had an instinctive feel for the power of symbols. In 1994 he changed the motto on the number plates of the state's cars from 'Victoria—The Garden State' (in green on white) to 'Victoria— *On the Move*' (in Liberal blue). 'The Garden State' had been Dick Hamer's slogan, selected in the 1970s when 'quality of life' was the issue of the day. Even then, the slogan was not new. A New South Wales politician had once called Victoria, derisively, 'the Cabbage Patch'. In the 1930s the Victorian Tourist Bureau had advertised Melbourne as the 'dignified' and 'stately' 'Garden City of a Garden State'.[5] The title called to mind Melbourne's glorious green belt of public parks, its neat suburban gardens and nature strips, its aspiration to blend urban and industrial progress with the softening influence of nature. Hamer's successors, both Liberal and Labor, happily stuck with it. By exhorting Victorians to get 'On the Move' Kennett signalled his determination to break sharply with his moderate predecessors. From being to doing, from vegetating to accelerating, from gridlock to full throttle, Kennett not only wanted to change how Victoria was ruled, but how its people thought about themselves and their metropolis.[6]

The change of character was more than skin deep, but less than fundamental. In the 1950s and 1960s, Bolte's heyday, Melbourne had become the main Australian beachhead for the adoption of modern American-style patterns of industrial organisation, consumerism, management and urban development, a paradigm sometimes called 'Fordism'. This was also the period when modernism, the aesthetic movement that patterned itself upon the values of the machine age, was also in the ascendant in the city's architecture, art, film and social commentary.[7]

In the 1990s, some commentators suggest, Melbourne entered a second revolution, away from the old production-line manufacturing industries, and the model of Keynesian economic management on which they rested, towards a more decentralised service economy, based on new information technologies and on the ever-accelerating global flows of money, goods, information and people. This structural shift, from a Fordist to a post-Fordist economy, produced corresponding changes in how the city was governed as well as how it looked. While the modernist city was shaped by processes of rational planning and civic participation, the postmodernist city exhibited a preference for market mechanisms and state partnerships with private corporations. Modernism had promoted a functionalist aesthetic governed by the principle that 'less is more'. Kennett's new Melbourne was 're-imaged as a city of spectacle', designed in accordance with a postmodernist aesthetic of playfulness, fragmentation, pastiche and illusion. The 'Kennett Revolution', the argument goes, mirrored a change in the structure of the city itself.[8]

This is a persuasive perspective, although the relationship between the shifts in Melbourne's economy and those in its politics and culture may have been more complex than in the Los Angeles from which this theorising derives.[9] By the 1980s the Hawke Government's phased withdrawal of protection for the local car industry was beginning to reconfigure the city's industrial belt. The shift from trade to service occupations apparent in all Australian cities was especially marked in Melbourne.[10] From my window in Monash's Ming Wing I look towards the now-empty carparks of the Nissan manfacturing plant at Westall. But if the city's first industrial revolution was on the wane, the shift to the new information economy had still not progressed far. The flows of investment and tourism that would sustain the new 'city of spectacle' were still only a trickle, compared, for example, with those already coursing through contemporary Sydney.[11] The Kennett Revolution was not a manifestation of structural change so much as a political campaign to hasten its arrival.[12]

THE DREAM EVENT

Kennett was a politician in a hurry, and he instilled his government with an almost manic commitment to change. Determined to shake off the crippling inertia of his predecessors, the new premier sometimes seemed more interested in generating momentum than in plotting a direction. 'Kennett's was the politics of perpetual motion', his biographer Tony Parkinson acutely observes.[13]

If the Kennett Revolution had a natural symbol it was the automobile. The historic link between economic liberalism and automobility had always been strong, but Kennett exploited the symbolism of the car more provocatively than any previous Australian leader. The smell of benzine seemed to rouse his native recklessness. On a European tour, he made a point of visiting the Ferrari plant and took a spin in the latest model. At a ceremony to mark the first turning of the sod for CityLink, his new privatised toll road, he impulsively took up a shovel and sprayed sand over the attending journalists and television crews. Cars even seemed to play a part in the political accidents that dogged his erratic drive to power. In 1987 an electronic eavesdropper's report of an uninhibited carphone conversation with his friend Andrew Peacock brought Kennett's contempt for Liberal leader John Howard embarrassingly into the open. A controversy occasioned by the free 'loan' of a BMW car to his wife Felicity highlighted the sometimes hazy line he drew between business and government.[14]

In 1994 Kennett's close associate, casino proprietor and Liberal Party treasurer Ron Walker, scored a promotional coup by luring the

Australian Formula One Grand Prix from Adelaide to Melbourne. This, said Kennett, was his 'dream event', the pick of the program of major events that Walker had selected to put Melbourne on the map.[15] 'It will add energy to our society, build confidence among the people, create jobs, add to our economic wealth and position this city internationally as no other event could', he enthused. Just to make sure the message was clear, Kennett and Walker located the race as close to the city centre as possible, in picturesque Albert Park, within sight of the CBD.

The park had once been a swamp but in the 1840s Victoria's first governor, Charles Joseph La Trobe, set it aside as a park for 'the Recreation of the People'. The swamp was drained and planted with trees, a billabong was shaped into an ornamental lake and serpentine carriage drives were wrapped around the shore. In the booming 1880s fashionable couples drove around the lake in imitation of London's famous equestrian promenade, Rotten Row. In the twentieth century organised sport began to compete with more passive recreations for use of the park. Rowing and sailing clubs erected their clubhouses by the water while cricket, football and tennis players annexed small sections from the still-ample acres of unspoiled parkland. In the 1950s, the golden age of mass motoring, when Kennett and Walker were still schoolboys, Albert Park was briefly used as a motor racing track. British ace Stirling Moss, Australia's Jack Brabham and Frenchman Jean Behra chased each other around the lake in a memorable contest for the 1956 Australian Grand Prix. But local residents were restive and after the 1958 Grand Prix, Henry Bolte banished the open-wheel racers to Sandown on the south-eastern fringe of the metropolis.[16]

Now the cars and drivers were about to return, noisier and smellier than ever. Soon rows of pits and grandstands would appear beside the lake. Three hundred trees would be felled to make way for a new indoor sports and aquatic centre. The carriage road would be reshaped into S-bends and chicanes. The scent of eucalypts would be drowned by petrol fumes and the warble of magpies by the deafening whine of racing engines.

Seldom in Melbourne's long car wars had the Machine so rudely invaded the Garden. Melbourne's favourite cartoonist Michael Leunig fashioned a whimsical symbol of protest, by planting a flower garden in an old car.[17] Local residents began what became a 1500-day vigil guarding a children's playground in the path of the builders.[18] In December 1994, over six thousand people attended a 'Save Albert Park' rally to oppose the felling of further trees. Over 100 protesters were arrested.[19]

To the protesters, the Grand Prix was not just an unwelcome invasion of their park. It was, one observed, 'part of an ethos that I find abhorrent—the ethos of speed, waste, noise, thrill-seeking, danger and death'.[20] Not everyone shared his abhorrence. 'Get a job', 'Shoot the bloody lot of them', passing motorists sometimes shouted at the dogged protesters. 'Keep Albert Park for the people' the saviours of Albert Park had demanded. But many people—perhaps even a majority—preferred speed, danger and thrill-seeking to quiet rambles and birdsong. They had a powerful ally. 'The park is not the possession of a few, it is for the enjoyment of many', the populist premier declared.[21]

THE ELECTRONIC SUPERHIGHWAY

'On the Move' was a slogan that expressed Melbourne's aspiration to become a part of the emerging global economy. In the age of the internet and 'just in time' technology, there was no more vital indicator of a city's economic health than the timely movement of people, goods and information along its roads, and through its docks and airport. As Australia's largest container port and a major manufacturing base, Melbourne was more dependent than most cities on the smoothness of these linkages. Yet by the early 1990s, after a decade of paralysis in transport policy, the congestion on the city's roads was reportedly growing worse. The RACV, which had been measuring traffic delays since the 1940s, claimed that peak travel on the Tullamarine Freeway had increased by 28 per cent between 1986 and 1992.[22] Every morning and evening long columns of stationary cars choked its freeways. Businessmen grew apoplectic at the sight of heavily loaded trucks queued on the Swan Street Bridge, the tightest bottleneck on the conduit between the city's eastern and western industrial zones. The South-Eastern Arterial, the freeway with traffic lights, even became known as 'The South-Eastern Carpark'.

In 1993 Kennett announced an ambitious plan to get Melbourne once more 'on the move'. When it first assumed office, his government had recoiled from the financial costs of enacting its Labor predecessor's expensive highway plans. Then it found a solution that would give the city its new road without the government having to pay for it. CityLink, as the $1.2 billion project was known, would become the world's largest privately constructed, privately owned and privately operated toll road. It would ease movement between the airport, city and docks, and dramatically cut car travel times. The Tullamarine and Westgate freeways would be widened and upgraded. The South-Eastern Arterial would become a six-lane freeway. All three highways would be linked via cross-city tunnels and bridges into an integrated metropolitan highway system. The most ambitious and expensive features of the scheme were the twin tunnels linking the South-Eastern and Westgate between Burnley and South Melbourne. Motorists would pay a toll for access to the road, not by stopping to pay coins at a toll booth, but through a newly developed electronic system that monitored patrons' passage along the road through transponders ('e-TAG' devices) fitted to their cars. Each month the cost of travel would be billed to the user's account. Like that other electronic superhighway, the internet, CityLink demonstrated the capacity of digital technology to increase the speed and volume of communications. Like the internet, too, it produced changes, at first subtle and increasingly profound, in the social geography and outlook of the city.[23]

As striking as the technology of the new road were its boldly postmodern aesthetics. Visitors arriving at Melbourne International Airport approached the city along Melbourne's first freeway, now upgraded as part of CityLink. Widening the road had removed the trees, rocks and grassy verges designed in the 1960s by the landscape architect Ellis Stones for the old Tullamarine Freeway. Sheer concrete walls now reared on either side, shielding neighbouring residents from the thunder of cars and lorries, and screening motorists from the sight of the Moonee Ponds Creek that still ran invisibly along the valley behind the concrete walls. At Flemington Bridge, the boundary of the City of Melbourne, architect John Denton, designer of several other Kennett monuments, created a symbolic gateway to the city. On the right, a row of tilting red sticks suggested a postmodern avenue of honour, while, from the left, a massive yellow beam leant across the carriageway in an ironic salute.

Functionality and illusion were cunningly entwined in the architecture of CityLink. Its purpose was to deceive as well as to display. The red poles and yellow beam drew the visitor's eye away from an untidy jumble of roads, bridges, drains and railway viaducts. Veering west, the highway threaded an elliptical metal tube, perforated like an enormous

'Designed to be seen at the speed we live our lives', this striking sculptural gateway greets visitors travelling down CityLink from Melbourne Airport to the city, diverting their gaze from ancient Moonee Ponds Creek flowing, more sluggishly, through a concrete drain underneath.

cheese-grater and angled to deflect traffic noise from the nearby Debney's Park high-rise public housing estate. From the elevated carriageway motorists glimpsed the monuments of Kennett's new Melbourne: the apartment towers of the revived Docklands, Colonial Stadium, the Exhibition Centre, popularly known as 'Jeff's Shed', and Crown Casino. Then soaring above the Yarra, between the giant goalposts of Bolte Bridge, they surveyed the city from an exciting new angle. CityLink was both symbol and a scenic gateway for the new Melbourne of spectacle and play.

It was also the product of a unique political moment. In 1993, when the project was announced, the government had recently shaved the state's budget by 9 per cent. Within four years, the budget was back in balance. In the meantime, however, it was impossible, politically if not financially, for the state to borrow funds for such a massive project. It could not pour millions of tonnes of concrete while it was sacking schoolteachers and closing hospital wards. Financial exigency alone might not have required the great privatisation experiment. But both

Kennett and his Treasurer, Alan Stockdale, were firmly committed to an 'enterprise culture' that preferred private enterprise to public. The state's financial necessity provided the opportunity to put those beliefs into action.

CityLink was a frontal attack on the long Victorian tradition of public enterprise, and became the self-defined 'high-water mark' of the government's reform agenda.[24] For as long as anyone remembered, state or local governments had built the city's roads, using day labour and raising the funds from rates, taxes, federal grants or loans. CityLink was a radical application of a free market recipe for the provision of infrastructure known, for short, as BOOT. Governments should steer, not row, argued the neo-liberals. They should get out of the business of building and operating urban infrastructure, and contract with private companies to Build, Own, Operate and, at the end of the contract period, Transfer the asset back into state ownership. The government would set the terms of the contract and monitor the company's compliance, but otherwise leave the private sector to run the business as it thought fit.

Kennett had embarked on the nation's biggest and boldest private road project at the very moment when other state governments were beginning to rue their own more modest experiments in privatisation. Sydneysiders were shocked when their state's Auditor-General revealed that they would pay more than $4 billion in tolls before the Harbour Tunnel constructed by the Transfield-Obayashi consortium was paid off. In Queensland, Labor premier Wayne Goss had proposed the construction by private contractors of a new toll road linking Brisbane and the Gold Coast. Conservationists mounted an impassioned campaign to save the coastal forests and their furry inhabitants from the new highway. The koalas were saved but the votes of the protesters tipped the Goss Government from office.[25]

Selling CityLink to a sceptical press and public was one of the government's biggest political challenges. In May 1995 the Melbourne CityLink Authority, the body appointed to oversee the project, placed full-page advertisements in the Melbourne dailies. A vividly coloured map depicted the city of Melbourne in the form of a gigantic, and apparently sclerotic, human heart joined by three large arteries labelled 'Tullamarine Freeway', 'Westgate Freeway' and 'South-Eastern Arterial'. 'LIFE WILL CERTAINLY IMPROVE ONCE WE HAVE A TRIPLE BY-PASS', it read.

Premier Jeff Kennett surveys his 'dream project'. (AGE PHOTOS)

> The major arteries leading to the very heart of our city are becoming increasingly clogged. The traffic delays increasingly unproductive. And the exhaust fumes, noise and fuel wastage increasingly difficult to swallow—for businesses and commuters alike.
>
> It's a situation that poses a threat not only to our traditionally high living standards but also to our personal and financial health. And it won't be improved by the estimated 250 000 additional vehicles that will be on our roads by the year 2000.

The message was clear: without an urgent bypass operation Melbourne would suffer a heart attack, perhaps even die.[26]

It was an arresting and, some considered, tasteless image. In 1969, the Melbourne Transportation Study had produced a promotional film with uncannily similar imagery. Against a crescendo of discordant traffic noises, the film alternated rapidly between images of chaotic peak-time traffic and a graphic of a rapidly pulsing heart. As it reached its climax, the noise grew louder, the pulse more rapid, and the heart swelled ominously as the city teetered on the edge of cardiac arrest. Both propaganda exercises drew, perhaps too obviously to be plausible, upon the classic image of the city as a human body. Some readers were

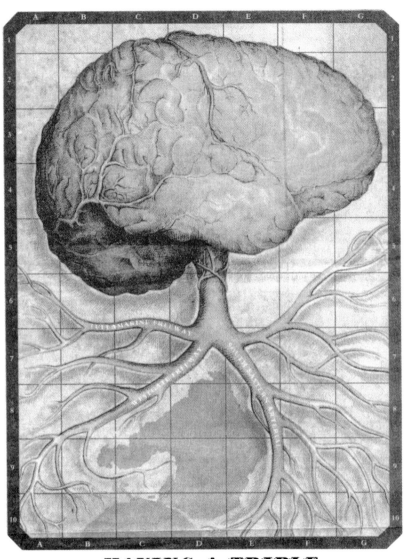

HAVING A TRIPLE BY-PASS WILL DO WONDERS FOR YOUR SANITY.

By offering surgical treatment for Melbourne's congested 'heart', CityLink promised to extend the city's life as well as 'do wonders' for its motorists' sanity.
(MELBOURNE CITYLINK AUTHORITY)

troubled by the anatomical explicitness ('awful offal') of the CityLink advertisement. Others challenged its political implications. A city is not just a heart, some objected. What about its lungs that were slowly being poisoned with petrol fumes? A bypass was not a cure, others added, but only a temporary reprieve. Did Melbourne need the 'high-tech' surgery of a bypass or some urban naturopathy? Certainly the patient was sick, another reader agreed. But perhaps the diagnosis was mistaken. 'My diagnosis suggests that Melbourne is suffering from an addiction peculiar to the 20th century. An addiction to the car.'[27]

After a short run, Kennett intervened to abort the $500 000 campaign. Ministers racked their brains for an alternative slogan. 'We're fixing up Labor's mess' was one suggestion. But by September, when the new billboards began to appear along the South-Eastern Arterial, the premier was back on message: 'We're clearing this carpark to get you . . . *ON THE MOVE*.'[28]

The symbolic convergence between CityLink and the government's neo-liberal political agenda was dramatised early in 1996 as the Kennett Government approached its first election. Transurban, the proprietor of CityLink, became the main sponsor of the first Melbourne Grand Prix. The Albert Park protesters were 'outraged' by the idea that this assault on their neighbourhood would be financed from motorists' toll revenues. Government ministers denied responsibility for the arrangement but expert observers were in no doubt about its benefits. 'It's a terrific opportunity and the Grand Prix has associations that are suitable for a road maker—speed, efficiency, hi-tech', observed advertising agent Peter Hickox.[29]

On the big day, 16 March, Kennett and Walker revelled in the high-octane excitement of their 'dream event'. 'Jeff, Jeff, Jeff' someone began to shout as they noticed the smiling premier. 'Jeff, Jeff, Jeff' the crowd took up the chant, as the revheads' hero looked down imperiously from the grandstand. Two weeks later the Kennett Government swept back to power.[30]

CityLink—For and Against

Like all revolutions, Kennett's incorporated old elements as well as new. Critics of CityLink portrayed it as a throwback to the 1950s and 1960s. It revived 'the dreams of 1950s road planners', said Ro Krivanek.

Public transport advocate Paul Mees saw it as a 'resurrection of the freeway plans of the 1960s'. Environmentalist John Stone feared that Melbourne was heading 'further down the old Los Angeles path'. They agreed that Melbourne had adopted an outdated solution to problems that other more progressive cities (Toronto was the critics' favorite model) had long since abandoned. Even Los Angeles, they argued, had lost faith in the urban freeway and was now reinvesting in public transport.[31]

Whether CityLink should be regarded as 'grandiose and obsolete' or 'bold and innovative' depended less on Melbourne's position in relation to other cities, than where the observer thought it *ought* to stand. Supporters of CityLink believed that Melbourne had long outgrown the centralised radial pattern of the old public transport city. It was now a decentralised metropolis where relatively few journeys were capable of being made by public transport. Only automobility could meet the transportation needs of the new world of electronic communication, information-based industries and just-in-time technology, and of a workforce increasingly geared to part-time, casual and mobile employment. 'Privacy', 'individuality' and 'flexibility' were the watchwords of the new urban paradigm. Transport planning must begin by examining individuals' actual travel demands, not by trying to fit their travel plans around an antiquated public transport system.[32]

Critics of CityLink began with different premises and reached opposing conclusions. Their planning horizon was dominated, not by the production and labour needs of global capitalism, but by the challenge of social and environmental sustainability. Their fears were not that Melbourne would be outpaced in the race for economic prosperity, but that it might become hostage to a dirty, wasteful and ultimately unsustainable technology, the automobile. Instead of strengthening community ties, the electronic superhighway reinforced a tendency to retreat into the privatised world of the home.[33] In approaching urban issues, the critics' natural bias was holistic. They began, not with the demands of the individual city-dweller, but with the characteristics of the urban system itself. Freeways, they argued, only reinforced the dependence of Melburnians on the car. Individuals' journey preferences were not the result of their own unmediated desires, but of previous locational decisions by firms, public institutions and transport providers. CityLink did not just satisfy the travel preferences of the city as it was; it was itself a powerful generator of longer and more wasteful journeys. While defenders of CityLink emphasised values of flexibility and opportunity, the critics' code-words were 'coordination', 'integration', 'equity', 'sustainability' and 'community'.

The lines of argument were not always as clear-cut as this. A few defenders of CityLink saw it as the first step towards a comprehensive system of road pricing that would finally force drivers to pay the full costs of motoring, including its social and environmental costs. Once every motorist had an e-TAG, the principle of 'user-pays' could be applied to every part of the road system, not just CityLink. They could be charged more to drive through congested parts of the city, so pushing some motorists to switch to public transport. For years public transport advocates had complained that motorists got a free ride by not having to pay the full costs of motoring. Here, some argued, was a way of evening up the competition.[34]

But CityLink was at best a partial and inequitable application of the doctrine of 'user-pays'. While some Melburnians would pay as they

Cartoonist Leunig contemplates potential new applications for the e-TAG, the electronic transponder that monitors motorists' usage of CityLink. (Courtesy Michael Leunig)

drove, the vast majority would continue to ride the city's high-speed roads for free. Rather than pay the toll, motorists could just take a little longer and pay no toll at all. In order to make the road system work, therefore, the government had to tilt the playing field heavily in the tollway's favour, with results—both economic and political—that could not easily be foreseen. Traffic on public roads would be regulated, not just to optimise travel times for everyone, but to enhance profitability for the company.

In a penetrating critique of such schemes economist John Quiggan argued that 'very few road schemes can be successfully financed by tolls unless the scope of the toll is extended to cover existing elements of the road network'. If the toll was high enough to generate enough revenue it was likely to be too high to encourage use without support-ing measures. This was especially so if the road was privately owned, since private investors would require a higher rate of return on their borrowings than the public sector which traditionally borrowed at lower rates over a longer term.[35] In order to secure Transurban's investment, and reassure the bankers, the government was obliged to make two major concessions. It agreed to abolish peak-time parking restrictions on nearby arterial roads in order to increase the attractiveness of the toll road. And it indemnified the company against the effects of future government-sponsored improvements in the public transport system, such as an airport rail link, that might affect the profitability of CityLink.

As they sized up the costs and benefits of the new toll road, and its likely impact on their daily lives, Melburnians recognised a radical realignment of forces in the city's car wars. CityLink pitted car-driving working-class battlers from the outer suburbs against cycling yuppies from the inner city. It won support from residents of outer suburban Knox, who continued to drive the toll-free outer section of the South-Eastern (Monash) Freeway, but antagonised middle- and working-class voters in Strathmore and Tullamarine, who now paid a toll to drive on a road they previously used without charge.[36] It pleased truckies and eastern suburbs holidaymakers seeking quick egress from the city onto the Westgate Freeway, but it infuriated the drivers and tram passengers creeping along arterial roads, such as Toorak Road and Mount Alexan-der Road, now clogged with toll-avoiding motorists. (This problem was only made worse by an agreement between Transurban and the govern-ment to remove clearways along a number of main roads in order to 'force' motorists onto the tollway. Soon the newly privatised tramways were threatening to sue the government for recovery of funds lost through their inability to meet the running schedules specified in their service agreements.)[37]

In the run-up to the 1996 election, many of Kennett's backbenchers feared that voter discontent with CityLink could unseat them. Polls predicted that the member for Tullamarine, Bernie Finn, the only Liberal representative on the north-west side of the city, would lose his seat. As the party room became more restive, ministers hinted at possible modifications of the scheme. Perhaps tolls could be left off existing roads like the Tullamarine Freeway, Planning Minister Robert Mac-Lellan suggested.[38] In November 1994 Kennett had faced a possible party room revolt over the tolls, but six months later his opponents had gone to water. There would be no deals or compromises. CityLink would be implemented as planned. Victorians would have to trust the hard-driving Man behind the Wheel or eject him from the driver's seat.

LEAKS AND GLITCHES

In 1996 the Kennett Revolution was still unfolding and Victorian voters, still reeling from its effects, were prepared nevertheless to give their premier the benefit of their mounting doubts. Despite the pain of public service sackings, the cuts to government services, the down-sizings and outsourcings, the people endorsed the premier's appeal for a second term. The hated CityLink tolls caused less political damage than the pundits had predicted. Even Bernie Finn, Liberal member for Tullamarine, miraculously survived.

During 1997 and 1998 work proceeded steadily on the survey and construction of the new road. Pleasure cruises on the Yarra were suspended while the river was diverted to facilitate work on the first of the cross-city tunnels. Residents in Richmond and South Melbourne protested against the environmental impact of the huge towers being erected to disperse polluted air from the Burnley Tunnel. Members of the Public Transport Users' Association planned legal challenges to the complex financial arrangements under which Transurban claimed federal government tax credits.

By mid-1999, as Kennett approached his third election, work on CityLink was lagging four months behind schedule. Construction costs, originally estimated at $1.2 billion, had blown out to nearly $2 billion. In order to reassure the public, and generate revenue for nervous investors in Transurban, Kennett authorised the opening of the western section of CityLink in August, six months ahead of the rest of the project.[39] Thousands of motorists crawled at 20 km/h single-file across the Bolte Bridge to take in a view that, as regular users, they would scarcely glimpse. 'Today is a red letter day for this state', the premier exulted. 'The believers have won and the doubting Thomases have got egg all over their faces.' It was the most satisfying day of his 23 years in politics, he told radio interviewer Neil Mitchell—better even than his two election victories, for CityLink was an achievement that would live for 500 years.[40]

Recent news had offered little to reassure the doubting Thomases. Motorists who phoned for e-TAGs were angered by mistakes, delays and overcharging. There were so many glitches in the sophisticated computer system designed to monitor traffic on the toll road that the company eventually decided to let customers ride toll-free until the problems were corrected.[41] Then came the worst news of all: the Burnley Tunnel, the most expensive and critical section of the road, had sprung a leak. Building a tunnel through wet and unstable ground deep below the Yarra was an inherently risky operation. Almost from its beginning the project was beset by accidents and delays. In order to contain costs, the constructors, Transfield-Obayashi Joint Venture (TOJV) had decided on a flat-bottomed tunnel rather than an inherently stronger cylindrical one. Now groundwater had begun to pour through the seams of the tunnel and buckle the concrete plates along the floor. Engineers quizzed international experts on how to fix the problem while Transurban began legal proceedings against TOJV to recover damages for the delay. Opposition Transport spokesman Peter Batchelor predicted that the whole of the road surface of the Burnley Tunnel might have to be replaced.[42]

Despite these setbacks, Kennett entered the 1999 election campaign a firm favourite. He had weathered the shocks of his first term, and now seemed poised to reap the electoral benefits of Melbourne's new dynamism and growth. The bold plan to privatise the city's public transport system had been realised and the last publicly operated train drew out of Flinders Street station just two weeks before polling day.[43] Undeterred by the setbacks of CityLink, Kennett was eager to maintain the pace of reform. In his next term he promised to complete the

Scoresby Bypass, the eastern section of a new outer suburban ring-road, and to engage private developers to build, own and operate a new toll road joining the Eastern and Tullamarine freeways. Rather than disturb the magpies and possums of the Mullum Mullum Valley or the gentry of Carlton, these new roads would be buried, like CityLink, in long underground tunnels.

For all its flaws, CityLink probably had more friends than enemies among Melbourne voters. But the more attention the premier, and the metropolitan press, lavished on big projects in the capital, the more resentful became electors in country and regional Victoria. Labor had recently elected a new leader, the modest Ballarat-born Steve Bracks, who astutely pitched his campaign to the disenchanted regions as well as the swinging voters in Melbourne suburbs. CityLink was not a major factor in the campaign and, when the results were in, only one seat—Tullamarine—seems to have changed hands because of voters' discontent with the road.[44] But rural resentment of the premier's fixation on Melbourne, and neglect of country Victoria, was enough to unseat the government. While the government's vote fell in working-class electorates, its support in the party's middle-class heartland held firm.[45] Melburnians had grown so accustomed to their premier's 'crash-through' political style that when he finally spun off the track, and retired from the political race, they were not quite sure whether to be disappointed or relieved.

In opposition, Labor had promised to renegotiate the CityLink agreement. Perhaps the new government would even buy the company out, and restore the road to the people. But the Kennett Revolution was not to be so easily rolled back. It would cost at least $7 billion to buy back CityLink, Labor's Transport Minister Peter Batchelor estimated. Like his predecessor, he recognised that public roads came well behind public schools and hospitals in the eyes of most voters. 'I can't cancel the tolls, but I'm not going to fall in love with them', he admitted.[46] Riding his bike to work each day, Batchelor was the very model of a modern Labor transport minister. But even he was unwilling to challenge the hegemony of the car.

The new government arm-wrestled the federal government for the funds to build the Scoresby Bypass and the Ringwood extension of the Eastern Freeway. After receiving the results of an economic feasi-bility study of the Tullamarine rail link, it quietly buried the project. On the most costly and contentious of Kennett's election promises—a new tunnel linking the Eastern and Tullamarine freeways under Carlton and Royal Park—the minister played for time. Extending the Eastern Freeway and linking it to the Scoresby Bypass would only increase the volume of traffic disgorging into the inner city. Already over 60 000 vehicles a day (60 per cent more than when the freeway opened in 1978) were crossing the river in each direction. A Northern Central City Corridor Study was established, with representation from community groups, to examine a range of alternative proposals.

Environmental and public transport activists, traditionally hostile to freeways, were almost as reluctant to sanction a freeway under their own backyards as they had been to have one running through them. A tunnel might divert traffic from their streets, but it only reinforced the city's unhealthy dependence on the car. The anti-freeway campaigners of the 1970s were united in a cause that was both local and global: defence of the neighbourhood (and their own real estate) was also a blow against the environmental dangers of mass automobilisation. Now, it seemed, the engineers had come up with a scheme that offered the locals protection from traffic but only at massive cost and by reinforcing the city's already heavy dependence on the car.

The mood within the reference groups established to gauge community reaction was cautious rather than angry. Much had changed since the *grand journées* of 1977, when indignant inner city residents had barricaded Alexandra Parade with the carcases of old cars, and dared police and road officials to remove them. It was hard to see the owners of the BMWs and Range Rovers now parked outside the terraces of Carlton and Fitzroy as potential protesters. Even harder to believe that they would oppose an underground freeway that actually dispersed traffic from their streets. The activists might win some concessions— more bus routes, for example—but sooner or later, it seemed, the engineers would have their way and the loose ends of the city's truncated freeway system would be tied up.[47]

Little by little, the map of the metropolis was changing as businesses and people reoriented themselves to the new equations of time, money and opportunity presented by the city's mix of toll roads, freeways, arterial roads and public transport. By freeing the motorist from the tyranny of the public transport timetable, the freeway offered the prospect of high-speed movement across the metropolis. By the 1990s many Melburnians regularly travelled 30 or 40 kilometres a day from home to work. Public transport became the transport mode of choice only for children, old people and the poor. CityLink created a new class distinction, between those motorists who could afford, or were obliged to pay, for access to an exclusive form of high-speed transport, the tollway, and those who were obliged to negotiate the increasingly crowded freeways and arterial road system. Some workers were supplied with e-TAGs by their bosses; others, who needed them just as much, paid them as a non-tax-deductible cost of employment out of their own pockets. Life may have improved, thanks to the city's triple bypass, but it had also become more complicated.

Most people, including the government, believe that Melbourne should lessen its dependence on the car. The city's latest plan, Melbourne 2030, anticipates a doubling of the proportion of people using public transport over the next 30 years. The privatisation of the system carried through by the Kennett Government, however, has gradually unraveled, and private operators have either relinquished their franchises or demanded a massive increase in the state subsidy to stay in business. The increased costs of saving the public transport system ($2.5 million per annum) were enough to jeopardise the Bracks Government's long-declared commitment to maintaining public funding of the road system. When the Commonwealth finally provided the funds to subsidise the construction of the Scoresby Bypass, the Victorian Government was no longer able to afford to contribute its share of the project's increased cost. It had faced an invidious choice: build the road and let the public transport system collapse, or maintain the public transport system and either cut the new road or follow the example of Labor's loathed predecessor and privatise it. Not building the road would enrage voters in the marginal outer suburban electorates; allowing the public transport system to collapse would alienate the party's inner suburban heartland. In April 2003 Premier Bracks apologetically announced an abrupt U-turn: the government would proceed with the Scoresby Bypass as a privatised toll road, built on the same basis as CityLink, save that no changes would be made to the arterial road system to force drivers onto the new road.[48] Now, unexpectedly, both sides of politics were committed, with varying degrees of enthusiasm, to the principle of requiring motorists, as well as public transport users, to pay as they go. Neo-liberalism had made an improbable alliance with environmentalism. Was this decision the last step towards realising the dreams of the 1960s highway planners, or the first step towards a more comprehensive system of road pricing?

ON THE MOVE—WHERE?

Everyone knows the story of the motorist driving down a country road who stops to ask an old-timer the way. 'Well', the oldster says, scratching his head, 'if I wanted to go *there*, I wouldn't have started out from *here*'. In the half-century since the advent of mass motoring most Melburnians cheerfully embraced the spirit of automobilism, confident that they were heading somewhere they wanted to go.

The pleasures of the car are mostly instant pleasures. Sit behind the wheel, feel the exhilarating sense of speed and power, enjoy the inviting prospect of the open road. Only later, as the road fills with traffic and your life is locked into drivetime, as the scenery changes and neighbourhood ties begin to fray, do you realise that the road you thought you took is not the road on which you are now driving.

The enemies of the car believe that we are already too far down the wrong road to turn back. The costs of recovering the world's already depleted supplies of oil will soon become prohibitive. Holes in the ozone layer will kill off the car if they don't kill off the motorists first. The car's defenders, on the other hand, point to the significant reduction in pollution through cleaner-burning engines and more efficient exhausts. Before the world's oil runs out, they say, engineers will have developed new cars that run on hydrogen, sugar cane or solar batteries. Only if you can foretell the destination of the road can you decide whether it is the wrong one.

In fact we don't have to wait till we reach the end of the road, or spin disastrously off it, to review the journey so far. CityLink was a vivid demonstration of the enormous sacrifices that Melburnians have been prepared, or persuaded, to make in order to keep their city on the move. Even its costs pale beside the countless billions more that have been spent on vehicles, roads, traffic engineering and policing since World War II. Some of the biggest costs cannot be measured in dollars at all. How should we weigh the almost 40 000 lives lost and the approximately three-quarters of a million injuries sustained in car accidents on Victoria's roads since 1945? Or assess more subtle changes, such as the slow transformation of our streets from places of play and gossip to lifeless traffic corridors? What price do we put on the loss of personal safety and community feeling? And how do we calculate the costs to our health through the steady accumulation of hydrocarbons in the atmosphere? Then, having totted up the massive costs of automobility, how will we balance them against the equally incalculable benefits: the opportunities given, friends met, deals done, dollars earned, dreams fulfilled? Or set that balance against the unknown pains and pleasures of the road we did not take?

As I have shown in these pages, Melbourne did not succumb to the charms of the car without vigorous, and sometimes bitter, debates. With hindsight, the triumph of the car may seem effortless, even inevitable. By the 1990s more than 80 per cent of daily journeys in Melbourne were made by car, and more than 50 per cent of households had two or more cars. But the victory of the car was neither uncontested nor absolute.

Melbourne is not the most automobilised city in Australia— that dubious honour is shared by Brisbane and Perth. Thanks to the retention of its historic tramway system, the eighth largest in the world, its inner suburbs retain some of the most pleasant strip shopping centres and attractive housing in Australia, and their attractions are increasing. European ideals of density and cosmopolitanism have displaced American ideals of space and segregation in the middle-class imagination.[49]

From the beginning, cars were sources of contention as well as objects of desire. Whether they were debating drink-driving or joy-riding, drive-ins or freeways, petrol taxes or electronic tolls, people were coming up against the same dilemma: how to reconcile the new freedom of automobilism with personal safety, social cohesion and environmental survival. Glancing in the rear-view mirror to see how we settled those debates may help us navigate the road ahead.

At the moment, freedom seems to have won the battle of ideas. The car is now as triumphant as the liberal ideals with which it has danced so intimately these past twenty years. Together they have become so deeply entwined in our consciousness that we find it hard to think them away.

But our long drive is not over yet. Already there are signs that the rich are tiring of the long commute and embracing the delights of urban density. Walking or cycling to work from a warehouse apartment, drinking caffe latte in a sidewalk café, sociability rather than seclusion are the new urban ideals. Now it is the poor, marooned in far suburbs, who are most dependent on their cars, and most vulnerable to the rising costs of urban sprawl. Slowly we are turning the steering wheel towards a new urban destination. We may all still arrive safely, but there could be better places to start than here.

Abbreviations

ANU   Australian National University
ARRB   Australian Roads Research Board
CPP   Commonwealth Parliamentary Papers
MUP   Melbourne University Press
OUP   Oxford University Press
PRO   Victorian Public Record Office
SLV   State Library of Victoria
VPD   Victorian Parliamentary Debates
VPP   Victorian Parliamentary Papers
VPRS   Victorian Public Record Series

AAA   Australian Automobile Association
CAF   Citizens Against Freeways
CBD   central business district
CDA   City Development Association
CRB   Country Roads Board
CUA   Committee for Urban Action
DMR   Department of Main Roads (NSW)
GMH   General Motors Holden's
MCC   Melbourne City Council
MTC   Metropolitan Transportation Committee
MTP   Metropolitan Transportation Plan
MTS   Melbourne Transportation Study
MMTB   Melbourne and Metropolitan Tramways Board

MMBW Melbourne and Metropolitan Board of Works
NRMA National Roads & Motorists' Association
RACV Royal Automobile Club of Victoria
TAC Transport Accident Commission
TCPA Town and Country Planning Association
TRB Transport Regulation Board
VFAG Valley Freeway Action Group

Notes

Introduction

1 *Royalauto*, May 1966, p. 21.

2 A. D. Hope, *Poems*, Viking Press, New York, 1961, p. 114.

3 Stephen Bayley, *Sex, Drink, and Fast Cars: The Creation and Consumption of Images*, Pantheon Books, Faber & Faber, London, 1986, p. 8.

4 Peter Marsh and Peter Collett, *Driving Passion: The Psychology of the Car*, Jonathan Cape, London, 1986, p. 5.

5 Wolfgang Sachs, *For Love of the Automobile: Looking Back into the History of Our Desires*, University of California Press, Berkeley, 1992, p. vii.

6 Charles Pickett (ed.), *Cars and Culture: Our Driving Passions*, Harper-Collins/Powerhouse Museum, Sydney, 1998

7 Marshall Berman, *All That Is Solid Melts into Air: The Experience of Modernity*, Verso, London, 1983, pp. 15–16. For a parallel discussion see Graeme Davison, 'The Modern and Melbourne' in Lynette Finch and Chris McConville (eds), *Gritty Cities: Images of the Urban*, Pluto Press, Sydney, 1999, pp. 45–64.

8 Graeme Davison, *The Rise and Fall of Marvellous Melbourne*, Melbourne University Press, Melbourne, 1978, p. 16.

9 Edward Soja, *Postmodern Geographies: The Reassertion of Space in Critical Social Theory*, Verso, London, 1989, chapters 7–8; David Harvey, *The Condition of Postmodernity*, Blackwell, Oxford, 1989, pp. 121–72. For local commentaries within this theoretical frame see Michael Berry, 'The Political Economy of Australian Cities' and Louise Johnson, 'The Postmodern Australian City' in Louise Johnson (ed.), *Suburban Dreaming: An Interdisciplinary Approach to Australian Cities*, Deakin University Press, Waurn Ponds, 1994, pp. 33–72.

10 Graeme Davison, Tony Dingle and Seamus O'Hanlon, *The Cream Brick Frontier: Histories of Australian Suburbia*, Monash Publications in History no. 19, Clayton, 1995.

Chapter 1: Dream Machines

1 The appeal of modernism in the 1950s is one of the themes of essays in Judith O'Callaghan (ed.), *The Australian Dream: Design of the Fifties*, Powerhouse Museum, Sydney, 1993. The postwar pursuit of the dream house is discussed in Alastair Greig, *The Stuff Dreams Are Made Of: Housing Provision in Australia 1945–1960*, Melbourne University Press, Melbourne, 1995; Barbara Davison and Graeme Davison, 'Suburban Pioneers' in Graeme Davison, Tony Dingle and Seamus O'Hanlon (eds), *The Cream Brick Frontier: Histories of Australian Suburbia*, Monash Publications in History no. 19, Clayton, 1995, pp. 41–50.

2 Kate Darian-Smith, *On the Home Front: Melbourne in Wartime 1939–1945*, OUP, Melbourne, 1990, p. 45 and passim.

3 Donald Cochrane, 'Travelling to Work', *Economic Record*, vol. 22, Dec. 1946, pp. 199–218.

4 P. Spearritt and J. Wells, 'The Rise and Decline of the Public Transport City', *Australian Historical Statistics Bulletin*, no. 8, 1984.

5 Morgan Gallup Polls no. 56, (23 March 1942), no. 109 (30 Jan 1943), *Australian Motorist*, March 1944.

6 On modern house design see Tony Dingle and Seamus O'Hanlon, 'Modernism versus Domesticity: The Contest to Shape Melbourne's Homes, 1945–1960', *Australian Historical Studies*, vol. 28, no. 109, October 1997, pp. 33–48; Alastair Greig, *The Stuff Dreams Are Made Of: Housing Provision in Australia 1945–1960*, MUP, Melbourne, 1995, Chapter 7.

7 *Argus*, letter columns for 1, 4, 5, 7, 8 December 1944, 27 January 1945 (Weekend Magazine).

8 *Australian Motor Manual*, April 1950, p. 5; December 1952, p. 594.

9 *Royalauto*, July 1958; *Modern Motor*, July 1958, p. 42.

10 *Herald*, 14 July 1945, *Sun*, 25 August 1945.

11 *Sun*, 13 May 1949.

12 *Argus*, 15 May 1949.

13 *Age*, 13, 16 May 1949; Sheryl Yelland, 'Motor Shows and Marketing Manoeuvres' and 'Transports of Desire: Motor Shows 1949–1995' in David Dunstan, *Victorian Icon: The Royal Exhibition Building Melbourne*, The Exhibition Trustees, Melbourne, 1996, pp. 350–6, 422–8.

14 *Sun*, 12 May 1949, *Radiator*, 15 June 1949.

15 *Argus*, 22 May 1947.

16 *Victorian Yearbooks*.

17 *Queensland Yearbook*, 1945 Government Printer, Brisbane, pp. 178–81.

18 *Town and Country Planning Board, Vehicular Traffic Census* (1948); Gallup Polls nos 746 (March 1951) and 851 (April 1952).

19 *Argus,* 12, 15 February 1949.
20 L. J. Hartnett, *Big Wheels and Little Wheels,* Lansdowne Press, Melbourne, 1964, chs. 28, 29; *Sun,* 26 April 1945; *Motor Manual,* 1 June 1955; *Modern Motor,* August 1958.
21 *Australian Motor Manual,* June 1946, pp. 18–19.
22 John Wright, *Heart of the Lion: The 50 Year History of Australia's Holden,* Allen & Unwin, Sydney, 1998, pp. 52–72.
23 *Argus,* 1 September 1948.
24 *The Automotive Market of Australia,* United States Department of Commerce, 1929, pp. 4–5.
25 *Argus,* 1 February, 19 July 1947, 17 September, 15 October, 17 December 1948, 26 March 1949; Geoffrey Bolton, *The Oxford History of Australia, vol. 5 1942–1988 The Middle Way,* OUP, Melbourne, 1990, pp. 61, 75, 80.
26 *Australian Motor Manual,* February 1947, p. 21.
27 *Australian Motor Manual,* February 1952, p. 777.
28 *Australian Automobile Trade Journal,* vol. 43, 1960, p. 118.
29 *Wheels,* October 1954, February 1955.
30 *Motor Manual: The Australian Monthly,* 1 September 1954, *Royalauto,* August 1957, pp. 3, 7.
31 Holden Booklet Report, February 1955, compare Survey of Australians who Own & Drive Motor Cars conducted for Ford Motor Co. May 1949 and Third Annual Survey of Australians who Own & Drive Motor Cars . . . June 1950 (Morgan Research Centre Archives).
32 Second Public Relations Survey for General Motors-Holden's, Opinion Research Centre for George Patterson, July 1953, p. 11 (Morgan Research Centre Archives).
33 Morgan Gallup Poll no. 969c (November–December 1953), compare nos 1060 (December 1954) and 1116 (September–October 1955).
34 *Australian Automobile Trade Journal,* 1 July 1954.
35 Ford Motor Company of Australia, Review Part 2, March 1960, Ford Company Archives.
36 'The Truth about Hire Purchase', *Wheels,* July 1955.
37 Wray Vamplew (ed.), *Australian Historical Statistics,* Fairfax, Syme and Weldon, Sydney, 1987, pp. 157, 213.
38 Gallup Poll no. 1208B, 1957; Australian Sales Research Bureau, *The Housewife's Day,* Melbourne 1960, p. 14.
39 J. M. Hill, 'Launching a New Car', *Journal of the Market Research Society of Australia,* January 1963, p. 9.
40 John B. Rae, *The American Automobile: A Brief History,* University of Chicago Press, Chicago 1965, ch. 12; James J. Flink, *The Automobile Age,* MIT Press, Cambridge Mass., 1988, pp. 281–7; David S. Hopkins, 'Estimating Demand for Durable Consumer Goods', *Journal of the Market Research Society of Victoria,* 1956, pp. 24–37.
41 E. Charles Edwards, *Dynamics of the United States Automobile Industry,* University of South Carolina Press, Columbia, 1965, pp. 201–16.

42 Bill Tuckey, *True Blue: 75 Years of Ford in Australia*, Focus Publishing, Edge-cliff NSW, 2000, pp. 94–7; John Wright, *The History of the Ford Falcon, 1960–1994*, Marque, Sydney, 1994, p. 26.

43 Judith Brett, *Robert Menzies' Forgotten People*, Macmillan, Sydney, 1992, pp. 46–7; John Murphy, *Imagining the Fifties: Private Sentiment and Political Culture in Menzies' Australia*, UNSW Press, Sydney, 2000, pp. 13–30.

44 C. Wright Mills, *White Collar: The American Middle Classes*, OUP, New York, 1951, pp. 256–7; Vance Packard *The Status-Seekers: An Exploration of Class Behaviour in America*, Penguin, London, 1960, pp. 313–17.

45 *Sun*, 11 April 1956; Robin Boyd, *The Australian Ugliness*, Melbourne 1960, Penguin 1963, p. 81.

46 *Wheels*, November 1955, pp. 6–7.

47 Ford Motor Company, Dealers' Confidential Bulletin, vol. 4, no. 10, September 1953, Ford Company Archives.

48 *Sun*, 11 April 1956; *Royalauto*, April 1956, p. 53; compare Reyner Ban-ham, 'The Machine Aesthetic', *Architectural Review*, vol. 117, April 1955, pp. 225–8.

49 *Royalauto*, 1 June 1954.

50 Survey on Standard Cars, August 1957, Opinion Research Centre, p. 8 (Morgan Research Centre Archives).

51 *Herald*, 26 March 1953; *Sun*, 11 April 1956; *Royalauto*, April 1954.

52 Albert Walker, Diary, 2, 7 July 1955, Ms 11509, SLV.

53 Alastair Greig, *The Stuff Dreams Are Made Of: Housing Provision in Australia 1945–1960*, Melbourne University Press, Melbourne, 1995; Don Garden, ' "Type 15", "Glengarry" and "Catalina": The Changing Space of the A. V. Jennings House in the 1960s' in Graeme Davison, Tony Dingle and Seamus O'Hanlon (eds), *The Cream Brick Frontier*, pp. 140–153.

54 *Wheels*, January 1959, p. 16; compare the more detailed analysis of station wagon sales in Ford Motor Company of Australia, Review Part 2, March 1960, Ford Company Archives.

55 *Motor Manual*, 1 Febuary 1955, p. 17.

56 *Royalauto*, April 1958, p. 30; *Motor Manual*, 1 August 1954, p. 51.

57 Precis of the Proceedings . . . of the Fifth National Dealer Council Meeting, November 26, 27 and 28 1957; Preliminary Confidential Infor-mation 1959 Consul/ Zephyr/ Zodiac Range 1959, Ford Motor Company Archives.

58 *Wheels*, December 1957, pp. 19–21, 67; April 1957, pp. 48–51; January 1959, pp. 14–15.

59 Metropolitan Transportation Committee, *Melbourne Transportation Study, vol. 1: Survey*, pp. 98–117; Car ownership returns for 1964, 1966, 1971 in Metropolitan Transport Study Papers, VPRS 10090–60–20A.

60 *Royalauto*, August 1964, p. 5.

61 R. Stephenson, 'Women's impact on motoring', *Royalauto*, September, 1968, p. 6.

62 Based on figures recorded in Victoria Police Licensing Branch, 'New Drivers: Statistics, 1964–1970'. Copy made available by Vicroads.

63 *Royalauto*, November 1964, pp. 20–21; also *Wheels*, February 1959, p. 56.

64 News Release, 'Girls Now Taking the Wheel', 27 March 1972, Ford Motor Company Archives; also see *Herald*, 19 April 1972 for story based on this release.

65 Car Owners' Survey in Australia, April 1980, Morgan Research Centre Pty Ltd January 1981 (Morgan Research Centre Archives).

66 *Melbourne Transportation Study, vol. 1: Survey*, p. 100; Max Neutze, *Urban Development in Australia*, Allen & Unwin, Sydney, 1977, p. 125; *Transporting Melbourne: A Summary for Public Consultation*, Department of Infrastructure, Melbourne, 1996, p. 6.

67 *Age*, 3 March 1970; *International Motor Show Catalogue 1976*, p. 12.

Chapter 2: Women Take the Wheel

1 *Royalauto*, November 1968, p. 36.

2 Leonore Davidoff and Catherine Hall, *Family Fortunes: Men and Women of the English Middle Class 1760–1850*, Hutchinson, London, 1987, chapter 3.

3 On the 'semi-public sphere' see Mary Ryan, *Women in Public: Between Banners and Ballots, 1825–1880*, Johns Hopkins University Press, Baltimore, 1990.

4 Kimberley Webber, 'Women at the Wheel' in Charles Pickett (ed.), *Cars and Culture: Our Driving Passions*, HarperCollins/Powerhouse Museum, Sydney, 1998, pp. 86–103; Georgine Clarsen, 'Women, Modernity and Cars in Interwar Victoria' in Martin Crotty and Doug Scobie (eds), *Raiding Clio's Closet: Postgraduate Presentations in History*, 1997, University of Melbourne, 1997, pp. 61–75; Mimi Colligan, 'Alice Anderson, Garage Proprietor' in Marilyn Lake and Farley Kelly (eds), *Double Time Women in Victoria—150 Years*, Penguin, Melbourne, 1985, pp. 305–11.

5 Susan Priestley, *The Crown of the Road: The Story of the RACV*, Macmillan, South Melbourne, 1983, pp. 9, 21, 36; compare Webber, p. 91.

6 *Sydney Morning Herald*, 19 June 1947 as quoted Rosemary Broomham, *On the Road: The NRMA's First Seventy-Five Years*, Allen & Unwin, Sydney, 1996, p. 91.

7 *Radiator*, 15 April 1943, p. 2.

8 *Women's Weekly* 19 October 1955; Figures from Victorian Police Licensing Branch, 'Statistics: Drivers' Section, 1953–1955', now held by Vicroads.

9 Fifth (1952) Annual Survey of Australians Who Own & Drive Motor Cars, Ford Motor Company of Australia, conducted by Opinion Research Corporation, June 1950, p. 7; Survey on Standard Cars, August 1957, Opinion Research Centre, p. 41.

10 *Royalauto*, June 1960, p. 18, May 1961, p. 6, April 1968, p. 12.

11 Richard White, 'The Importance of Being *Man*', in Peter Spearritt & David Walker (eds), *Australian Popular Culture*, Allen & Unwin, Sydney, 1979, pp. 145–168.

12 For example, 'Back Seat Drivers, By Torque', *Radiator*, 17 September 1947, p. 2; K. Norman, 'Back Seat Driving . . . as she is did!', *Motor Manual*, 15 May 1954, p. 60.

13 *Royalauto*, July 1955, p. 24; *Sun*, 27 October 1954; *Wheels*, November 1955, pp. 12–13, 82–4; Mrs. B. K. of Pascoe Vale South, *Royalauto*, June 1959, p. 2.

14 Ann Clifford, *Royalauto*, September 1959, p. 8; ibid., May 1961, p. 6, June 1961, p. 3.

15 *Radiator*, 13 August 1947, p. 12.

16 *Argus*, 12–17 May 1947.

17 See discussion in P. Jackson, 'Towards a Cultural Politics of Consumption', in J. Bird, B. Curtis, T. Putnam, G. Robertson & L. Tickner (eds), *Mapping the Futures: Local Culture, Global Change*, Routledge, London, 1993, pp. 208–28.

18 E. J. Harman, 'Women and Consumer Capitalism', in C. V. Baldock and Bettina Cass (eds), *Women, Social Welfare and the State in Australia*, Allen & Unwin, Sydney, 1983, pp. 85–163.

19 Australian Sales Research Bureau, *The Housewife's Day*, Melbourne, 1960.

20 Interviews with Waverley and Clayton suburban pioneers.

21 Compare E. J. Harman, 'Capitalism, Patriarchy and the City', in Baldock & Cass (eds), *Women, Social Welfare and the State*, pp. 104–29.

22 *Radiator*, 13 August 1947, p. 12.

23 *Victorian Automobile Chamber of Commerce Journal*, 1 February 1950, p. 22.

24 *Australian Automotive Trade Journal*, 1 September 1950, p. 20.

25 Gail Reekie, 'Market Research and the Post-War Housewife', *Australian Feminist Studies*, vol. 14, Summer 1991, pp. 15–27.

26 Advertisement, *Age*, 12 January 1956.

27 Virginia Scharff, *Taking the Wheel: Women and the Coming of the Motor Age*, University of New Mexico Press, Albuquerque, 1991, pp. 59–63; compare Georgine Clarsen, 'The "Dainty Female Toe" and the "Brawny Male Arm": Conceptions of Bodies and Power in Automobile Technology', *Australian Feminist Studies*, vol. 15, no. 32, 2000, pp. 153–63.

28 *Australian Automobile Trade Journal*, 1 November 1950, p. 15.

29 *The Australian Motor Manual*, April 1952, p. 1; Sheryl Yelland, 'Transports of Desire: Motor Shows 1949–95' in David Dunstan (ed.), *Victorian Icon: The Royal Exhibition Building*, Exhibition Trustees, Melbourne, 1996, pp. 422–8; Roland Marchand, *Advertising The American Dream: Making Way for Modernity, 1920–1940*, University of California Press, Berkeley, 1985, pp. 66–9.

30 Frank Mort, 'Politics of Consumption', in S. Hall & M. Jacques (eds), *New Times: The Changing Face of Politics in the 1990s*, Lawrence & Wishart, London, 1989, pp. 160–72.

31David Bottomley, *Introduction to Market Analysis*, Market Research Society of Australia, Melbourne, 1959.

32M. Frostick, *Advertising the Motor Car*, Lund Humphries, London, 1970, p. 124.

33Vanguard 'Spacemaster' Advertisement, loc. cit.; and see Reyner Banham, 'The Machine Aesthetic' (first published in *Architectural Review*, April 1955), in P. Sparke, *Design By Choice: Ideas in Architecture*, Academy Editions, London, 1981, p. 45.

34*Australian Women's Weekly*, 10 September, p. 33; 1 October, p. 30; 25 November, p. 12; and 5 November, p. 4.

35*Royalauto*, December 1954, p. x.

36For a discussion of the Holden as a masculinist national icon see M. Taussig, 'An Australian Hero', *History Workshop Journal*, vol. 4, Autumn 1987, pp. 111–33; ' "Old Soldiers Never Die": A Re-survey of Early Holdens', *Motor Manual*, 1 December 1954, pp. 48–49; and compare, for example, GMH's advertisements in *Australian Motor Manual*, November 1948, p. 53, and in the *Women's Weekly*, 28 December 1953, p. 26; the promotional article in *Australian Automobile Trade Journal*, December 1953, p. 28; and *Motor Manual*, 15 February 1955, p. 12.

37*Royalauto*, April, pp. 12–13, June 1968, pp. 6–7; compare Chapter 1.

38Interview with Denise and Brian Hurley, 20 April 1995.

39Interview with Ursula Draper, 26 April 1995.

40See for example, *Herald*, 30 June 1956.

41Interview with Jessie Reed, 20 April 1995.

42Interview with Clem and Nina Harris, February 1995.

43Interview with Don and Shirley Knights, March 1995.

44Compare Martin Wachs, 'Men, Women and Urban Travel: The Persistence of Separate Spheres' in Martin Wachs and Margaret Crawford (eds), *The Car and the City: The Automobile, the Built Environment and Daily Urban Life*, University of Michigan Press, Ann Arbor, 1992, pp. 86–100.

45*The Patterson Report*, Sydney, 1972, pp. 68–71.

46Anonymous interviewee, 16 January 1995. Pseudonyms replace the interviewees' real names.

47Anonymous interviewee, 22 February 1995. Pseudonyms replace the interviewees' real names.

48See for example, Graham Keogh, *The History of Doncaster and Templestowe*, City of Doncaster and Templestowe, Doncaster, 1975, pp. 64–6.

49Interview with Olive Barker, 26 April 1995.

50Ruth Bence, *Socio-economic Characteristics and Travel Patterns of Non-Drivers Resident in Metropolitan Melbourne*, Australian Road Research Board, Report No. 30, November 1974, p. 26; and see Melbourne Metropolitan Transportation Study '1964 Data Summary', p. 1.

51ibid., pp. 31–9.

52Patrick Troy, *Environmental Quality in Four Melbourne Suburbs*, Urban Research Unit, RSSS, ANU, Canberra, 1972, pp. 98–9.

53 Bence, *Socio-economic Characteristics*, p. 29; and Harman, 'Capitalism, Patriarchy and the City', in Baldock & Cass, pp. 120–25.

54 Bence, *Socio-economic Characteristics*, pp. 4, 8, 24–6, 75; and for comment on the current American context, see S. Rosenbloom, 'Why Working Families Need a Car', in Wachs and Crawford (eds), *The Car and the City*, pp. 37–56; for an Australian perspective see Margo Huxley, 'Ecologically Sustainable Cities, Environmentally Friendly Transport or Just "More Work for Mother"?', unpublished paper to Women on the Move Conference, Adelaide, 1995.

55 *Royalauto*, July 1967, p. 9.

56 ibid., November 1966, p. 11.

57 ibid., August 1968, p. 10.

58 ibid., October 1968, p. 29.

59 Michael L. Berger, 'The Car's Impact on the American Family', in Wachs and Crawford (eds), *The Car and The City*, pp. 68–72; and 'Women at the Wheel' *Sun*, 20 November 1964.

60 *Royalauto*, June 1961, p. 31.

61 Between 1969 and 1973, Anne Raymond and Ruth Bence published the results of several such research projects which they had carried out for the Australian Road Research Board in their journal, *Australian Road Research*.

62 Compare Ann Summers, *Damned Whores and God's Police*, Penguin, Ringwood, 1975.

63 *Women's Weekly*, 5 October 1955, p. 80; see also *Royalauto*, September 1965, p. 2; August 1967, p. 6; and October 1969, p. 18.

64 *Royalauto*, June 1970, pp. 6–7.

65 ibid., August 1967, p. 11.

66 ibid., December 1967, p. 9.

67 ibid., September 1967, pp. 6–7.

68 ibid., October 1971, p. 13.

69 Marilyn Lake, *Getting Equal: The History of Australian Feminism*, Allen & Unwin, Sydney, 1999.

Chapter 3: Sex, Speed and Power

1 *Australasian*, 23 January 1897 as quoted in Margaret Indian, 'Leisure in City and Suburb: Melbourne 1880–1900', PhD thesis, ANU, 1980, p.21.

2 Graham McInnes, *Humping My Bluey*, Hamish Hamilton, London, 1966, chs 2, 3.

3 *Argus*, 6 September 1924. Complaints of reckless driving and immoral behaviour among the young were common in Australia as well as the United States in the 1920s. See for example *Argus*, 8 February 1926 and Peter Ling, 'Sex and the Automobile in the Jazz Age', *History Today*, vol. 18, November 1989, pp. 17–29.

4 Anonymous boy as quoted in *Social Issues of the Seventies*, Australian Broadcasting Commission, Sydney, 1976, p. 98.

5 Gallup Polls, nos 746, March 1951 and 851, April 1952.

6 Wray Vamplew (ed.), *Australians: Historical Statistics*, Fairfax, Syme and Weldon, Sydney 1987, p. 433; compare David Hilliard, 'God in the Suburbs: The Religious Culture of Australian Cities in the 1950s', *Australian Historical Studies*, vol. 25, no. 97, October 1991, pp. 399–419.

7 On cars, clothes, hairstyles etc in the self-definition of adolescent gang members see D. C. Dunphy, *Cliques, Crowds and Gangs: Group Life of Sydney Adolescents*, Cheshire, Melbourne, 1969, p. 114.

8 Based on an analysis of the addresses (usually the parents') given in engagement notices published in the *Age* and *Sun* over four corresponding Saturdays in March, June, September and December of 1950 and 1970. We have excluded notices where one or more sets of parents gave a country address or where no suburb was given for either couple.

9 'Holdin' you in my Holden' (Words by Norma Hall and Music by Don Bennett, 1952), Holden Ltd.

10 John R. Seeley, R. Alexander Sim and Elizabeth W. Loosley, *Crestwood Heights: A Study of the Culture of Suburban Life*, (1956), John Wiley, New York, 1963, p. 109.

11 *Victorian Yearbooks*, Government Printer.

12 Jack Hibberd, 'White with Wire Wheels' in Alexander Buzo et al., *Four Australian Plays*, Penguin, Melbourne, 1970, pp. 149–230.

13 Henry Williams, *My Love had a Black Speed Stripe*, Macmillan, Melbourne, 1973, pp. 10, 76.

14 *Social Issues of the Seventies*, p. 99.

15 See 'Tom Corrigan', *Australian Dictionary of Biography*, vol. 3, Melbourne University Press, Melbourne, pp. 405–6.

16 Harry Gordon, *Young Men in a Hurry*, Lansdowne, Melbourne, 1961, pp. 27–36.

17 The popularity of speedway racing among working-class youths is hinted at in W. F. Connell, E. P. Francis and Elizabeth Skilbeck, *Growing Up in an Australian City*, Australian Council for Educational Research, Melbourne, 1957, pp. 127–8.

18 *Age*, 26 November, 3 December 1956.

19 Tony Thomas, 'The Man Who Made a Mountain', *Business Review Weekly*, 22 August 1994, pp. 68–73; *Australian*, 10 August 1971.

20 *Herald*, 23 November 1962.

21 *Herald*, 1 Jan 1962, *Motor Manual*, March 1962.

22 *Motor Manual*, 1 April 1962, p. 30

23 *Royalauto*, November 1968, p. 19; February 1969, p. 5; October 1969, pp. 16–17.

24 See for example Lesley Johnson, *The Modern Girl: Girlhood and Growing Up*, Allen & Unwin, Sydney, 1993, ch. 3.

25 Report of Advisory Committee on Juvenile Delinquency, *VPP*, vol. 2 1955–56, p. 11.

26 *Wheels*, August 1957, p. 40.

27 Report of the Select Committee appointed to inquire into and report upon Road Safety, *Journal of the Senate*, 1960–61, vol. 1, pp. 26–27. The statistics quoted are from a special report compiled for the committee by the Commonwealth Statistician based on returns from Queensland. The published Victorian figures, which are grouped in broader age categories, are nevertheless consistent with these conclusions.

28 Calculated from Road Fatality Statistics, *Victorian Statistical Registers*, Government Printer.

29 Charles Stamp, 'Remember Dad?', *Royalauto*, May 1967, p. 19.

30 ibid.

31 *Royalauto*, May 1962, pp. 7–8.

32 *Royalauto*, July 1962, p.7.

33 *Royalauto*, November 1969, p. 20.

34 *Royalauto*, January 1967, p. 5.

35 *Royalauto*, January 1967, p. 5; March 1967, p. 15; April 1967, p. 4; June 1967, p. 4.

36 *Radiator*, 18 February 1948.

37 *Age*, 10 February 1955.

38 *Age*, 4 August 1955.

39 *Age*, 30 January 1959.

40 Report of Committee on Larceny and Illegal Use of Motor Vehicles and Associated Matters, *VPP*, vol. 2, 1964–5, pp. xi, 34.

41 Compare recent studies of car-related law-breaking among young men in Sydney's West: Linley Walker, 'Chivalrous Masculinity among Juvenile Offenders in Western Sydney: A New Perspective on Young Working Class Men and Crime', *Current Issues in Criminal Justice*, vol. 9, no. 3, March 1998, pp. 279–93; Kate Hartwig, 'Claiming the Freeway: Young Male Drivers in Pursuit of Independence, Space and Masculinity', *Journal of Interdisciplinary Gender Studies*, vol. 5, no. 1, June 2000, pp. 36–50.

42 I draw here on the interesting discussion in Philip Butterss, 'Becoming a Man in Australian Film in the Early 1990s: *The Big Steal, Death in Brunswick, Strictly Ballroom* and *The Heartbreak Kid*', *Australian Studies*, vol. 14, nos 1 & 2, Summer/Winter 1999, pp. 81–3.

Chapter 4: The New Landscape

1 Peter Spearritt, 'The Rise and Decline of the Public Transport City', *Australian Historical Statistics*, no. 8, 1984, pp. 61–79.

2 I rely here on memories disciplined mainly by the entries in *Sands and McDougall Melbourne Directories*.

3 'In the New Landscape' in Bruce Dawe, *Sometimes Gladness: Collected Poems 1954–1987*, Sydney, 1988, p. 100.

4 Peirce F. Lewis, 'Axioms for Reading the Landscape' in D. W. Meinig (ed.), *The Interpretation of Ordinary Landscapes: Geographical Essays*, Oxford University Press, New York, 1979, pp. 18, 22.

5 Kenneth Jackson, *Crabgrass Frontier: The Suburbanization of the United States*, Oxford University Press, New York, 1985, chapter 14.

6 Reyner Banham, *Los Angeles: The Architecture of Four Ecologies*, University of California Press, Berkeley, 2001, p. 213.

7 Robin Boyd, *The Australian Ugliness*, Penguin, Melbourne, 1960, pp. 78–9.

8 For a more extended discussion of Boyd's Austerica see Graeme Davison, 'Driving to Austerica: The Americanization of the Postwar Australian City' in Harold Bolitho and Chris Wallace-Crabbe (eds), *Approaching Australia: Papers from the Harvard Australian Studies Symposium*, Harvard University Committee on Australian Studies/Harvard University Press, Cambridge, Mass., 1998, pp. 159–84. Compare Mark Rolfe, 'Suburbia' in Philip and Roger Bell (eds), *Americanization and Australia*, UNSW Press, Sydney, 1998, pp. 1–8.

9 Jackson, *Crabgrass Frontier* , pp. 255–60.

10 *Australian Automobile Trade Journal*, 1 May 1950, p. 13.

11 Notes of Interview between Rootes representatives and John Cain, 18 December 1945, Manufacture of Motor Vehicles in Australia, Premier's Office, VPRS 1163/776.

12 John Wright, *Heart of the Lion: The 50 Year History of Australia's Holden*, Allen & Unwin, Sydney, 1998, pp. 87, 96, 110; *Australian Automobile Trade Journal*, September 1955; *Royalauto*, September 1955, p. 15; *Wheels*, May 1959, pp. 18–21; P. J Rimmer, *Manufacturing in Melbourne*, Australian National University, Canberra, 1969, pp. 17–19, 43, 120; Lois Bryson and Faith Thompson, *An Australian Newtown: Life and Leadership in a New Housing Suburb*, Penguin, Melbourne, 1972, pp. 19–22.

13 *Australian Automobile Trade Journal*, 1 December 1954, 1 June 1956, November 1956; *Royalauto*, May 1956, January 1959.

14 Ken Johnson, *People and Property in Clayton*, Australian National University, Canberra, 1979, pp. 18, 65; *Sands and McDougall Melbourne Directories*, 1955, 1961, 1970.

15 Patrick Troy, 'Introduction' in Patrick Troy (ed.), *Technological Change and the City*, Federation Press, Sydney, 1995, p. 2.

16 Geoff Easdown, *Ford: The Story of the Ford Motor Company in Australia*, Golden Press, Sydney, 1987, p. 85.

17 Andrew Lemon, *Broadmeadows: A Forgotten History*, Hargreen, Melbourne, 1982, pp. 188–9; *VPD* vol. 250, 1956, pp. 5580 ff for parliamentary debate on the arrangement; also see May Keeley, *A Journey into Yesterday – A History of Clayton*, Clayton, 1980.

18 Mark Peel, *Good Times Hard Times: The Past and Future in Elizabeth*, MUP, Melbourne 1995, esp. ch. 3.

19 Edward Soja, *Postmodern Geographies: The Reassertion of Space in Critical Social Theory*, Verso, London, 1989, chs 6–9; David Harvey, *The Condition of Postmodernity*, Blackwell, Oxford, 1989; also compare Alastair Greig, *The Stuff Dreams Are Made Of: Housing Provision in Australia*, MUP, Melbourne, 1993.

20 On the democratic grid see Andro Linklater, *Measuring America: How the United States was Shaped by the Greatest Land Sale in History*, Harper-Collins, London, 2002, pp. 111 ff.

21 Compare Martin Daunton, 'Public Space and Private Space: The Victorian City and the Working Class Household' in Derek Fraser and Anthony Sutcliffe (eds), *The Pursuit of Urban History*, Edward Arnold, London, 1983, pp. 212–33.

22 Michael Southworth and Eran Ben-Joseph, 'Street Standards and the Shaping of Suburbia', *Journal of the American Planning Association*, vol. 61, no. 1, Winter 1995, pp. 65–81.

23 Robert Freestone, *Model Communities: The Garden City Movement in Australia*, Nelson, Melbourne, 1989, pp. 187–99.

24 Don Garden, *Builders to the Nation: The A. V. Jennings, Story*, MUP, Melbourne, 1992, p. 161.

25 A. V. Jennings, 'Project Management Housing', *The Australian Builder*, July 1960, p. 490.

26 Ron Smith, 'Culs-De-Sac A. V. Jennings' Contribution', *Australian Planner*, vol. 27, no. 3, September 1989, pp. 12–16; Ray Brindle, 'Two Steps Forward and One Step Back: The Hesitant Progress of Australian Subdivision and Road Planning (1988)' in his *Living with Traffic*, Australian Road Research Board Special Report 53, 1986, pp. 335–47; M. G. Lay, *Sourcebook for Australian Roads*, ARRB, Melbourne, 1985, pp. 61–70.

27 Sally Wilde, City of Monash Environmental History, typescript, 1996, pp. 68–73.

28 G. R . Broadbent, ' Garaging the Car', *Argus*, 4 July 1925.

29 *Australian Monthly Motor Manual*, January 1947, p. 12; also see Karen Olson, 'Laying the Yellow Brick Road: The Rise of the Suburban Driveway' in Australia ICOMOS (International Council on Monuments and Sites), Victorian Conference Papers, March 1996.

30 Robin Boyd, *Australia's Home*, Melbourne University Press, Melbourne, 1952, p. 91.

31 *Royalauto*, July 1959, p. 16.

32 See advertisments in *Royalauto*, July 1958, July 1959.

33 Compare J. B. Jackson, 'The Domestication of the Garage', *Landscape*, vol. 20, no. 2, 1976, pp. 10–17.

34 Compare designs in Don Garden, ' "Type 15", "Glengarry" and "Catalina": The Changing Space of the A.V. Jennings Home in the 1960s' in Davison et al. (eds),*Cream Brick Frontier*, pp. 140–53.

35 'Service Stations: Temples of Monetary Plenty?', *Wheels*, September 1959, pp. 12–13, 84–87; 'Service Stations: Riches or Ruins?', *Wheels*, October 1959, pp. 20, 75–8.

36 *Australian Automobile Trade Journal*, 1 February 1950, p. 13.

37 Daniel Catrice and Michelle Summerton, The Motor Garage & Service Station in Victoria: A Survey, National Estate Grants Programme, Department of Infrastructure, Melbourne, February 1997, pp. 32–41.

38 Survey of Garages, March 1951, Roy Morgan Research Centre, p. 9; Garages and Service Stations: Survey of Motorists' Opinions, March 1951, p. 11, both conducted for Shell Oil Company by Roy Morgan Research Centre.
39 *Royalauto*, August 1960, p. 15.
40 *Australian Motor Manual*, 15 October 1955, p. 13.
41 'Service Stations: Riches or Ruins?', *Wheels*, October 1959, *Australian Automobile Trade Journal*, 1 July 1954.
42 'Destruction of houses', *Australian Automobile Trade Journal*, 1 August 1954, p. 12; 1 October 1954, p. 13; 1 May 1960, p. 57.
43 *Australian Automobile Trade Journal*, 1 July 1954, p. 14.
44 *Radiator*, 13 February 1946, p. 2; RACV Council Minutes, 13 February 1946.
45 *Australian Motor Manual*, 1 February 1955, p. 49.
46 Robin Boyd, *The Australian Ugliness*, p. 80.
47 I have described the stringent timetabling of interwar society in my *The Unforgiving Minute: How Australia Learned to Tell the Time*, Oxford University Press, Melbourne, 1993, pp. 124–38.
48 *Radiator*, 20 September 1950.
49 *Royalauto*, 1 October 1954, p. 11.
50 *Australian Women's Weekly*, 14 December 1955, p. 20; on the wider Australian story see Jim Davidson and Peter Spearritt, *Holiday Business: Tourism in Australia since 1870*, MUP, Carlton, 2000, pp. 179–86.
51 From listing in *Motor Manual*, 1 February 1960, p. 56.
52 *Motor Manual*, 16 May 1955, pp. 8–9.
53 *Herald*, 16 December 1959.
54 RACV Guide to Motels, cyclostyle October 1959.
55 Cyril Lewis to Henry Bolte, 16 January 1956; Bolte to Arthur Fadden, 8 March 1956; Fadden to Bolte, 22 March 1956 in 'Motels', VPRS 1163/1174.
56 *Royalauto Journal*, January 1957, pp. 36–7; August 1957.
57 Robin Boyd, *The Australian Ugliness*, pp. 76–7.
58 Personal communication from David Yencken 1 April 1995; Geoffrey Serle, *Robin Boyd: A Life*, MUP, Carlton, 1995, pp. 193–6; *Nation*, 28 July 1962, p. 17.
59 *Wheels*, January 1959, p. 7.
60 *Herald*, 17 April 1957.
61 *Herald*, 24 October 1958, 19 February 1959, 2 June, 3 November 1960, 13 October 1961; *Motor Manual*, 1 February 1960, pp. 56–7, 1 August 1961, p. 58; RACV Guide to Motels, cyclostyle, November 1959.
62 *Royalauto*, May 1963, p. 11.
63 *Radiator*, 18 January 1950, p. 13.
64 *Herald*, 24 June 1950.
65 *Herald*, 25 June 1957, 27 February 1958.
66 *Herald*, 7 June 1954, 7 January, 23 May 1956; for developments elsewhere in Australia see John Richardson, 'Movies under the Stars: Drive-ins and

Modernity', *Continuum: An Australian Journal of the Media*, vol. 1, no. 1, 1987, pp. 111–15; Steve Bedwell, *Suburban Icons: A Celebration of the Everyday*, ABC Books, Sydney, 1992, pp. 112–16.

67 *Motor Manual*, 15 July 1955, pp. 16–17; *Royalauto*, December 1954, p. 27.

68 *Motor Manual*, April 1954, p. 45.

69 Peter Spearritt, 'I Shop, Therefore I Am' in Louise C. Johnson (ed.), *Suburban Dreaming: An Interdisciplinary Approach to Australian Cities*, Geelong, 1994, pp. 129–140; Peter Spearritt, 'Suburban Cathedrals: The Rise of the Drive-in Shopping Centre' in Graeme Davison et al. (eds), *The Cream Brick Frontier*, Melbourne, 1995, pp. 88–107; Beverley Kingston, *Basket, Bag and Trolley: A History of Shopping in Australia*, Oxford University Press, Melbourne 1994, ch. 6.

70 *Motor Manual*, 1 February 1955, p. 17.

71 *Royalauto*, April 1958, p. 32.

72 *Herald*, 3 October 1960.

73 Ambrose Pratt, *Sidney Myer: A Biography*, Quarter Books, Melbourne, 1978, pp. 104–12; Alan Marshall, *The Gay Provider: The Myer Story*, F. W. Cheshire, Melbourne, 1961, pp. 28–36.

74 Interview with S. B. Myer, 22 November 1995.

75 *Herald*, 3 October 1960.

76 Lisabeth Cohen, 'From Town Center to Shopping Center: The Reconfiguration of Community Marketplaces in Postwar America', *American Historical Review*, vol. 101, no. 4, October 1996, pp. 1056–60.

77 George McCahon, A Regional Shopping Centre at Chadstone, Progress Report to Mr A. H. Tolley, December 1958, (Coles Myer Archives); R. J. Johnson and P. J. Rimmer, 'The Competitive Position of a Planned Shopping Centre', *Australian Geographer*, vol. 10, no. 3, 1966, pp. 160–8; P. J. Rimmer, 'A Survey of Chadstone Shopping Habits', *Australian Planning Institute Journal*, vol. 4, no. 3, July 1966, pp. 75–7.

78 *Chadstone* (Melbourne News Group), 28 September 1960.

79 *Age*, 3 October 1960.

80 *Herald*, 3 October 1960.

81 *Chadstone*, 28 September 1960.

82 *Age*, 20 February 1959 and compare *Sun*, 4 October 1960.

83 The Editors of Fortune, *The Exploding Metropolis*, Doubleday, New York, 1957, pp. 32, 140. Jane Jacobs' classic *Death and Life of Great American Cities* appeared in 1962.

84 Lewis Mumford, *The City in History*, (1961), Penguin, Harmondsworth, 1966, pp. 575–6; also compare Mumford, 'Highway and the City' (1958) in *The Highway and the City*, Greenwood Press, Westport, 1963, pp. 234–46.

Chapter 5: The Freedom of the Road

1 *Argus, Age, Sydney Morning Herald*, 11 November 1949; *Sydney Morning Herald*, 18 November 1949. Also see Judith Brett, *Robert Menzies' Forgotten*

People, Macmillan, Melbourne, 1992; John Murphy, *Imagining the Fifties*, UNSW Press, Sydney, 2000, Chapters 1, 10.

2 *Sydney Morning Herald*, 9 February 1950 as quoted Rosemary Broomham, *On the Road: The NRMA's First Seventy-Five Years*, Allen & Unwin, Sydney, 1996, p. 96.

3 *Royalauto*, 1 July 1965 and annual reports.

4 Notice the significance accorded car-based patterns of mobility in Eric Campbell, *The Rallying Point: My Story of the New Guard*, MUP, Melbourne, 1965, p. 70.

5 Elizabeth Kenworthy Teather, 'The Taylors, Sir Charles Rosenthal, and Protofascism in the 1920s' in Robert Freestone (ed.), *The Australian Planner*, University of New South Wales, May 1993, pp. 102–11.

6 John William Knott, ' "The Conquering Car": Technology, Symbolism and the Motorisation of Australian before World War II', *Australian Historical Studies*, vol. 31, no. 114, April 2000, pp. 1–26.

7 *Radiator*, 18 June 1947, p. 3; 12 November 1947, p. 7; G. F. James, 'Broadbent, George Robert', *Australian Dictionary of Biography*, MUP, Melbourne, vol. 7, pp. 416–17.

8 *Argus*, 28 October 1924.

9 Wolfgang Sachs, *For the Love of the Automobile: Looking Back into the History of Our Desires*, University of California Press, Berkely, 1992, p. 2.

10 *Radiator*, 10 September 1950.

11 *Argus*, 8 April 1924, 3 June 1924. Emphasis added.

12 ibid., 6 January 1925.

13 ibid., 23 September 1924, 16 September 1921.

14 Compare Mark H. Rose, *Interstate: Express Highway Politics, 1941–1956*, Regents Press of Kansas, Lawrence Ks, 1979.

15 RACV Minutes 18 February 1944, RACV 1/21.

16 ibid., June 1945.

17 ibid., October 1946, March 1947,

18 'T. G. Paterson, 'The Voice of the Man at the Wheel', *Rydge's*, May 1945, p. 350.

19 RACV Minutes, 6 January, 13 March, 10 July 1946.

20 Susan Priestley, *The Crown of the Road: The Story of the RACV*, Macmillan, Melbourne, 1983, pp. 101–2, 107, 119, 133, 141; Annual reports in *Radiator* and *Royalauto*.

21 On the 'progressive' character of Liberal Party ideology, see Marian Simms, *A Liberal Nation: The Liberal Party and Australian Politics*, Hale & Iremonger, Sydney, 1982, chs 4–5; Gerard Henderson, *Menzies' Child: The Liberal Party of Australia, 1944–1994*, Allen & Unwin, Sydney, 1994, ch. 3.

22 T. G. Paterson, 'Voice', p. 350.

23 ibid., p. 333.

24 ibid., p.334.

25 *CPD*, vol. 192, 1947, p. 2679.

26 *Radiator*, 16 October 1946, p. 2.

27 *Argus,* 29 May 1947; compare Richard White, ' "The Australian Way of Life" ', *Historical Studies,* vol. 18, no. 73, October 1979, pp. 528–45.

28 *Radiator,* 11 December 1946, p. 7;

29 T. G. Paterson, 'Voice', p. 349.

30 *CPD,* vol. 190, 19 March 1947, p. 847; vol. 192, 21 May 1947, p. 2695.

31 Susan Priestley, *Crown of the Road,* p. 115; compare Broomham, *On the Road,* pp. 69, 108.

32 Tony Dingle and Carolyn Rasmussen, *Vital Connections: Melbourne and its Board of Works 1891–1991,* Penguin, Ringwood, 1991, pp. 243–4.

33 Julie P. Smith, *Taxing Popularity: The Story of Taxation in Australia,* ANU, Canberra, 1993, pp. 81–3.

34 Dingle and Rasmussen, *Vital Connections,* pp. 339–52.

35 A. W. Martin, *Robert Menzies: A Life,* vol. 1, Melbourne University Press, Melbourne, 1993, pp. 102–4.

36 For workforce statistics see Michael Keating, *The Australian Workforce 1910 to 1960–1,* Department of Economic History, ANU, Canberra, 1973, p. 236.

37 Colin A. Hughes and B. D. Graham, *Australian Government and Politics 1890–1964,* ANU Press, Canberra, 1968, p. 136; *Who's Who,* Herald and Weekly Times Ltd, Melbourne, 1947.

38 S. E. Doran and R. G. Henderson, *The Electric Railways of Victoria,* Electric Traction Society, Sydney, 1979, p. 39.

39 H. W. Clapp, 'Railway Problems', address to Young Nationalists Association, 29 July 1934, p. 34; PRO (Lav) VPRS 10214, Unit 25 as quoted by Vicki Plant, 'Rights of Passage Public Transport in Postwar Melbourne', MA Thesis, Monash University, 1994, p. 11.

40 Peter Spearritt, 'The Privatisation of Australian Passenger Transport' in John Halligan and Chris Paris (eds), *Australian Urban Politics: Critical Perspectives,* Longman, Melbourne, 1984, pp. 198–9.

41 *Age,* 4 September 1959 as quoted in Plant, p. 39.

42 On the history of underground proposals see Nicholas Clark, Ieuan Richards and K. W. Ogden, 'Analysis of the Proposed Melbourne Underground Railways' in Nicholas Clark (ed.), *Analysis of Urban Development Tewkesbury Symposium,* Melbourne, 1970, 4.89–4.119.

43 Stewart Joy, 'The Evaluation of Comprehensive Metropolitan Plans, and their Uses in Predicting Demand for Individual Facilities', Report for Minister for Transport, 6 November 1967, 5.10.

44 Melbourne and Metropolitan Tramways Board, *Annual Report,* 1958.

45 Victorian Railways Board, *Annual Report,* 1981.

46 For a more recent statements of the case for public transport see Clive S. Beed, *Melbourne's Development and Planning,* Clewara Press, Melbourne, 1981, passim; Paul Mees, *A Very Public Solution: Transport in the Dispersed City,* Melbourne University Press, Melbourne, 2000, esp. Chapter 1.

47 Andrew Brown-May, *Melbourne Street Life,* Australian Scholarly Publishing, Melbourne, 1998, p. 38; compare similar responses in Sydney and

Adelaide: Peter Morton, *After Light: A History of the City of Adelaide and its Council*, 1878–1928, Adelaide City Council, Adelaide, 1996, pp. 242–7; Shirley Fitzgerald, *Sydney 1842–1992*, Hale & Iremonger, Sydney, 1992, pp. 240–4.

48 *Argus*, 9 October 1948.

49 *Argus*, 3 March 1925; compare Andrew Brown-May, *Melbourne Street Life*, p. 40.

50 *Age*, 1 February 1947; *Argus*, 1, 6, 7 March, 1947; 4 June, 4 November 1948; Town and Country Planning Board, *Traffic Census of Melbourne*, Government Printer, Melbourne, 1948, p. 20.

51 *Radiator*, 12 February 1947; *Argus*, 26 February 1947, 30 January, 3 February 1948; compare similar conflicts in Sydney, Broomham, *On the Road*, pp. 104–7.

52 *Radiator*, 17 March 1948, p. 7.

53 *Radiator*, 12 February 1947, 20 June 1951.

54 *Radiator*, 20 February 1952.

55 *Argus*, 5 September 1947, 14 July 1948; *Radiator*, 21 July 1948, 19 January 1949, 21 February 1951, 23 April 1952; RACV Council Minutes 30 January, 27 February 1952; compare the similar proposals being debated in London: see William Plowden, *The Motor Car and Politics 1896–1970*, Bodley Head, London, 1971, pp. 327–30.

56 *Radiator*, 23 April 1952, p. 3.

57 *Argus*, 26 February 1946; *Radiator*, 13 February 1946, *Royalauto*, October 1965, pp. 2–3.

58 *Radiator*, 17 March 1948, 22 November 1950.

59 John M. Bayley, 'Parking in the City of Melbourne', *Traffic Quarterly*, July 1965, pp. 458–76.

60 Andrew Brown-May, *Melbourne Street Life*, Australian Scholarly Publishing, Melbourne, 1998, pp. 36–41.

61 For the Melbourne modern movement, and examples of Myer's influence, see Geoffrey Serle, *Robin Boyd: A Life*, Melbourne University Press, Carlton, 1996; Graeme Davison, 'Welcoming the World: The 1956 Olympic Games and the Re-presentation of Melbourne' in John Murphy and Judith Smart (eds), *The Forgotten Fifties*, *Australian Historical Studies*, vol. 28, no. 109, October 1997, pp. 64–76; Graeme Davison, 'The Modern and Melbourne—Self-imaging in Photography, Journalism and Film' in Lynette Finch and Chris McConville (eds), *Gritty Cities: Images of the Urban*, Pluto Press, Sydney, 1999, pp. 45–64.

62 Town and Country Planning Association, *Meet Mr Muddle*, Melbourne, 1954, pp. 6, 15.

63 *Herald*, 17 November 1953.

64 Michael Robinson, 'The Melbourne Movers: The City Development Association 1953–1961', BA Hons thesis, University of Melbourne, 1981.

65 *Age*, 4 August 1953.

66 RACV Minutes, 27 June 1954.

67 *Sun*, 8, 19, 30, October 1954; *Wheels*, January 1955, p. 34.
68 D. Grant Mickle, *Melbourne's Traffic Problem*, City Development Association, Melbourne, October 1954.
69 *Sun*, 8 October 1954.
70 *Royalauto*, June 1957, p. 6.
71 *Sun*, 26 October 1954.
72 *Sun*, 19, 27, 30, October, 1954, *Royalauto*, August, December 1954, January 1955.
73 City Development Association, *Parking in the City of Melbourne*, Melbourne 1955, p. 2.
74 Compare Clay McShane, *Down the Asphalt Path: The Automobile and the American City*, Columbia University Press, New York, 1994, pp. 203–28; Paul Barrett, *The Automobile and Urban Transit: The Formation of Public Policy in Chicago 1900–1930*, Temple University Press, Philadelphia, 1983, pp. 154–63.
75 *Parking in the City of Melbourne*, pp. 20–3.
76 *Victorian Yearbooks* 1961, p. 700, 1969, p. 614; 1970, p. 778.
77 Colin Buchanan, *Traffic in Towns: A Study of the Long Term Problems of Traffic in Urban Areas*, HMSO, London, 1963.
78 *Living with the Motorcar: A Traffic Symposium*, RACV, Melbourne, 24/26 February 1964.
79 Richard Sennett, *Flesh and Stone: The Body and the City in Western Civilization*, W. W. Norton, New York, 1994, Chapter 10.
80 Graeme Davison, 'The City as a Natural System: Theories of Urban Society in Early Nineteenth Century Britain' in Derek Fraser and Anthony Sutcliffe (eds), *The Pursuit of Urban History*, Edward Arnold, London, 1983, pp. 349–70.
81 *Living with the Motorcar*, pp. 18–20, 26, 131, 134, 136, 138, 143.
82 ibid., p. 263.

Chapter 6: Blood on the Bitumen

1 *Argus*, 27 August 1947.
2 *Herald*, 15 October 1946.
3 Dean Wilson, 'On the Beat: Police Work in Melbourne, 1853–1923', PhD thesis, Monash University, 2000, pp. 367–73; compare John W. Knott, 'Speed, Modernity and the Motor Car: The Making of the 1909 Motor Traffic Act in New South Wales', *Australian Historical Studies*, vol. 26, no. 103, October 1994, pp. 221–41.
4 *Argus*, 26 May 1925.
5 *Radiator*, 16 March 1949.
6 *Argus*, 21 August 1947; 1 March 1949, and compare *Argus*, 29 April 1947, edit, *Herald*, 25 November 1950.
7 *Radiator*, 14 June 1950, p. 1.
8 In 1953 the motor licensing branch sent out a pledge with license renewals, see *Herald*, 9 November 1953.

9 *Argus,* 13 November 1950; *Australian Automobile Trade Journal,* 1 January 1950.

10 *Herald,* 17, 20 November 1950.

11 *Herald,* 24 February 1951.

12 *VPD,* vol. 227, 1948, pp. 3137–8.

13 *Herald,* 9 November 1953, 28 May 1954.

14 *Argus,* 16 November 1921.

15 ibid., 9 July 1954.

16 *Herald,* 27 April 1949.

17 *Victorian Yearbooks,* and compare the similar trends described by John Knott, 'Road Traffic Accidents in New South Wales, 1881–1991', *Australian Economic History Review,* vol. 34, no. 2, September 1994, pp. 80–116.

18 *Argus,* 23 September 1924.

19 *Royalauto,* August 1964, p. 32. For an interesting discussion of Canadian parallels see Stephen Davies, ' "Reckless Walking Must be Discouraged": The Automobile Revolution and the Shaping of Modern Urban Canada to 1930', *Urban History Review/Revue d'histoire urbaine,* vol. 18, October 1989, pp. 123–38.

20 *Australian Monthly Motor Manual,* July 1947.

21 *Argus,* 8 May 1946; *Radiator,* 13 March 1946, 17 September, 7 November 1947.

22 Robert Haldane, *The People's Force: A History of the Victoria Police,* MUP, Carlton, 1986, p. 249.

23 Victoria Police Annual Report 1967, *VPP,* vol. 3, no. 22, 1967–68, p. 28.

24 *Herald,* 21 June 1955; also see *Australian Automobile Trade Journal,* 1 March 1955, p. 35; *Royalauto,* September 1965, p. 23.

25 *Herald,* 22 April 1951.

26 See the annual returns in *Victorian Yearbooks* and the summaries published in the press, e.g. *Herald,* 30 August 1949, 8 March 1953.

27 J. H. W. Birrell, 'Alcohol as a Factor in Victorian Road Accidents', *Medical Journal of Australia,* vol. 1, no. 19, 7 May 1960, pp. 713–29; also see Birrell, 'Some Experiences with Cases of Driving Under the Influence of Intoxicating Liquor in Victoria: An Essay on Drunk Driving', *MJA,* vol. 2, no. 11, 9 September 1961, pp. 417–22.

28 *Herald,* 2 October 1951, 12 July 1954.

29 *Herald,* 2 September 1954.

30 Haldane, *The People's Force,* pp. 239–43.

31 Interview with Dr John Birrell, 8 October 1999.

32 *Herald,* 25 September 1957.

33 *Herald,* 21 December 1957.

34 *Age,* 19, 20, 21 June 1959.

35 Under the Victorian Licensing Act hotels beyond the city limits were permitted to serve alcohol to 'bona fide travellers' after six o'clock, or on Sunday, when city hotels were closed. This loophole was notoriously

exploited by both publicans eager for trade and Melburians seeking a Saturday evening or Sunday tipple. By combining the incentive to drink with the necessity to drive it was in itself a major contributor to the drink-driving problem.

36 John Birrell, *Drink Driving and You*, Sun Books, Melbourne, 1974, p. 20.
37 *Herald*, 17 September 1957.
38 Interview with Dr John Birrell, 8 October 1999; John Birrell, 'Public Education and Mass Communications Aspects' in *Alcohol and Traffic Safety 4th Conference Bloomington Indiana*, 1965.
39 *Herald*, 2, 3, 4 October 1959.
40 *Herald*, 15, 18, 25, 27 November 1957; 8 June 1959.
41 Summary of his report in *Royalauto*, May 1960, pp. 22–3.
42 *Herald*, 5, 6 October 1960; 9 September 1961.
43 John Birrell, 'Alcohol as a Factor in Road Accidents', *Medical Journal of Australia*, vol. 1, no. 19, May 1960, pp. 713–29.
44 Select Committee on Road Safety, *Senate Journal*, vol. 1, 1960–1, p. 24.
45 *VPD*, vol. 264, pp. 738–46, 767.
46 *Herald*, 19, 23 December 1961; 4 January 1962.
47 Peter Blazey, *Bolte: A Political Biography*, Jacaranda, Milton, Qld, 1990, pp. 132–4.
48 Royal Commission into the Sale, Supply, Disposal or Consumption of Liquor in the State of Victoria, *VPP*, vol. 2, 1964–5, p. 29. Note also Phillips' eugenic argument that excessive alcohol consumption sapped the 'efficiency' of the nation, *Herald*, 31 January 1966.
49 *Herald*, 26, 27 January 1965.
50 *Herald*, 27 January 1966.
51 On the liberal thread see Stuart Macintyre, *A Colonial Liberalism: The Lost World of Three Victoran Visionaries*, OUP, Melbourne, 1991.
52 *Royalauto*, January 1966, p. 4.
53 Anne Raymond, 'Ten O'clock Closing—The Effect of the Change in Hotel Bar Closing Time on Road Accidents in the Metropolitan Area of Melbourne', *Australian Road Research*, vol. 3, no. 10, June 1969, p. 15.
54 *Royalauto*, July 1967, pp. 6–7; Anne Raymond, 'A Comparison of Breathalysed Drivers with the General Driving Population', *Australian Road Research*, vol. 4, no. 8, March 1972, pp. 52–61.
55 Anne Raymond, 'What Shall We Do With the Drunken Driver?' *Australian Road Research Board Newsletter*, no. 2, April 1972, pp. 2–3; P. D. Phillips. 'Time to Remove Alcoholic Driving Risks', *Royalauto*, August 1969, pp. 8–9.
56 *Royalauto*, December 1968, pp. 22–3.
57 Graydon Brown, 'The Wrong Way Up to Road Safety', Royal Australasian College of Surgeons Road Trauma Committee Report, 1971, p. 1.
58 Joint Select Committee on Road Safety Third Progress Report on . . . Compulsory Wearing of Seat Belts, *VPP*, vol. 1, no. D1, 1969–70.
59 *Herald*, 28 October 1953, 16 July 1954; *Royalauto*, October 1959, p. 20.
60 J. D. Thorpe, 'The Use and Effect of Car Seat Belts in Victoria', *Australian*

Road Research, June 1964, pp. 49–54; *Royalauto*, July 1964, p. 28; November 1964, p. 40.

61　*VPD*, vol. 300, 1970–1, pp. 2314 ff; vol. 301, 1970–1, pp. 2793 ff.

62　Joint Select Committee on Road Safety, Sixth Progress Report, *VPP*, vol. 1, no. 3, 1970–1; Summary in *Royalauto*, July 1971, p. 3.

63　*VPD*, vol. 302, 1970–1, pp. 5192 ff.

64　*VPD*, vol. 327, 1976, p. 1902.

65　Victoria Police Annual Report, *VPP*, vol. 3, no. 30, 1972–3, p. 10. For critical evaluations of the random breath testing measures see Glen Sullivan, Antonietta Cavallo and Alan Drummond, *An Overview of Random Breath Testing Operations in Victoria 1989–1991*, Accident Research Centre Report no. 40, Monash University, October 1992; Antonietta Cavallo and Max Cameron, *Evaluation of a Random Breath Testing Initiative in Victoria 1990 and 1991*, Accident Research Centre, Monash University [1992], Mary Sheehan et al., *Alcohol Controls and Drink Driving: The Social Context*, Federal Office of Road Safety, Canberra, 1994.

66　*Road Trauma: The National Epidemic: A Survey of Australian Road Crash Statistics 1983*, Royal Australasian College of Surgeons, 1983, p. 16.

67　P. N. Troy and N.G. Butlin, *The Cost of Collisions*, Cheshire, Melbourne, 1971.

68　Motor Accident Board, *Annual Report*, 1984–5.

69　Transport Accident Commission, Fourth Annual Report 1990, p. 18.

70　TAC Sixth Annual Report 1992, p. 41.

71　ibid., p. 40 and compare Max Cameron et al., *Evaluation of Transport Accident Commission Road Safety Television Advertising*, Accident Research Centre, Monash University, Report no. 52, September 1993.

72　Compare J. Henstridge, R. Homel and P. Mackay, *The Long-term Effects of Random Breath Testing in Four Australian States: A Time Series Analysis*, Federal Office of Road Safety, Canberra 1997, pp. 114–16 and Cameron et al., *Evaluation*, p. 34.

Chapter 7: Dream Highways

1　I draw here upon the valuable discussion in John D. Fairfield, 'The Scientific Management of Urban Space: Professional City Planning and the Legacy of Progressive Reform', *Journal of Urban History*, vol. 20, no. 2, February 1994, pp. 179–204; also compare my *The Unforgiving Minute: How Australia Learned to Tell the Time*, Melbourne, 1993, ch. 4.

2　Leonie Sandercock, *Cities for Sale: Property, Politics and Planning in Australia*, MUP, Carlton, 1975, pp. 155–9. For other critiques of the MTS see Ian Manning, *The Open Street: Public Transport, Motor Cars and Politics in Australian Cities*, Sydney, 1991, pp. 71–5; Clive S. Beed, *Melbourne's Development and Planning*, Cleward, Melbourne, 1981, pp. 77–85.

3　J. Michael Thomson, *Great Cities and their Traffic*, Penguin, London, 1977,

p. 137; Paul Mees, *A Very Public Solution: Transport in the Dispersed City*, MUP, Melbourne, 2000, p. 74.

4 William Calder, *Report on his Investigations of Road Problems in Europe and America during 1924,* Government Printer, Melbourne, 1925, p. 2.

5 US Bureau of Public Roads as quoted in W. T. B. McCormack, *Report on his Investigation of Road Problems in the United States and Canada in 1937,* Government Printer, Melbourne, [1937], p. 38.

6 *Radiator,* 22 June 1947, p.12.

7 ibid., 16 February 1949, p. 7; also see ibid., 14 June 1950, p. 4.

8 *A Detailed City Plan for Melbourne,* City Development Association, Melbourne n.d.[1959?], p. [6]; compare Cliff Ellis, 'Professional Conflict over Urban Form: The Case of Urban Freeways, 1930–1970' in Mary Corbin Sies and Christopher Silver (eds), *Planning the Twentieth Century City,* Johns Hopkins University Press, Baltimore, 1996, pp. 262–79.

9 Louis Ward Kemp, 'Aesthetics and Engineers: The Occupational Ideology of Highway Design', *Technology and Culture,* vol. 27, October 1986, pp. 759–97.

10 *Herald,* 13 June 1974.

11 See for example the pictures in *Modern Motor,* July 1954; *Wheels,* June 1957.

12 *CRB News,* vol. 1, no. 28, December 1973, Supplement.

13 *Radiator,* 19 September 1951, p. 4.

14 *Australian Automobile Trade Journal,* 1 August 1955; *Royalauto,* November 1956, p. 28; also see similar plea by C. A. Smith of the Ford Motor Company, *Motor Manual,* September 1955, p. 7.

15 *Royalauto,* October 1957.

16 *Royalauto,* October 1956, pp. 12–13.

17 *Modern Motor,* July 1954, pp. 8–14; November 1954, pp. 44–6; *Wheels,* March 1955, pp. 38–9, 89–91; September 1957, pp. 16–17, 94.

18 Interview with John Bayley, 25 May 1994.

19 *Bureau of Highway Traffic, Yale University, Biennial Report and Roster of Graduates, 1963–1964,* pp. 15–33.

20 Of the six engineers interviewed for this study four were born in the country—Barton (Yackandandah) Underwood (Lismore, Vic), Delaney (Warrnambool), Bayley (Bega, NSW)—one (Saggers) was born in Melbourne but educated in Ballarat, and another (Guerin) was born in Melbourne but served as a shire engineer in Kerang.

21 Interviews with Joe Delaney, 7 June 1994 and Neil Guerin, 11 May 1994.

22 *Royalauto,* February 1957.

23 The influence of American models and Fordist methods on the development of the house building industry can be charted in the history of A.V Jennings, Australia's largest project builders and developers; see Don Garden, *Builders to the Nation: The A. V. Jennings Story,* MUP, Carlton, 1992, pp. 91, 159, 161 and compare with the career of the major American project builder Abraham Levitt, as described in Jackson, *Crabgrass Frontier,*

pp. 234–8. For a discussion of the dimensions of Fordism in the Australian house building industry see Alastair Greig, *The Stuff Dreams Are Made Of: Housing Provision in Australia 1945–1960*, Melbourne, 1995, pp. 22–8 and ch. 3 and ibid., *Housing and Social Theory: Testing the Fordist Models or Social Theory and AfFORDable Housing*, Urban Research Program Working Paper, no. 45, February 1995.

24 *Wheels*, July 1955, p. 44.

25 For examples of Smith's pro-freeway advocacy in the United States see Wilbur Smith and Associates (WSA), *Future Highways and Urban Growth*, WSA, New Haven, 1961, and ibid., *Transportation and Parking for Tomorrow's Cities*, WSA, New Haven, 1966.

26 Interview with Robin Underwood, 23 June 1994.

27 In his book *Masculinity and the British Organisation Man Since 1945*, Michael Roper identifies this code of toughness, on which young businessmen modelled themselves, as a clue to the masculine ethos of the managerial elite as a whole. 'He was a formidable bugger, but he was also an exciting man to work for', one of Roper's interviewees remarks, p. 83.

28 *Herald*, 22 May 1955.

29 Interview with Joe Delaney, 1 June 1994.

30 Joe Delaney, 'The Relationship between Land Use and the Movement of People in Urban Areas', unpublished paper 1964.

31 *Australian Motor Manual*, 15 July 1955.

32 *Metropolis*, vol. 2, no. 1, September 1957.

33 Tony Dingle and Carolyn Rasmussen, *Vital Connections: Melbourne and its Board of Works*, MUP, Melbourne, 1991, pp. 242–3.

34 Rosemary Broomham, *Vital Connections: A History of NSW Roads from 1788*, Hale & Iremonger, Sydney, 2001, pp. 148–9, 155; David Ball, *The Road to Nowhere? Urban Freeway Planning in Sydney to 1977 and in the Present Day*, Urban Research Program Working Paper no. 51, Australian National University, Canberra, February, 1996; Peter Spearritt, *Sydney's Century: A History*, UNSW Press, Sydney, 2000, pp. 131–57.

35 *Victorian Yearbook*, 1968, pp. 257–67.

36 *Royalauto*, September 1957, pp. 6–8; July 1958, pp. 29–31; October 1959, pp. 13–15. Tony Dingle and Carolyn Rasmussen, *Vital Connections*, pp. 250–6; W. K. Anderson, *Roads for the People: A History of Victoria's Roads*, Hyland House, Melbourne, 1994, pp. 195–210.

37 MTC Minutes, 14 August 1964 (copy in possession of John Bayley).

38 Interview with Joe Delaney, 1 June 1994.

39 *Future Highways and Urban Growth*, Yale University Press, New Haven, 1961, p. 57.

40 MTC Minutes, August 1963.

41 The progress of the survey is outlined in the MTC's bulletin *Transreport*, February, June 1964; June 1965, VPRS 10090/18.

42 MTC Minutes, 30 August 1963; Metropolitan Transportation Committee,

Melbourne Transport—1985, Metropolitan Transportation Committee, Melbourne 1969.

43 John Kain, 'A Reappraisal of Metropolitan Transport Planning' in *The Economics of Roads and Road Transport*, Commonwealth Bureau of Roads, Occasional Paper no. 1, Melbourne 1968; compare the similar local critique by Pat Troy, 'Transportation Studies, Anyone?', *Australian Planning Institute Journal*, vol. 5, no. 1, 1967, pp. 13–17. The gravity model remained the basis of MTS planning throughout the first phase of the study. In 1967 John Bayley was still defending it against the criticisms of economist Stewart Joy (see John Bayley to Chairman, Technical Committee, 23 November 1967, VPRS, 100090–16) but in 1973, as work began on a revised and reduced version of the plan the committee chairman Sir Louis Loder travelled to California where he interviewed representatives of two firms, Alan Voorhees and De Leuw Cather, whose modelling techniques were believed to supercede Smith's (see Executive Director to Technical Director, 4 December 1973, VPRS—100090–13); Sir Louis Loder to John Bayley, 31 October, VPRS 10090–18.

44 *Sun*, 12 February 1965.

45 Graeme Davison, *The Rise and Fall of Marvellous Melbourne*, MUP, Carlton, 1978, pp. 156–72; *Plan of General Development, Melbourne: Report of the Metropolitan Town Planning Commission*, Melbourne: H. J. Green, Govt. Printer, 1929, pp. 115, 212.

46 *Melbourne Metropolitan Planning Scheme 1954, Report*, Melbourne and Metropolitan Board of Works, Melbourne, 1954, pp. 97–102.

47 Interviews with Joe Delaney, 1 June 1994; Bill Saggers, 20 April 1994.

48 RACV, *Living with the Motor Car*, 1964, p. 100.

49 ibid.

50 Interviews with Joe Delaney and John Bayley.

51 Interview with Neil Guerin, 11 May 1994.

52 *The Transportation Plan*, p. 3.

53 Interview with Bill Saggers, 20 April 1994.

54 Interview with Ted Barton, 27 April 1994. Some later students of the Melbourne transport system have sometimes argued that Toronto afforded a more appropriate model for the city than the more fashionable US models: See Paul Mees, *A Very Public Solution*, Chapters 6 and 7; though compare Ray Brindle, 'Toronto-Paradigm Lost?', *Australian Planner*, vol. 30, no. 3, 1992, pp. 123–30.

55 Melbourne Transportation Study, vol. 3, *The Transportation Plan*, pp. 58–60.

56 Ian Manning, *The Open Street*, p. 84.

Chapter 8: The Walls of Jericho

1 R. G. Menzies, *The Forgotten People*, Melbourne, 1942 as quoted in Judith Brett, *Robert Menzies' Forgotten People*, Sydney, 1992, p. 73.

2 John R. Kellett, *Railways and Victorian Cities*, Routledge, London, 1979, pp.327–36; Gareth Stedman Jones, *Outcast London*, Oxford University Press, London, 1971, pp. 152–78.

3 Peter Curson and Kevin McCracken, *Plague in Sydney: The Anatomy of an Epidemic*, NSW University Press, Sydney, n.d; Shirley Fitzgerald and Christopher Keating, *Millers Point: The Urban Village*, Hale & Iremonger, Sydney, 1991, pp. 67–79.

4 M. A. Jones, *Housing and Poverty in Australia*, MUP, Carlton, 1972, pp. 72–3.

5 *Age*, 19 December 1969, editorial.

6 *Herald*, 30 October 1972; *Sun*, 30 October 1972; RACV Public Affairs Department, *The Effects of Traffic Noise from Freeways*, Melbourne 1972.

7 Commonwealth Bureau of Roads, *Report on Roads in Australia*, 1973, p. 135.

8 MMBW, *Melbourne Metropolitan Planning Scheme*, Melbourne, 1954, p. 99.

9 MMBW, *Social Dysfunction and Relative Poverty in Metropolitan Melbourne*, Melbourne, 1974; MMBW, *Melbourne's Inner Area—A Position Statement*, April 1977, pp. 57–63.

10 [Chris Wallace-Crabbe], 'Melbourne', *Current Affairs Bulletin*, vol. 32, no. 11, 14 October 1963, p. 170.

11 William Stewart Logan, *The Gentrification of Inner Melbourne: A Political Geography of Inner City Housing*, University of Queensland Press, St Lucia, 1985, pp. 39–40.

12 Examples: Holding in *Age*, 15 September 1972; Merilyn White in *Herald*, 20 November 1972. Anti-freeway meeting in *Sun*, 24 September 1971; D. Bornstein in *Sun*, 20 December 1971; Holding in *Sun*, 12 October 1972.

13 For a still-pertinent analysis of 'community politics' see Andrew Jakubow-icz, 'The New Politics of Suburbia', *Current Affairs Bulletin*, 1 April 1972, pp. 338–50.

14 *Newsday*, 3 November 1969.

15 *Sun*, 20 December 1971, *Herald*, 27 December 1972.

16 See for example Lois Bryson and Faith Thompson, *An Australian Newtown: Life and Leadership in a New Housing Suburb*, Penguin, Ringwood, 1972, ch. 11.

17 This paragraph draws on the testimony of 1960s inner city activists who participated in a one-day conference organised by Renate Howe and Graeme Davison at Richmond Town Hall, 1 April 2000.

18 Interview with Trevor Huggard, 10 August 1999.

19 George Tibbitts, ' "The Enemy Within": Slum Clearance and High-Rise Flats' in Renate Howe (ed.), *New Houses for Old: Fifty Years of Public Housing in Victoria, 1938–1988*, Ministry of Housing and Construction, Melbourne, 1988, pp. 123–62; Logan, *The Gentrification of Inner Melbourne*, pp. 184–190; compare David Ball, *The Road to Nowhere? Urban Freeway Planning in Sydney to 1977 and in the Present Day*, Urban Research

Program Working Paper no. 51, February 1996, Australian National University, Canberra, pp. 20–22; Zula Nittim, 'The Coalition of Resident Action Groups' in Jill Roe (ed.), *Twentieth Century Sydney: Studies of Urban and Social History*, Hale & Iremonger, Sydney, 1980, pp. 231–47.

20 *Carlton News*, 6 May 1969.

21 Committee for Urban Action, *Transport Melbourne ... The Inner Area Crisis, Part 1, A Transport Policy for the Inner Areas An Evaluation and Submission*, Melbourne 1970.

22 Town and Country Planning Association of Victoria, *Melbourne Transportation*, Nunawading, 1971.

23 Undated clipping in Citizens against Freeways Files, SLV.

24 George MacLeod, *Only One Way Left*, Iona Community, Glasgow, 1956, p. 141.

25 Interview with Andrew McCutcheon, 1 September 1999.

26 *Carlton News*, 14 October 1970

27 ibid., 6 October 1971.

28 *Carlton News*, 20 January 1971.

29 W. S. Logan, *The Gentrification of Inner Melbourne*, pp. 40–51.

30 *Sun*, 24 December 1971.

31 *Age*, 18 November 1971.

32 *Freeway Crisis: A Carlton Association Report*, 29 March 1972.

33 *Herald*, 29 March 1972; *Carlton News*, 12 April 1972.

34 *Age*, 28 July 1972.

35 *Herald*, 20 November 1972.

36 *Age*, 12 October 1972, *Herald*, 20 November 1972; interview with Sally Browne, 28 May 1996.

37 Tom Lewis, *Divided Highways: Building Interstate Highways, Transforming American Life*, Viking, New York, 1997.

38 David Ball, *The Road to Nowhere?*, pp. 22–6.

39 Donald Horne, *Time of Hope: Australia 1966–1972*, Angus & Robertson, Sydney, 1980.

40 *VPD*, 21 November 1972, p. 2229 as quoted in Jean Holmes, 'Political Chronicle—Victoria', *Australian Journal of Politics and History*, vol. 9, no. 1, April 1973, p. 85.

41 *Melbourne Times*, 13 December 1972; John Bayley, 'United Freeway Action Group', 13 December 1972, MTS Papers, VPRS 10090/6.

42 Statement of Policy on Transport in Melbourne by the Premier (Mr Hamer), 21 December 1972, VPRS 10090/6/19; *Sun*, 22 December 1972.

43 Robert Risson to Hon. Vernon Wilcox, 7 December 1972, VPRS 10090/6/19.

44 *Royalauto*, May 1973, p. 3.

45 R. J. Roscholler to Technical Director, 13 December 1972, VPRS 10090/6/19.

46 This memo was leaked by a former CRB engineer and published in the *Age*, 14 October 1974.

47 Robert Caro, *The Power Broker: Robert Moses and the Fall of New York*, Vintage Books, New York, 1974, p. 318.

48 *Sun*, 10 May 1973.

49 *Age*, 15, 17, 25 October 1974.

50 *Sun*, 15 October 1974.

51 *Melbourne Times*, 29 October 1975, p. 3; *Sun*, 30 October 1975; *Age*, 5 November 1975.

52 John Bayley (Technical Director) to Robert Risson (Executive Director), MTS 25 June 1973, VPRS, 100090–6–19.

53 Bernard Barrett, *The Inner Suburbs: The Evolution of an Industrial Area*, MUP, Carlton, 1971, pp. 45, 74.

54 *Collingwood Courier*, 10 April 1974.

55 ibid., 20 March, 3, 10 April 1974.

56 ibid., 10 April 1974; *Sun*, 27 April 1974.

57 *Herald*, 14 September 1974.

58 *Age*, 19 June 2002 (Marion Miller obituary).

59 *Collingwood Courier*, 18 September 1974.

60 *Herald*, 14 September 1974.

61 Compare Manuel Castells, *The Urban Question: A Marxist Approach*, Edward Arnold, London, 1977; C. G. Pickvance (ed.), *Urban Sociology*, Tavistock Publications, London, 1976.

62 Meredith and Verity Burgmann, *Green Bans, Red Union: Environmental Activism and the New South Wales Builders Labourers Federation*, UNSW Press, Sydney, 1998.

63 *Age*, 31 October 1975.

64 Neil Wilkinson, 'Conflict over Transport in Melbourne' in John Halligan and Chris Paris (eds), *Australian Urban Politics: Critical Perspectives*, Longman, Melbourne, 1984, pp. 204–11.

65 *Stop Freeways* [n.d.] Citizens Freeway Coalition Papers, State Library of Victoria.

66 *Express*, (Albert Park) March, April 1974.

67 *Freeway Fighter*, September 1977.

68 *Age*, 28 June 1974.

69 *Melbourne Times*, 19 May 1976.

70 *Freeway Fighter*, September 1977.

71 *Age*, 15 September 1977.

72 Interview with Marion Miller, 23 November 1995.

73 The following account of the barricade draws on local and metropolitan press reports, oral testimony and the anonymous near-contemporary history, *Barricade! The Resident Fight against the F19 Freeway*, Australian Independence Movement, Melbourne, 1978.

74 *Barricade*, p. 9.

75 *Freeway Fighter*, April 1977.

76 *Barricade*, p. 10.

77 Summary of residents' working group proposals in *The Freeway Survival Kit*, supplement to *Melbourne Times*, December 1977.

78 Interview with Andrew McCutcheon.
79 *Herald*, 25 November 1977.
80 *Age*, 23 December 1977.
81 *Sun*, 4 July 1973.
82 *Herald*, 24, 25 August 1978; R. Bookman, An Assessment of the Social Disruption on Alexandra Parade Residents caused by the Opening of the Eastern (F19) Freeway, [Melbourne] 1979.
83 Brian Howe became Labor MHR for Batman and later Deputy Prime Minister of Australia in the Hawke and Keating governments; Trevor Huggard became Lord Mayor of Melbourne; Andrew McCutcheon and Barry Pullen were ministers in the Cain and Kirner Labor governments, Bob Hogg became federal secretary of the Australian Labor Party.
84 I draw here on the testimony of a number of former inner city activists who exchanged recollections at a one-day conference organised by Graeme Davison and Renate Howe and held at Richmond Town Hall on 1 April 2000.
85 Thomas Bender, *Community and Social Change in America*, Johns Hopkins University Press, Baltimore, 1978, p. 6.

Chapter 9: The Serpent in the Garden

1 Leo Marx, *The Machine in the Garden: Technology and the Pastoral Ideal in America*, OUP, New York, 1964, p. 353.
2 Robert A. Caro, *The Power Broker: Robert Moses and the Fall of New York*, Knofp, New York, 1974, pp. 161–2
3 Marshall Berman, *All That is Solid Melts into Air*, Verso, London, p. 299.
4 Graeme Davison, *The Rise and Fall of Marvellous Melbourne*, MUP, Melbourne, 1978, p. 156.
5 *Plan of General Development, Melbourne: Report of the Metropolitan Town Planning Commission*, Melbourne: H. J. Green, Govt Printer, 1929, pp. 115. 122.
6 *Melbourne Metropolitan Planning Commission Planning Scheme 1954, Report*, Melbourne 1954, p. 99.
7 Ray Brindle, 'It's Obvious when you Know the Answer: the "Analysis of Predetermined Solutions" in 20th Century Transport Planning', in Robert Freestone (ed.), *The Twentieth Century Urban Planning Experience*, 8th International Planning History Conference, University of New South Wales, July 1998, pp. 68–73.
8 W. K. Anderson, *Roads for the People: A History of Victoria's Roads*, Hyland House, Melbourne, 1994, pp. 207, 266.
9 Tony Dingle and Carolyn Rasmussen, *Vital Connections*, p. 325; W. K. Anderson, *Roads for the People*, pp. 191, 246–7.
10 *Sun*, 29 March 1973.
11 Helen Topliss, *The Artists' Camps: Plein Air Painting in Melbourne 1885–1898*, Monash University Gallery, Melbourne, 1984.

12 Graham Butler, *Heidelberg Conservation Study, Part 1 Heidelberg Historic Buildings and Area Assessment*, Heidelberg, 1985, pp. 28, 67, 121, 132; Marilyn McBriar and Loder and Bayly, *Heidelberg Conservation Study, Part 2.*

13 *Valley Freeway Action Newsletter*, October 1972. In a press article at about this time Ann Bunbury claimed a membership of 400. *Herald*, 1 November 1972.

14 *VFAG Newsletter*, October, November 1972; June 1973; Victorian Electoral Roll, 1972. The group included several prominent lawyers including criminal advocate Frank Galbally and QC Hartog Berkeley and a few stray Leftists including Communist planning advocates Maurie and Ruth Crow and Monash historian Ian Turner.

15 *Herald*, 1 November 1972; A. I. Bunbury to V. F. Wilcox, 15 November 1972, VPRS 10090–6–21.

16 *VFAG Newsletter*, August 1972, p. 3.

17 ibid., October 1972.

18 Tom Prior, *Bolte by Bolte*, Craftsman Publishing, Melbourne, 1990, p. 201.

19 *VFAG Newsetter*, February 1973.

20 Colin A. Hughes, *Voting for the Australian State Lower Houses 1965–1974*, ANU Press, Canberra, 1981.

21 Victorian Public Interest Research Group, *The Merri Creek Study*, Melbourne, 1975, p. 94.

22 Letters from M. L. Ostrowski, 10 November 1975; John Beezley, 6 November 1975; Dr J. Sandford, 8 November 1975, VPRS 10450, MV File.

23 Alan M. Voorhees, *Planning in the Koonung Creek Corridor Phase 1 Report Problem Definitions*, 1975, pp. 19–21. Also see Summary of Research Meeting, Box Hill High School 20 October 1975, VPRS 10450.

24 *Freeway Fighter*, November 1978.

25 *Gardiner's Creek Valley Let It Be*, n.d. [c. 1986], p. 1.

26 For a more complete narrative of the dispute see Lyn Strahan, *Private and Public Memory: A History of the City of Malvern*, Hargreen Publishing, Malvern, 1989, ch. 11.

27 Gardiner's Creek Valley Study, *Bulletin*, no. 1, May 1977.

28 *CRB News*, no. 34, December 1976, p. 8.

29 Gardiner's Creek Valley Study, *Bulletin*, no. 1, May 1977, *Bulletin*, no. 3, n.d.

30 Gardiner's Creek Valley Study, *Bulletin*, no. 2, n.d.

31 *Gardiner's Creek Valley Study Report on Noise Studies Part 2 Noise Assessment of Road Alternatives*, 1977.

32 J. S. B. Rosair to Hon. A. J. Hunt MLC 24 Jan 1978 [copy], Gardiner's Creek Association Papers, MS 11841, Box 2179/1, LaTrobe Library.

33 Gottstein to Lindsay Thompson, 21 April 1980; Robert Maclellan to Lindsay Thompson, 22 October 1979; Gottstein Objection to Amendment No. 120, 10 July 1980; Road Construction Authority to Gottstein, 4 April 1984, Gardiner's Creek Association Papers, 2179/2.

Chapter 10: On the Move?

1   J. Michael Thompson, *Great Cities and their Traffic*, Penguin, London, 1978, p. 133–40.

2   Minister for Manufacturing and Industry Development, Media Releases, 22 May 1992; 3 August, 18 September 1992; *Herald–Sun* 3 April 1992.

3   Mark Considine and Brian Costar (eds), *Trials in Power: Cain, Kirner and Victoria 1982–1992*, MUP, Carlton, 1992, Chapters 2, 3; John Cain, *John Cain's Years: Power, Parties and Politics*, MUP, Carlton, 1995, pp. 218–40.

4   Brian Costar and Nicholas Economou (eds), *The Kennett Revolution: Victorian Politics in the 1990s*, UNSW Press, Sydney, 1999, chapters, 10, 12, 13.

5   Graeme Davison, 'The Picture of Melbourne, 1835–1985' in A. G. L. Shaw (ed.), *The Heritage of Victoria*, Allen & Unwin, Sydney, 1985, pp. 12–36.

6   *Age*, 13 September 1994.

7   Graeme Davison, 'The Modern and Melbourne: Self-Imaging in Photography, Journalism and Film' in Lynette Finch and Chris McConville (eds), *Gritty Cities: Images of the Urban*, Pluto Press, Sydney, 1999, pp. 50–1.

8   Louise Johnson, William S. Logan and Colin Long, 'Jeff Kennett's Melbourne: Postmodern City, Planning and Politics' in Robert Freestone (ed.), *The 20th Century Urban Planning Experience*: 8th International Planning History Conference Proceedings, University of New South Wales, Sydney, 1998, pp. 436–41.

9   Central to this interpretation are the writings of members of the UCLA Planning School, such as Edward Soja and Manuel Castells. For a cautionary view about the dangers of uncritical adaptation of Los Angeles models to Australian circumstances see Mark Peel, 'The Urban Debate: From "Los Angeles" to the Urban Village' in Patrick Troy (ed.), *Australian Cities: Issues, Strategies and Policies for Urban Australia in the 1990s*, Cambridge University Press, Melbourne, 1995, pp. 39–64.

10 Clive Forster, *Australian Cities: Continuity and Change*, OUP, Melbourne, 1995, pp. 45–7.

11 Robert Fagan, 'Industrial Change in the Global City: Sydney's New Spaces of Production' in John Connell (ed.), *Sydney: The Emergence of a World City*, OUP, Melbourne, 2000, pp. 144–66. Compare Peter Murphy and Sophie Watson, *Surface City: Sydney at the Millennium*, Pluto Press, Sydney, 1997, chapter 2.

12 Edward Soja, *Postmodern Geographies: The Reassertion of Space in Critical Social Theory*, Verso, London, 1989, esp. Chapters 8, 9; Mike Davis, *City of Quartz: Excavating the Future in Los Angeles*, Verso, London, 1990; compare Chris McConville, 'Learning from Venturi—and Melbourne' in Lynette Finch and Chris McConville (eds), *Gritty Cities*, pp. 228–32.

13 Tony Parkinson, *Jeff: The Rise and Fall of a Political Phenomenon*, Penguin, Melbourne, 2000, p. 6.

14 ibid., pp. 248, 282–6.

15 *Age*, 16 November 1994.
16 Jill Barnard and Jenny Keating, *People's Playground: A History of Albert Park*, Chandos Publishing, Melbourne, 1996, pp. 12, 13, 51, 141–5.
17 *Age*, 22 October 1994.
18 *Age*, 5 November 1994.
19 *Sunday Age*, 9 July 1995.
20 *Age*, 27 March 1995 (letter).
21 *Age*, 16 November 1994.
22 *Sunday Age*, 28 March 1993, *Age*, 24 April 1993.
23 David Holmes, 'The Electronic Superhighway: Melbourne's CityLink Project', *Urban Policy and Research*, vol. 18, no. 1, March 2000, pp. 65–76.
24 *Age*, 30 July, 1 August 1995.
25 *Australian*, 23–24 July 1994; *Age*, 19 November 1994.
26 *Age*, 23, 25 May 1995.
27 Letters to the *Age*, 29, 31 May; 2, 15, 16 June 1995.
28 *Sunday Age*, 10 September 1995.
29 *Herald-Sun*, 15 November 1995.
30 Tony Parkinson, *Jeff*, pp. 202–3, *Sunday Age*, 24 March 1996.
31 *Age*, 19 Jan 1995 (Stone), 30 Jan 1995 (Mees), 21 November 1994 (Burt, TCPA), 30 January 1995 (Krivanek).
32 See for example, Kevin O'Connor, *Age* 10 May 1995.
33 See for example, David Holmes, 'The Electronic Superhighway', pp. 65–76.
34 Peter Hone, *Age*, 3 August 1995; Bruce Tobin, *Age*, 11 September 1995; Graeme Davison, 'Melbourne's Triple By-pass', *Arena Magazine*, no. 22, April–May 1996, pp. 19–25.
35 John Quiggan, 'Public Pays Price for Private Infrastructure', *Age*, 22 November 1994.
36 *Age*, 1 August 1995; *Sunday Age*, 6 August 1995.
37 *Age*, 22 April 2000.
38 *Age*, 29 January 1995.
39 Mark Skulley, 'One for the Roads Scholars', *Australian Financial Review*, 13 August 1999.
40 *Age*, 21 August 1999.
41 *Age*, 31 August 1999.
42 Ivor Ries, 'It's a Rollercoaster Ride', *Australian Financial Review*, 20 November 1999.
43 *Age*, 14 September 1999.
44 *Age*, 18 September 1999.
45 Nicholas Economou, 'Political Chronicle—Victoria, June to December 1999', *Australian Journal of Politics and History*, vol. 46, no. 2, 2000, pp. 226–37.
46 *Age*, 12 March 2000.
47 Vicroads, Northern City Corridor Study, August 1999; Reports of the Northern Central City Corridor Study, Community Reference Group,

Discussion Notes, 2001–2002, *http://www.doi.vic.gov.au/doi/internet/ transport.nsf/headingpagesdisplay/transport+projectsnorthern+central+ city+corridor+study*

48 *Age*, 14 April 2003.
49 Graeme Davison, 'The European City in Australia', *Journal of Urban History*, vol. 27, no. 6, September 2001, pp. 779–93.

Select Bibliography

Anderson, W. K. *Roads for the People: A History of Victoria's Roads*, Hyland House, Melbourne, 1994.

Ball, David. *The Road to Nowhere? Urban Freeway Planning in Sydney to 1977 and in the Present Day*, Urban Research Program Working Paper no. 51, Australian National University, Canberra, February 1996.

Banham, Reyner. *Los Angeles: The Architecture of Four Ecologies*, University of California Press, Berkeley, 2001.

Bayley, Stephen. *Sex, Drink, and Fast Cars*, Pantheon Books, New York, 1986.

Bedwell, Steve. *Suburban Icons: A Celebration of the Everyday*, ABC Books, Sydney, 1992.

Beed, Clive S. *Melbourne's Development and Planning*, Clewara Press, Melbourne, 1981.

Berman, Marshall. *All That Is Solid Melts into Air: The Experience of Modernity*, Verso, London, 1983.

Boyd, Robin. *The Australian Ugliness*, Penguin, Melbourne, 1963.

—— *Australia's Home*, Melbourne University Press, Melbourne, 1952.

Brett, Judith. *Robert Menzies' Forgotten People*, Macmillan, Melbourne 1992.

Broomham, Rosemary. *On the Road: The NRMA's First Seventy-Five Years*, Allen & Unwin, Sydney, 1996.

Brown-May, Andrew. *Melbourne Street-Life*, Australian Scholarly Publishing, Melbourne, 1998.

Bryson, Lois and Thompson, Faith. *An Australian Newtown: Life and Leadership in a New Housing Suburb*, Penguin, Melbourne, 1972.

Caro, Robert. *The Power Broker: Robert Moses and the Fall of New York*, Vintage Books, New York, 1974.

Catrice, Daniel and Summerton, Michelle. *The Motor Garage & Service Station in Victoria: A Survey*, National Estate Grants Programme, Department of Infrastructure, Melbourne, February 1997.

Clarsen, Georgine. 'The "Dainty Female Toe" and the "Brawny Male Arm"': Conceptions of Bodies and Power in Automobile Technology', *Australian Feminist Studies*, vol. 15, no. 32, 2000, pp. 153–63.

—— 'Women, Modernity and Cars in Interwar Victoria', in Martin Crotty and Doug Scobie (eds), *Raiding Clio's Closet: Postgraduate Presentations in History*, University of Melbourne, Melbourne, 1997, pp. 61–75.

Cohen, Lisabeth. 'From Town Center to Shopping Center: The Reconfiguration of Community Marketplaces in Postwar America', *American Historical Review*, vol. 101, no. 4, October 1996, pp. 1056–60.

Darian-Smith, Kate. *On the Home Front: Melbourne in Wartime 1939–1945*, Oxford University Press, Melbourne, 1990.

Davidson, Jim and Spearritt, Peter. *Holiday Business: Tourism in Australia Since 1870*, Melbourne University Press, Melbourne, 2000.

Davison, Graeme. 'Driving to Austerica: the Americanization of the Postwar Australian City', in Harold Bolitho and Chris Wallace-Crabbe (eds), *Approaching Australia: Papers from the Harvard Australian Studies Symposium*, Harvard University Committee on Australian Studies/ Harvard University Press, Cambridge, Mass, 1998, pp. 159–84.

—— 'Melbourne's Triple By-pass', *Arena Magazine*, no. 22, April–May 1996, pp. 19–25.

—— 'The Modern and Melbourne—Self-imaging in Photography, Journalism and Film', in Lynette Finch and Chris McConville (eds), *Gritty Cities: Images of the Urban*, Pluto Press, Sydney, 1999, pp. 45–64.

—— *The Rise and Fall of Marvellous Melbourne*, Melbourne University Press, Melbourne, 1978.

—— *The Unforgiving Minute: How Australia Learned to Tell the Time*, Melbourne, 1993.

—— 'Welcoming the World: The 1956 Olympic Games and the Representation of Melbourne', in John Murphy and Judith Smart (eds), *The Forgotten Fifties*, *Australian Historical Studies*, vol. 28, no. 109, October 1997, pp. 64–76.

Davison, Graeme, Dingle, Tony and O'Hanlon, Seamus. *The Cream Brick Frontier: Histories of Australian Suburbia*, Monash Publications in History no. 19, Clayton, 1995.

Dingle, Tony and O'Hanlon, Seamus. 'Modernism versus Domesticity: The Contest to Shape Melbourne's Homes, 1945–1960', *Australian Historical Studies*, vol. 28, no. 109, October 1997, pp. 33–48.

Dingle, Tony and Rasmussen, Carolyn. *Vital Connections: Melbourne and its Board of Works 1891–1991*, Melbourne University Press, Melbourne, 1991.

Easdown, Geoff. *Ford: The Story of the Ford Motor Company in Australia*, Sydney, 1987.

Ellis, Cliff. 'Professional Conflict over Urban Form: The Case of Urban Freeways, 1930–1970', in Mary Corbin Sies and Christopher Silver (eds), *Planning the Twentieth Century City*, Johns Hopkins University Press, Baltimore, 1996, pp. 262–79.

Fairfield, John D. 'The Scientific Management of Urban Space: Professional City Planning and the Legacy of Progressive Reform', *Journal of Urban History*, vol. 20, no. 2, February 1994, pp. 179–204.

Finch, Lynette and McConville, Chris (eds). *Gritty Cities: Images of the Urban*, Pluto Press, Sydney, 1999.

Fitzgerald, Shirley. *Sydney 1842–1992*, Hale and Iremonger, Sydney, 1992.

Flink, James J. *The Automobile Age*, MIT Press, Cambridge, Mass, 1988.

Freestone, Robert. *Model Communities: The Garden City Movement in Australia*, Nelson, Melbourne, 1989.

Frostick, M. *Advertising the Motor Car*, Lund Humphries, London, 1970.

Garden, Don. *Builders to the Nation: The A.V. Jennings Story*, Melbourne University Press, Melbourne, 1992.

Greig, Alastair. *The Stuff Dreams Are Made Of: Housing Provision in Australia 1945–1960*, Melbourne University Press, Melbourne, 1995.

Haldane, Robert. *The People's Force: A History of the Victoria Police*, Melbourne University Press, Melbourne, 1986.

Hartnett, L. J. *Big Wheels and Little Wheels*, Lansdowne Press, Melbourne, 1964.

Hartwig, Kate. 'Claiming the Freeway: Young Male Drivers in Pursuit of Independence, Space and Masculinity', *Journal of Interdisciplinary Gender Studies*, vol. 5, no. 1, June 2000, pp. 36–50.

Hilliard, David. 'God in the Suburbs: The Religious Culture of Australian Cities in the 1950s', *Australian Historical Studies*, vol. 25, no. 97, October 1991, pp. 399–419.

Holmes, David. 'The Electronic Superhighway: Melbourne's CityLink Project', *Urban Policy and Research*, vol. 18, no. 1, March 2000, pp. 65-76.

Howe, Renate (ed.). *New Houses for Old: Fifty Years of Public Housing in Victoria, 1938–1988*, Ministry of Housing and Construction, Melbourne, 1988.

Jackson, J. B. 'The Domestication of the Garage', *Landscape*, vol. 20, no. 2, 1976, pp. 10–17.

Jackson, Kenneth T. *Crabgrass Frontier: The Suburbanization of the United States*, Oxford University Press, New York, 1985.

Jakle, John A., Sculle, Keith and Rogers, Jefferson S. *The Motel in America*, Johns Hopkins University Press, Baltimore, 1996.

Johnson, Lesley. *The Modern Girl: Girlhood and Growing Up*, Allen & Unwin, Sydney, 1993.

Johnson, Louise, Logan, William S. and Long, Colin. 'Jeff Kennett's Melbourne: Postmodern City, Planning and Politics', in Robert Freestone (ed.), *The 20th Century Urban Planning Experience*, 8th International Planning History Conference Proceedings, University of New South Wales, Sydney, 1998, pp. 436–44.

Kemp, Louis Ward. 'Aesthetics and Engineers: The Occupational Ideology of Highway Design', *Technology and Culture*, vol. 27, October 1986, pp. 759–97.

Kingston, Beverley. *Basket, Bag and Trolley: A History of Shopping in Australia*, Oxford University Press, Melbourne, 1994.

Knott, John William. '"The Conquering Car": Technology, Symbolism and the Motorisation of Australian before World War II', *Australian Historical Studies*, vol. 31, no. 114, April 2000, pp. 1–26.

—— 'Road Traffic Accidents in New South Wales, 1881–1991', *Australian Economic History Review*, vol. 34, no. 2, September 1994, pp. 80–116.

—— 'Speed, Modernity and the Motor Car: The Making of the 1909 Motor Traffic Act in New South Wales', *Australian Historical Studies*, vol. 26, no. 103, October 1994, pp. 221–41.

Lake, Marilyn. *Getting Equal: The History of Australian Feminism*, Allen & Unwin, Sydney, 1999.

Lewis, Tom. *Divided Highways: Building Interstate Highways, Transforming American Life*, Viking, New York, 1997.

Logan, William Stewart. *The Gentrification of Inner Melbourne: A Political Geography of Inner City Housing*, University of Queensland Press, St Lucia, 1985.

McShane, Clay. *Down the Asphalt Path: The Automobile and the American City*, Columbia University Press, New York, 1994.

Manning, Ian. *The Open Street: Public Transport, Motor Cars and Politics in Australian Cities*, Transit Australia, Sydney, 1991.

Marchand, Roland. *Advertising the American Dream: Making Way for Modernity, 1920–1940*, University of California Press, Berkeley, 1985.

Marsh, Peter and Collett, Peter. *Driving Passion: The Psychology of the Car*, Jonathan Cape, London, 1986

Mees, Paul. *A Very Public Solution: Transport in the Dispersed City*, Melbourne University Press, Melbourne, 2000.

Meinig, D. W. (ed.). *The Interpretation of Ordinary Landscapes Geographical Essays*, New York, 1979.

Morton, Peter. *After Light: A History of the City of Adelaide and its Council, 1878–1928*, Adelaide City Council, Adelaide, 1996.

Murphy, John. *Imagining the Fifties: Private Sentiment and Political Culture in Menzies' Australia*, University of New South Wales Press, Sydney, 2000.

Neutze, Max. *Urban Development in Australia*, Allen & Unwin, Sydney, 1977.

O'Callaghan, Judith (ed.). *The Australian Dream: Design of the Fifties*, Powerhouse Museum, Sydney, 1993.

Olson, Karen. 'Laying the Yellow Brick Road: The Rise of the Suburban Driveway', in Australia ICOMOS, Victorian Conference Papers, March 1996.

Peel, Mark, *Good Times Hard Times: The Past and Future in Elizabeth*, Melbourne University Press, Melbourne, 1995.

—— 'The Urban Debate: From "Los Angeles" to the Urban Village', in Patrick Troy (ed.), *Australian Cities: Issues, Strategies and Policies for Urban Australia in the 1990s*. Cambridge University Press, Cambridge, Mass, 1995, pp. 39–64.

Pickett, Charles (ed.). *Cars and Culture: Our Driving Passions*, HarperCollins/ Powerhouse Museum, Sydney, 1998.

Plowden, William. *The Motor Car and Politics 1896–1970*, Bodley Head, London, 1971.

Priestley, Susan. *The Crown of the Road: The Story of the RACV*, Melbourne, 1983.

Rae, John B. *The American Automobile: A Brief History*, Chicago, 1965.

Richardson, John. 'Movies under the Stars: Drive-ins and Modernity', *Continuum: An Australian Journal of the Media*, vol. 1, no. 1, 1987, pp. 111–15.

Roe, Jill (ed.). *Twentieth Century Sydney: Studies of Urban and Social History*, Hale and Iremonger, Sydney, 1980.

Rolfe, Mark. 'Suburbia', in Philip and Roger Bell (eds), *Americanization and Australia*, University of New South Wales Press, Sydney, 1998, pp. 1–8.

Rose, Mark. *Interstate: Express Highway Politics, 1941–1956*, Regents Press, Lawrence, Ks., 1979.

Sachs, Wolfgang. *For Love of the Automobile: Looking Back into the History of Our Desires*, University of California Press, Berkeley, 1992.

Sandercock, Leonie. *Cities for Sale: Property, Politics and Planning in Australia*, Melbourne University Press, Melbourne, 1975.

Scharff, Virginia. *Taking the Wheel: Women and the Coming of the Motor Age*, University of New Mexico Press, Albuquerque 1991.

Serle, Geoffrey. *Robin Boyd: A Life*, Melbourne, 1995.

Soja, Edward. *Postmodern Geographies: The Reassertion of Space in Critical Social Theory*, Verso, London, 1989.

Spearritt, Peter. 'I shop, therefore I am', in Louise C. Johnson (ed.), *Suburban Dreaming: An Interdisciplinary Approach to Australian Cities*, Deakin University Press, Geelong, 1994, pp. 129–40.

—— 'The Privatisation of Australian Passenger Transport', in John Halligan and Chris Paris (eds), *Australian Urban Politics: Critical Perspectives*, Longman, Melbourne, pp. 193–203.

—— *Sydney's Century: A History*, University of New South Wales Press, Sydney, 2000.

Spearritt, Peter and Wells, J. 'The Rise and Decline of the Public Transport City', *Australian Historical Statistics Bulletin*, no. 8, 1984, pp. 61–79.

Strahan, Lyn. *Private and Public Memory: A History of the City of Malvern*, Hargreen Publishing, Malvern, Vic, 1989.

Taussig, M. 'An Australian Hero', *History Workshop Journal*, vol. 4, Autumn 1987, pp. 111–33.

Thompson, J. Michael. *Great Cities and their Traffic*, Penguin, London, 1978.

Toohey, Bill. *True Blue: 75 Years of Ford in Australia*, Focus Publishing, Sydney, 2000.

Troy, Patrick (ed.). *Technological Change and the City*, Federation Press, Sydney, 1995.

Wachs, Martin and Crawford Margaret (eds). *The Car and the City: The Automobile, the Built Environment and Daily Urban Life*, University of Michigan Press, Ann Arbor, 1992.

Walker, Linley. 'Chivalrous Masculinity Among Juvenile Offenders in Western Sydney: A New Perspective on Young Working Class Men and Crime', *Current Issues in Criminal Justice*, vol. 9, no. 3, March 1998, pp. 279–93.

White, Richard. '"The Australian Way of Life"', *Historical Studies*, vol. 18, no. 73, October 1979, pp. 528–45.

Wilkinson, Neil. 'Conflict Over Transport in Melbourne', in John Halligan and Chris Paris (eds), *Australian Urban Politics: Critical Perspectives*, Longman, Melbourne, 1984, pp. 204–11.

Wright, John. *Heart of the Lion: The 50 Year History of Australia's Holden*, Allen & Unwin, Sydney, 1998.

—— *The History of the Ford Falcon, 1960–1994*, Marque, Sydney, 1994.

Yelland, Sheryl. 'Motor Shows and Marketing Manoeuvres' and 'Transports of Desire: Motor Shows 1949–1995', in David Dunstan, *Victorian Icon: The Royal Exhibition Building Melbourne*, The Exhibition Trustees, Melbourne, 1996, pp. 350–6, 422–8.

Index

Captions in *italics*

Index by Russell Brooks